Visual Basic .NET
Code Security Handbook

Eric Lippert

® Wrox Press Ltd.

Visual Basic .NET Code Security Handbook

First published August 2002

Published by Wrox Press Ltd,
Arden House, 1102 Warwick Road, Acocks Green,
Birmingham, B27 6BH
United Kingdom
Printed in the United States
ISBN 1-86100-747-7

Trademark Acknowledgments

Wrox has endeavored to provide trademark information about all the companies and products mentioned in this book by the appropriate use of capitals. However, Wrox cannot guarantee the accuracy of this information.

Credits

Author
Eric Lippert

Editor
Benjamin Hickman

Technical Reviewers
Mark Horner
Michael Howard
Damien Foggon
Slavomir Furman

Indexer
Michael Brinkman

Production Coodinator
Sarah Hall

Proof Reader
Chris Smith

Cover Design
Natalie O'Donnell

Project Manager
Beckie Stones

Managing Editor
Jan Kolasinski

About the Author

Eric Lippert was born in southwestern Ontario, Canada. After studying mathematics at the University of Waterloo he moved to beautiful Seattle, Washington where he has worked for Microsoft since 1996.

Eric's primary focus during his six years at Microsoft has been on improving the lives of developers by designing useful programming languages and development tools. He is at least partially responsible (or as some would say, "to blame") for the VBScript and JScript languages, the Windows Script Host, and Windows Script Components. Odds are good that if the product has "Microsoft" and "Script" somewhere in the name then he had some hand in it.

He was also part of the teams that worked on designing JScript .NET and Visual Basic .NET, and until recently was a contributing member of the ECMAScript working group. He is presently thinking about how to design even better tools for developers who use applications such as those in the Microsoft Office suite as part of their development process.

Eric has long been interested in computer security issues, particularly with respect to the spate of highly destructive script-related viruses spread by malicious vandals over the last few years. He realized in 2001 that the excellent new security features in the .NET Framework designed to mitigate these sorts of problems would not do any good if they remained unused or poorly understood. Since then he has been somewhat obsessive about explaining to anyone who will listen how the security system works and why it is important to understand it.

Eric has written several magazine articles on scripting throughout the years and edited other books. This is his first published book as an author.

When he's not at work and not writing or editing books, Eric tries his best to keep the mast of his International 14 sailboat vertical rather than horizontal. (Puget Sound is awfully cold.) He also enjoys building kites, playing old songs on old pianos, collecting books, and talking his housemates into helping him fix up his hundred-year-old house.

Eric can be reached via e-mail at Eric@Lippert.com.

I would like to thank everyone who made this book possible. Though only one name goes on the cover, no book is ever published without the valuable time, expertise, and moral support of many diverse people.

First, many thanks to my reviewers and all the staff at Wrox Press for their patience in shepherding a first-time author from the outline to the final edit, their deep insights and their always-constructive criticisms. This book could not have been written without the assistance of Damien Foggon, Slavomir Furman, Ben Hickman, Mark Horner, Michael Howard, and Beckie Stones. They helped me remove many mistakes from this text; those that remain are my own.

Obviously, this book could not have been written without someone developing the security system which is its subject! Many thanks go to all the people at Microsoft who worked on the .NET Runtime and the Windows security systems. Many thanks also go to the entire scripting team; one could not ask for a better group of smart, dedicated people to have as coworkers. Particular mention must go to .NET Security team members Greg Fee, Loren Kohnfelder, Sebastian Lange, and Rudi Martin, Windows Security team members Praerit Garg, Phil Hallin, Michael Howard, and John Lambert, and Scripting team members Andrew Clinick and Peter "Evil Security Twin Powers… Activate!" Torr. All of these people are dedicated to the pursuit of writing great secure software, and have provided me with both expert advice and strong technical leadership.

Finally, thanks must go to all of my friends and family for their many kind words of encouragement. Special thanks to my partner Leah and my parents Linda and Bruce for their love, patience, and moral support.

Eric Lippert
Seattle, Washington
2002

For Mort

VB.NET

Code Security

Handbook

Table of Contents

Table of Contents

VB.NET

Code Security

Handbook

Introduction

Introduction

The .NET languages now allow you to explicitly express security concepts by making secure programming concepts available as a part of the framework. The rich security classes available to you give both the opportunity and the responsibility to write secure code.

By implementing these concepts in the form of classes in the framework, the .NET runtime makes these new security capabilities available to all .NET programming languages. Though we will concentrate on Visual Basic .NET in this book, the information about the security system applies to other .NET languages as well.

Who is This Book For ?

This book is intended for Visual Basic .NET (VB.NET) programmers who want to write robust, secure code. Since very few developers wish to write brittle, insecure code this should be pretty much all VB.NET programmers!

In the past, the majority of Visual Basic programmers used VB for four purposes:

- ❑ To add rich functionality behind Office documents (and other applications) with VBA

- ❑ To implement forms-based applications

- ❑ To implement components for use in web pages or other applications

- ❑ To implement server-side functionality using VBScript on Active Server Pages

Each of these kinds of development has various aspects concerned with security. Developers of controls usable by web pages, for example, must ensure that a hostile web page cannot use the VB control to delete files on the client, or access unauthorized information. Developers of server-side scripts on ASP pages must ensure that hostile clients cannot access unauthorized information on the server. .Net brings a powerful new security model that can make help all these types of applications secure, if it is used properly.

Throughout we assume that you have a good working knowledge of the VB.NET language, of object-based programming, and of the .NET Framework in general. However, we explain the concepts in detail where necessary.

What does This Book Cover?

❏ **Chapter 1 – Application Security:** gives an overview security issues, discussing what sort of attacks can be mounted against code and the motivation of attackers.

❏ **Chapter 2 – .NET and Security: An Overview:** this chapter introduces the concepts of code- and role-based security, relating them to the .NET and Windows security systems respectively. We cover the key concepts needed to understand the .NET security system, such as the managed stack but most of the chapter is taken up with the .NET code-based security model. In particular, we look at how security policy is applied to code based on evidence, that it turn determines which permissions are granted.

❏ **Chapter 3 – Advanced .NET Security:** here we dig into the more complex features of the .NET security system such as link-time demands, inheritance demands, and using role-based security with .NET.

❏ **Chapter 4 – Security and Customizable Applications:** we look at security and customizable applications, discussing custom evidence and custom policies along the way.

❏ **Chapter 5 – How to Write Insecure Code:** in this and the next chapter, we discuss specific coding patterns, good and bad. We show how to spot both common and rare vulnerabilities and how to fix them up, as well as how to avoid them in the first place. This chapter will concentrate on "worst practices" that produce vulnerabilities.

❏ **Chapter 6 – How to make Code Secure:** this chapter describes the "best practices" that help you prevent the problems we saw in Chapter 5. We conclude the chapter with a handy checklist summarizing the best and worst practices.

❏ **Chapter 7 – Spot the Security Bug:** Being able to put the knowledge contained in this book into practice and spot security bugs in your own and other code is vital. In this chapter, we take several short, realistic methods full of security holes and see if you can spot the vulnerabilities.

What does it Not Cover?

This book is intended to be a handbook for VB.NET programmers who need to understand the .NET security system, who need to understand what common coding mistakes lead to vulnerabilities, and who wish to write solid code that uses the security system to avoid those vulnerabilities. It specifically does not intend to cover:

❑ The architectural design problems inherent in securing large applications. For example: we **will** discuss methods of defending yourself against malicious user data intended to mess with a SQL back-end database. We **will not** discuss how the database should be configured. We will not discuss what encrypted protocols you should use to communicate with your database nor how to ensure that transactions are nonrepudiable, nor how to protect yourself from packet-sniffers capturing and replaying the packets to spoof the server and so on.

❑ The implementation details of the dozens of cryptographic algorithms and subtle differences between them all. For instance, we will discuss some common mistakes made when trying to keep secrets but will not get into the mind-numbing complexity of, say, the differences between various hash algorithms. We will not discuss when you should use, say, Triple DES and when you should use RSA; these choices are complex and far beyond the scope of this book.

❑ The details of properly configuring ASP or ASP.NET servers. The web server's authentication model mostly uses the Windows user-based security system, which we will not cover in great detail. We will discuss briefly how to use code-based security in ASP.NET as well as some common security errors made in server-side code. We will not discuss the differences between basic authentication and Windows authentication or any other ASP security configuration details.

VB.NET

Code Security

Handbook

1

1

Application Security

The intention of this chapter is to lay the groundwork and provide a basic mindset: that hostile people want to do your users harm and that you can help protect them by designing and implementing secure solutions. We will approach this by posing and answering some of the questions you might have about code security:

❑   What do we mean by **security, harm, attackers, vulnerabilities,** and so on?

❑   Who would want to attack my code?

❑   How will they attack my code?

❑   What can I do about it?

We'll start off, however, by looking at what sorts of applications people develop today and why in many cases code security is (or should) a much greater concern than ever before.

The Security Landscape

The applications being developed today are much more loose-knit than the traditional "shrink-wrapped" applications of the past. Applications today may be multi-tiered, running code on both clients and servers. Applications may be composed from disparate parts written by diverse sources. Data may be sent around the world via the Internet, crossing "trust boundaries" as it moves from one machine to another.

In the previous world of monolithic applications there was less need for code-level security because all parts of an application were written together. The data manipulated by these applications was under complete control from end to end. Developing modern applications requires that code security concepts such as permissions and policies must be made explicitly available to developers.

There are many general techniques for writing secure programs that we will discuss throughout this book. Techniques such as verifying that your inputs are well-formed, or running your code with the least privilege are useful in almost every scenario. More specifically, we will look at common scenarios for modern applications such as:

❏   You are writing an application for a user who trusts you, the developer. However, the application may call third-party "customization" components that the user does not trust.

   For example, as a user you probably trust that Internet Explorer was written by the benign developers at Microsoft, but that trusted application could download web pages written by hostile people whom you do not trust. Similarly, you probably trust that Microsoft Excel was written by people who wish you well, but the macros that it runs may contain viruses written by hostile third parties. You may be writing similar sorts of application in VB.NET. How do you protect your users from hostile content while still letting them get work done?

❏   If in the above situation your application provides an object model available to the potentially hostile customization code then your object model must be robust and secure when called by hostile callers. How do you limit the ability of untrustworthy code to take advantage of your object model?

❏   Perhaps you are the one writing a custom component for use in a third party's application and have to consider the case where the users do not fully trust your code. Now the problem is turned around: how do you write code that gets work done when in restricted security environments?

❏   We also cover some of the specific code-level security issues that arise when writing server-side ASP.NET pages. We will not go into the full details of configuring ASP.NET security, as that would take us far afield, but we will cover ways to avoid introducing commonly exploited vulnerabilities.

Note that "design and implementation of secure solutions" implies more than mere careful coding. A secure application is not only well written, but it also makes it easy for the administrators who install the application to make good decisions about its deployment. A secure application has features that make it easy for users to get their work done safely without requiring that they all be security experts.

The focus of this book is on teaching developers how to write secure code that is technically correct. Remember, however, that technical correctness is only one part of the whole security story. Ultimately, developers, administrators and end users all have to take security seriously. If administrators make poor policy decisions, or if users allow themselves to be taken advantage of by "social engineering" then all the technical correctness in the world will not help them.

Why Should I Care about Security?

Obviously, no one wants to write insecure, brittle code. The real question is then "how much should I care?" Unfortunately, in a world with hard deadlines, finding and fixing security problems is often left until it is too late to do a good job.

There are many reasons to make security a high priority. Let's climb up on a soapbox for a moment and proclaim them:

❑ The first and most important reason is that *you have a moral obligation to engineer code that cannot be used to hurt other people*. People depend on their applications and have an entirely reasonable expectation that when used properly the tools you provide will not be used to harm them. In a world where people and businesses depend on timely access to accurate, confidential data a denial of service, theft of data, or data tampering can be extremely harmful.

Unfortunately, due to widespread security problems such as e-mail and macro viruses, we now live in a world where some people literally live in fear of opening e-mails or viewing web pages. Users need to know that their regular, everyday actions will not end up causing themselves harm. Helping to build a secure, trustworthy infrastructure is everyone's responsibility.

❑ Second, *writing insecure code hurts your reputation*. Even if for whatever reason you personally are not vulnerable to the attacks made on your users, producing vulnerable applications is bad for your reputation. Attacks taint not only your code but also the whole platform, which slows adoption of the platform and hence cuts down on the number of customers.

❑ Third, *writing insecure code directly hurts your bottom line*. Having a reputation for writing insecure code will likely result in lower sales or contracts not being renewed. Furthermore, fixing any flaws after the code has shipped is orders of magnitude more expensive than fixing them beforehand. That is especially true of security vulnerabilities. If your code crashes and dies horribly, you can always postpone shipping a fix until the next release. You can find a workaround to keep customers happy until the release. However, serious security flaws in released code often need to be addressed immediately; the attackers will not wait for the next version to be released! Implementing, debugging, testing, and shipping security patches is expensive. Worse, rushed work under pressure often introduces more flaws. The alternative is frequently a Draconian workaround: having users disable major chunks of functionality – assuming that the vulnerable functionality even can be disabled!

❑ Fourth, *there are legal implications in our litigious society*. If your customers can make a case that the insecurities in your code were a result of negligence then they may decide to take legal action against you.

> The simple fact is this: if your code is deployed then it is
> open to attack. Plan for that attack before it happens.

What do we Mean by Security?

In order to enable developers to write secure code and deliver it to customers the .NET
Runtime provides a rather complex, highly configurable security system. It does not
matter whether the security system is the alarm system in your house, the vault at a
bank, or the .NET security system, the purpose of all of them is the same:

> The primary purpose of any security system is to try to
> prevent an attacker's attempts at deliberate harm from
> succeeding (or at least slow them down).

But how exactly do we characterize an attacker? And what exactly do we mean by
harm in the computer world?

Hostile Intent

A security system is concerned with **deliberate** attempts to cause harm; though it is a
useful side effect of a well-implemented security system that it prevents accidental
harm, a security system is intended to handle malicious attacks.

You might feel that no one would want to maliciously cause you or your users harm
but that is simply naïve; employees get disgruntled, unethical competitors engage in
espionage or sabotage, vandals with too much time on their hands write viruses, and
criminals would love to have access the name, address, and credit card numbers you
hold. These are a few possible scenarios; there are as many potential motivations for
attackers as there are potential victims.

Note that in this book we will use the term "attacker" to characterize the source of the
threat. This is generally a more accurate term than the more common "hacker".

> *A hacker is someone interested in gaining a deep understanding of the secrets
> of some system just for the sake of understanding. Hackers are security threats
> in the sense that anyone who can gain unauthorized access to data is a
> threat, but threats come in all shapes and sizes, not just stereotypical hackers.*

Many attackers have no desire whatsoever to understand systems for their own sake;
they just want to cause mayhem or they want to gain knowledge solely to increase
their ability to do harm. Some attackers are merely vandals, and others just want to
establish credibility amongst their peers, for example, by defacing a popular web site.
However, some attackers are outright criminals intent on financial gain.

Attackers come in all levels of sophistication. They may be sophisticated, highly knowledgeable experts or ignorant "script kiddies" running malicious programs written by others. Attackers may be well financed and organized or penniless students working alone. It is often much harder to find security vulnerabilities than it is to exploit them; conversely, even relatively unsophisticated attackers can use exploits found by others.

The best you can do is to design your systems to be resilient against both sophisticated, targeted attacks and the brute force attacks of the script kiddies.

> **Be conservative; overestimate your attackers. If you assume that your attackers are both brilliant and legion then you are more likely to write secure code.**

Surely They Would Not Attack Me!

Assuming that the problem does not exist (or is someone else's problem) is probably the biggest mistake you can make; any deployed software is venerable to attack. However, a number of factors do affect the risk your code is exposed to:

- ❑ How widely it is deployed
- ❑ The value or sensitivity of the information it handles
- ❑ The importance or notability of the organizations using it

You may feel that your project is low risk on all those fronts. However, that implies that your coding efforts will forever languish in obscurity, which in itself isn't a desirable outcome.

Furthermore, the popularity of the Internet and the corresponding rise in software designed to work in networked environments has worked in the attackers' favor. When was the last time you got attacked by a virus on a floppy disk boot sector? Attackers can now launch attacks against networked machines from anywhere in the world. They can move hostile software around extremely easily.

Time is Not on Your Side

Something extremely important to remember about all attackers is this: they have much, much more time on their hands than you do. Attackers will gladly spend days, weeks, or months poring over other people's code looking for vulnerabilities. Unlike you, they have no ship deadlines to meet, no team meetings to attend, and no last minute changes to implement. Attackers can use the same professional quality tools you use to inspect code looking for vulnerabilities, or they can write their own tools.

> **An interesting example of the lengths an attacker (albeit a benign hacker in this case) will go to in creating tools is the successful reverse-engineering of the hardware portion of the XBox security system.** See ftp://publications.ai.mit.edu/ai-publications/2002/AIM-2002-008.pdf **for details. If benign hackers can do it then so can hostile ones.**

Attackers will install your software and then monitor every byte written to or read from the registry and disk, every operating system API called, every string allocated until they know all your secrets. Unlike your users, they will read every word of the documentation, looking for weaknesses in the design.

This is why it pays to design security in to your code from the beginning. If you do not, the attackers will beat you to finding the vulnerabilities simply because they have more time to spend and more impetus to look hard.

Trust, Safety, and Intent

It is an equal failing to trust everybody and to trust nobody.
(18th-century English proverb)

Security experts often use word pairs such as **safe/dangerous, trusted/untrusted,** and **benign/hostile** without clearly distinguishing them from each other. These distinctions are both important and frequently misunderstood. Essentially the differences are these:

A particular assembly is **safe** if it is unable to harm you: modify your disk, steal your data, deny service, and so on. The safety or dangerousness of an assembly is fundamentally a **technical** question: what does the assembly attempt to do? For instance, does it read the disk? Then it might steal secrets. Does it create dialog boxes? Then it might create hundreds of them and make it hard to use your machine.

The level of **trust** you assign to an assembly is essentially the set of permissions you are willing to grant it based on evidence. For instance, if you believe that if an assembly from the Internet is granted permission to access your disk then it might misuse that ability to do you harm, you should not grant the permission. Administrators express their opinions about trust by configuring their policies appropriately. "Do not trust code from the Internet to access the disk" is an example of such a policy.

Whether an assembly is **hostile** or **benign** depends on the mindset and goals of the assembly's author. An assembly that creates a file might be perfectly benign, or it might be creating the file in order to consume all the hard disk space on your machine as a denial-of-service attack. An assembly that creates a dialog box that looks just like the Windows password dialog might be attempting to steal your password.

Unfortunately, there is no way to detect the intent of the programmer. If there were then security would be easy: use your magical ESP powers to see what the programmer was thinking and then just prevent code written by hostile people from running! In the real, non-magical world all that the .NET security system can do is restrict the abilities of an assembly based on the available evidence.

Notice that essentially we use these words technically in the same way we do in everyday speech. A tennis ball is inherently quite **safe** and an axe is inherently quite **dangerous**. Whether someone carrying an axe is **hostile** or **benign** has nothing to do with the axe, but everything to do with their intentions. And whether you **trust** them to do yard work has to do with what **evidence** you have that they're trustworthy. A **policy** that expresses this trust decision might be "Don't let unknown people carrying axes into the yard."

Harm

Now we've considered what motivates people to attack software, it is time look at what **harm** they can cause when they do. In computer security, there are three main categories of harm we need to consider. In order of increasing severity they are:

- ❑ **Denial of service**
- ❑ **Unauthorized access to data**
- ❑ **Data tampering**

These categories are extremely broad and each encompasses a considerable range of possible damage. All of them hurt the user in some way.

Denial of Service

If the attacker wants to keep legitimate users from doing something, they are mounting a Denial-of-Service (DoS) attack. There are many techniques for denying service. For example, a simple DoS attack might consist of providing bad input to a web server causing it consumes large quantities of resources such as memory or disk space. A successful DoS attack against a server could consume enough memory to prevent it from servicing legitimate users' requests.

DoS attacks often use this pattern of consuming all of a finite resource, whether it is memory, disk space, processor cycles, printer paper, file handles, network bandwidth, or screen real estate. The last is common on the World Wide Web; everyone has probably had the experience of going to a web page that constantly spawned off new full-screen windows *ad naseum*. Early versions of Internet Explorer allowed pages to print themselves as many times as the page author wanted.

Unfortunately these sorts of DoS attacks on client machines are practically impossible to stop, though the .NET Framework does have some safeguards protect your disk space and printer paper. Fortunately, they are usually merely annoyances, which can be dealt with by killing the offending process or rebooting the machine. Note, however, that what is an annoyance to a typical home user may be a very serious problem if the client in question is being used by an ambulance dispatcher.

Far more serious are DoS attacks against server machines. If an attacker can cause your server to stop serving up data to your users then that is potentially far more than an annoyance. If those users depend on timely access to data to do their jobs it could be extremely costly. Think about the cost of delaying stock quotes or other pricing data, for example. There are several techniques for mounting DoS attacks against servers. However, most of them are variations on two main patterns: attackers provide bad data that causes the server to misbehave, or they flood the server with bogus requests to slow it down to a crawl.

DoS attacks against servers are often **distributed attacks** (DDoS). In a DDoS the attacker causes many machines to attack the server at the same time, multiplying the effect of the attack. Usually the attacking machines have themselves been compromised by the attacker and are being used without authorization.

A good example is the famous "smurf" attack. The real-world analog to the ping attack is the irksome practical joke whereby the prankster fills out hundreds of "bill me later" magazine subscription cards in your name and then waits for you to be deluged with unwanted mail. In the smurf attack the attacker sends out thousands of "please tell me whether your machine is on the Internet" requests to thousands of machines, but with the sender's address forged to look like your server sent the request. When the thousands of recipients all attempt to tell the target machine that they are up the target machine spends all its time dealing with the unwanted traffic rather than servicing regular clients.

For more information on the specifics of the smurf attack, see
http://www.pentics.net/denial-of-service/white-papers/smurf.cgi.

Simple DoS attacks are easy to pull off and hard to prevent. Usually the heuristics used to mitigate DoS attacks on clients are somewhat arbitrary; for example, Internet Explorer allows web pages to create an unlimited number of message boxes but does not allow them to be created outside of the visible screen area or to fill the entire screen.

We will discuss some possible attacks and defenses in chapters to come, but will concentrate on the other two kinds of harm. The techniques of hardening servers against DDoS attacks is beyond the scope of this book, though we will discuss techniques for making your server-side code robust against attacks in general.

Unauthorized Data Access

It is fair to say that attackers are interested in any and all data they can obtain from your machine. There are many different kinds of data stored on every machine. We can break "data" down further into three classes of data: personal data, configuration data, and authorization data.

Personal data consists of all the information you store on your disk, such as Word documents, databases, or source code. Your files probably contain confidential information. Obviously, it would be harmful to you if attackers could read these files. The potential harm inflicted when data falls into the hands of unauthorized individuals ranges from the trivial (such as having your e-mail address harvested by a spammer) to catastrophic (such as having secret source code or confidential financial data stolen by rivals).

Attackers may also be after information such as personal income statements, credit reports, medical history, and other such highly personal data. Identity theft is a growing problem. Many countries now have laws mandating that companies must take adequate measures to protect such sensitive data.

Configuration data consists of all the information about how your machine is configured. What version of IIS do you have installed? What version of Office? What is your default e-mail client? And so on. Configuration data is usually not stolen for its own sake; rather, it is used as part of a broader attack. For instance, an attacker would certainly like to know what machines on a network have not been updated with the latest security patches! If an attacker knows about some vulnerability in a particular piece of software then an attack that harvests configuration data can make it much easier to successfully pull off the exploit.

This is not to say that attackers will not try to mount specific attacks without this information; additional configuration information just makes the attack easier. Having readily available configuration information is rather like having a complete list of all the people who are careless with their keys in a given neighborhood; you do not need that information to break into cars, but it makes it a lot easier if you do!

Most dangerous is theft of secret authentication and authorization data. These are the secret pieces of data used to authenticate users' identities and hence authorize their various privileges. Credit card numbers, user names and passwords, cryptographic keys, and so on are data used to authenticate users and thereby authorize various actions such as making purchases, gaining access to files, and decrypting secret documents.

Obviously, there is more valuable and less valuable data and the more valuable data should be more carefully protected. That is no excuse for giving away less valuable data free. Almost any information on a machine, such as user names, which applications and services are installed, the values of environment variables, and so on, is of interest to the attacker because it may give some clue as to how to launch a better attack the next time.

Data Tampering

Allowing unauthorized individuals to read your personal, configuration, and authorization data is bad. Allowing them to change it is far worse.

An attacker who can tamper with personal data can cause harm from the blatantly destructive (deleting your files) to subtle changes you'd never notice until it was too late (transposing a few vital numbers in some spreadsheet.)

Subtle attacks are in fact much more dangerous than blatant ones. At least if your files are deleted you know about it right away and can put your disaster recovery plan into effect. (You do have a recovery plan, right?) You can restore the files from your last backup and continue with your life. Even more important is the fact that you know you have been attacked. That means you can find the vulnerability, patch it, and start tracking down the attacker. However, if the attack is so subtle that you never know you were attacked then none of that is true.

If your machine configuration is compromised then it becomes extremely difficult to guard against future attacks. Once attackers can tamper with data by installing their own applications on your disk or by replacing your applications with Trojan horses it is very difficult to keep them from coming back to hurt you again. Clever attackers alter your machine configuration in subtle ways that make it easier for them to mount further attacks later.

The first thing a well-prepared attacker does once they have gained control of your machine through some vulnerability is install a "root kit". A root kit is some software that introduces vulnerabilities, which the attacker can exploit later. Should their present intrusion be detected and the vulnerability they exploited be fixed there will be another way in.

If authorization and authentication data is vulnerable to tampering, then again it becomes extremely difficult to keep the attacker from coming back. If the attacker can create new accounts, change your password, or perform other administrative tasks then securing the machine in the future is quite tricky.

Attackers will often use a particular form of data tampering, **repudiation**, as either part of the attack or the whole attack. Repudiation is tampering with specific data in such a way that it becomes impossible to prove who launched the attack. An attacker who can erase security logs is much harder to detect than one whose every move has been recorded permanently. An attacker who can write someone else's name into security logs can cause considerable harm to the innocent individual named.

Erasing the system logs after a successful attack is just one kind of repudiation. Another more dangerous kind is to actually cause harm through careful deletion; for instance, suppose you could transfer money from account Alpha to account Beta and then erase all record of the transaction from Alpha's computer but not Beta's computer. Banking systems are carefully designed so that transactions are non-repudiable. Multiple redundant systems attempt to ensure that you cannot plausibly say "I never took that money out." Transactions are carefully recorded, frequently reconciled, and audited; your identity is verified through possession of physical artifacts (credit cards), secrets (personal identification numbers), and ability to produce a reasonable facsimile of your signature.

Again, the more valuable the data is, the more carefully it should be protected from tampering. But even seemingly unimportant data should be protected; if unimportant data can be attacked, odds are good that more important data can also be attacked.

How do Attackers do It?

Many of the most widely publicized successful attacks (such as the famous "Code Red" attack) are attacks based on exploiting a single "gaping hole" vulnerability. However, some common attacks are based on a combination of smaller vulnerabilities that add up to a big one.

Before we look at some of the attack patterns used by attackers, however, we should get some jargon carefully defined.

Vulnerabilities and Exploits

> **A vulnerability is any flaw in a piece of software that may be exploited by a motivated attacker to cause harm.**

Note that vulnerabilities are by definition flaws. (We will mostly avoid the imprecise and colloquial term "bug" in this text.) Therefore vulnerabilities are seldom due to the intended behavior of a piece of code. A method that deletes a file is not a vulnerability if it can only be used to delete those files that the user wants deleted! However, if it can be used by hostile code to delete **any** files then it is potentially a very serious vulnerability.

Similarly, if you turn off the security settings in Internet Explorer then you are leaving yourself open to attack. Though that is not necessarily a wise thing to do, it is not a vulnerability in IE; that is by-design behavior. We are concerned with eliminating vulnerabilities that exist as part of the normal operation of a piece of software.

Vulnerabilities lead to **exploits:**

> **An exploit is a successful attack that takes advantage of a particular vulnerability.**

The point of this book is to teach you how to identify these vulnerabilities in your VB.NET code and then **mitigate** them by either making the exploit more difficult or by reducing the maximum possible harm to an acceptable level. There is no such thing as invulnerable software (that also does useful work); any tool can be misused. You can, however, make it difficult for attackers to misuse your software effectively.

Combined Attacks: ILOVEYOU Redux

This has been a very theoretical and general discussion so far. Let's consider a hypothetical situation from the days before the Outlook Security Patch:

Perhaps some attacker wishes to cause some large web site, say
www.SomeBigCompany.com to stop serving pages in an effort to discredit
SomeBigCompany and make them lose face, lose business, and lose value. Perhaps the
attacker has also recently shorted (making a bet that a stock will decline in value)
SomeBigCompany's stock and is looking to make a fast buck by causing investors to
lose confidence in the company.

The attacker writes up a hostile script, perhaps something along the same lines as the
famous ILOVEYOU worm. They then look up "anonymous usenet posting" on Yahoo
for tips on how to easily post information without revealing their identity or IP address.

They then anonymously post it out to USENET newsgroups with the description "Click on
me for free stock tips". Since the USENET posting is anonymous, the attacker can plausibly
repudiate any claim that they are responsible for authoring and spreading the virus.

Eventually someone clicks on the script, executing it. If the hapless victim is not using
a system that restricts the rights of e-mailed scripts (such as one with the Outlook
Security Patch or the Windows XP Software Restriction Policies) then the script runs
with the privileges of the user, not the script's author. The script's author is unknown
and hence should have very few (if any) privileges, but users have considerable
privileges such as the right to run programs, produce files, and write to the disk.
Essentially the script has elevated its privilege from that of an untrusted, unknown user
to that of a trusted, known user.

Attacks in which users or (the software they run) are fooled into believing that hostile
code is some harmless or trustworthy thing are called **spoof attacks.** This particular
kind of spoofing attack, where a human is tricked into performing some dangerous
action by some slick pitch is often called a **social engineering attack**.

The user has executed the untrustworthy code, giving it the privileges of a trusted
application. The script starts by using its elevated privileges to access the user's **data**,
reading the address book of the victim so that it can mail itself around further. It then
tampers with data, installing a small program onto the user's disk such that when the
machine is rebooted, the payload program runs. The payload program does nothing
but wait for the right time to launch the **distributed denial of service attack** against
SomeBigCompany. If the worm is successful and widespread then
www.SomeBigCompany.com gets millions of phony hits at within a short period and soon
becomes unresponsive to real requests.

If the attacker is thinking clearly they also make sure that, the hostile script gives the
user a few stock tips (such as "sell SomeBigCompany"). This both furthers their
ultimate goal of driving the stock price down and keeps the attacked user from
realizing that anything is amiss.

It Could be Worse

So far, we have all been fortunate that such attacks have been generally cruder than the above attack. A more sophisticated attack would take advantage of the elevation of privilege to steal other kinds of information. It would look through the web browser history to find what financial sites all the infected users browsed to recently. It could trap key presses and look for patterns that looked like user names and passwords.

The damage is limited only by the cleverness of the attacker. A cleverly written virus could search for financial data such as Quicken or Microsoft Money files and figure out who owned lots of BigCompany. Many of these files contain all the authorization and authentication information necessary to make trades. It could transmit that information to the attacker who could use it to sell lots of other people's stock BigCompany all at once to attempt to manipulate the price.

A clever worm would then erase all traces of itself once the payload was delivered. Ideally, you would never even know you had been attacked.

This scenario may sound somewhat implausible, but the point is this: attackers are increasingly sophisticated. They use multiple attacks that take advantage of many small mistakes. The complexity of the attack is limited only by the attacker's ingenuity.

Fortunately in reality the ILOVEYOU virus, though extremely destructive (costing businesses hundreds of millions of dollars all told) was not particularly sophisticated. The motivation of the attacker seems to have been random destructiveness rather than personal gain. What is notable about ILOVEYOU, however, (aside from its unprecedented destructiveness) is the variety of techniques used to encourage the continued spread of the virus. If you were to execute the ILOVEYOU virus, it would:

- ❑ E-mail itself to everyone in your address book. This fact led to massive denials of service as e-mail services became overtaxed.

- ❑ Delete all your image files and script files and replace them with copies of the virus. This is obviously destructive and serves to further the spread of the virus by tricking people into re-infecting themselves every time they attempt to open an image file.

- ❑ Hide all your music files and write copies of the virus with similar names to disk.

- ❑ Alter your Internet Relay Chat client configuration so that your IRC use could spread the virus via IRC chat rooms.

- ❑ Download a hostile executable from the Internet and save it to disk so that the hostile executable would start up when you next rebooted your machine.

- ❑ Modify other configuration data in your registry to change your file sharing security settings.

As you can see, it uses a whole litany of techniques to ensure that infected machines remain infected and vulnerable to further attacks. Ironically, its very virulence led to its rapid demise. It was so successful and so destructive that information about the attack was disseminated around the world extremely rapidly. A cleverer virus writer bent on more subtle harm would write a virus that spread slowly rather than announcing itself as an obvious attack.

For more information about the ILOVEYOU virus, see http://www.cert.org/advisories/CA-2000-04.html. The CERT advisory web page is an excellent site in general for obtaining accurate information on current and historical security issues.

What Can I Do about It?

Notice that the fictional combination attack described above depended on multiple failures working together. Addressing any one of them would have prevented this specific attack.

- ❏ If there were no way to post anonymously then the attacker could be easily tracked down and brought to justice. Unfortunately, USENET is fundamentally insecure; postings to USENET are easily repudiated.

- ❏ If all users were trained to not click on untrusted attachments then the virus would not be able to elevate itself to their level of privilege. Unfortunately, it is not reasonable to expect that all users will know this. Recall that a vulnerability is a flaw **in the normal operation** of a program. Clicking on attachments is a normal operation. If the e-mail client refused to run attached scripts on behalf of the user (as Outlook now does) or restricted the rights of that script to a safe subset of all possible behavior then the worm would not be able to spread.

- ❏ The untrustworthy script was able to steal data such as e-mail addresses. If the object model prevented untrustworthy code from accessing the e-mail addresses (again, as Outlook now does) then the worm would be unable to spread.

- ❏ The untrustworthy script was able to install a payload program. If the operating system denied the e-mail program the right to install new programs then the payload program would not be installed.

- ❏ SomeBigCompany's server did not handle many thousands of simultaneous requests well. With good DDoS mitigation features, such as bandwidth throttling, it might weather the storm better.

The ultimate aim of the attacker in this fictional example was to use a virus to launch a DDoS attack against SomeBigCompany. Would patching any one of these holes really be sufficient to prevent all future DDoS attacks against SomeBigCompany? Of course not! If you just fixed the e-mail client to prevent it from giving the contents of the address book to untrustworthy code then the worm writers would just find some other way to spread the worm.

Fixing all of the possible vulnerabilities by training users, securing the object model implementation, denying administration rights to users or processes, and mitigating attacks when they happen is far better than fixing one vulnerability to prevent one attack. This is the basis of the "nested vaults" model that we will advocate in the next section.

Furthermore, do not stop there! If you find a vulnerability in one place, look for vulnerabilities just like it in other places. Look for more vulnerabilities where you found the first one. Software testers know that if you find a flaw, the odds that you have just found the *only* such flaw are quite low.

> **Find every vulnerability you possibly can.**

Mission: Moderately Difficult versus Mission: Impossible

When you are designing new code or reviewing old code for vulnerabilities, think like a movie producer. The people who make caper movies know that a highly trained team breaking in to an ordinary suburban house to steal groceries is not a particularly compelling movie. It is far too easy. A house has dozens of ways into it: the front door, the attached garage, the chimney and windows all come to mind. Many houses have a simple alarm system, and that's about it. The reason people do not steal your groceries is because the reward is not worth the effort, not because the security systems are too strong to defeat.

Far more interesting is to have the Mission: Impossible secret agents penetrate multiple nested puzzles, each deadlier than the last: once they get past the guards and dogs they have to scale the fence, then defeat the locks, the pressure-sensitive floors and the deadly lasers before they obtain whatever treasure is in the vault.

As mentioned above, in the software world the "treasure" for an attacker need not be financial gain. Attackers have a variety of motives, such as malicious revenge or mere random destructiveness. Well designed, secure software mitigates attacks by raising the effort required to exploit vulnerabilities so high that it is not worthwhile to attempt an attack.

Let's continue to think about physical analogs to software security for a moment. Would you trust your assets to a bank that designed its vault like this?

Figure 1

With four locked doors, the attackers need only defeat the weakest of the locks to get at your assets. Like a typical home with many entrances, this design does not provide much difficulty for the attackers at all. The Mission: Moderately Difficult Team could probably handle this vault easily.

Realistic bank vaults are designed like this:

Figure 2

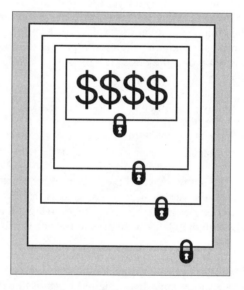

In such a vault, the attacker must penetrate all of the defenses from the weakest to the strongest. Such a system is inherently far more secure; it not only discourages attacks, it also slows down attackers, buying you time to detect and handled them. When we discuss how to write practical, real-world code that is secure against attack, we will use this model of multiple redundant defenses.

Raise the Bar

The aim of writing secure code is not to guarantee the safety of your user's data; there is no such guarantee short of turning off their computers and sinking the machines to the bottom of the ocean (and even that is not completely secure unless you demagnetize the hard disks first).

Rather, the aim is to raise the bar so high and make it so expensive (in money, time, and other resources) to attack your users via your code that the attacker either gives up or pursues some other avenue of attack.

Consider our virus example above. If you were able to lock down every link on that chain of failures then the attacker would have to first figure out how to make an untraceable posting. Then they would have to figure out some way to get the user's secure reader to download a hostile script. Then they would have to figure out how to trick the smart user into running the code. Then they would have to defeat the "sandboxing" system and turn off the system that informs the user that some program is accessing the address book. And so on, and so on.

You take the point by now I'm sure. Most attackers are not willing to go through the software equivalent of getting past the guards, the dogs, the pressure sensors, the motion detectors, the retinal scanners, and the boss monster. They will give up and look for easier vulnerabilities. Make sure those easier vulnerabilities are not in code for which you are responsible!

You Do Not Have to be a Cryptologist

You might find it surprising, but there is no need whatsoever to understand the gritty details of cryptography, the Kerberos authentication system, the implementation details of the .NET Runtime security system or any other heavy-duty **security** code in order to write **secure** VB.NET code. We will not cover the implementation details of any of these technologies in this book.

Writing **security** code requires years of study and training. Writing **secure** code requires the same skills as writing any correct code: knowledge of the system and attention to detail. Or, put another way:

> **Most attacks succeed because they exploit vulnerabilities caused by sloppy coding and/or incorrect assumptions found in code that has nothing to do with security features.**

To write secure VB.NET code you need to have only two things:

❑ First, a good working knowledge of the .NET security system. For example, it is not necessary to have a deep understanding of the cryptography of the strong assembly name algorithm. It is necessary to understand what strong names are and what they are for.

❑ Second, specific knowledge of common coding patterns that lead to vulnerabilities in your code plus the ability to carefully structure your code with multiple levels of defense against attackers. We will come back to this "nested vaults" concept repeatedly.

This book will give you specific knowledge of how to use the .NET Runtime security system (without delving too deep into its underlying implementation). We will also cover many possible vulnerabilities and the corresponding attacks that exploit them.

Remember, however, that the .NET Runtime security system is a tool, not a panacea. Like any tool, it is not useful until you know how to use it and then use it correctly. Once you understand how to use it, how to think like an attacker, and how to carefully build robust systems with many levels of defense you will not only be able to write really secure code, but your code will be more robust in general.

Take the Long View

Finally, if you take away only one thing from this book it should be this: Writing secure VB.NET code requires a process. Security is not a "feature" that can be easily tacked on at the end of the development cycle. Think about the entire life cycle of a piece of code, from the early design stages to the implementation, testing, release, service releases, and eventual replacement by future versions. At every stage, there are security implications.

❑ Good **designers** take security into account from the beginning of the design process.

❑ Good **developers** make writing secure code a priority and implement the code to handle attacks.

❑ Good **testers** look for vulnerabilities before the release.

❑ Good **release managers** have a plan for what to do if a security flaw is found after the product ships to customers.

The converses are obvious. An application that was not designed to be secure, which was implemented by sloppy developers who don't understand the security system and tested by testers who do not know how to attack code, will undoubtedly contain vulnerabilities. When (not if!) they are exploited your users will not be very happy if you do not have a plan to save them!

Summary

To briefly sum up the story so far: the modern world of ubiquitous, high-speed networking has led to a new style of application programming in which code and data from disparate locations can travel quickly and easily. Though this has obvious benefits to everyone, it also makes security a much higher priority since it also makes mounting attacks easier.

Any successful software tool that does something useful could be misused by a determined attacker. Attackers will likely probe your software looking for vulnerabilities that they can then exploit to cause harm to users. Attackers like to deny service to authorized, benign users. They like to read data they are not authorized to read, they like to tamper with data they are not authorized to write, and they like to get away with it undetected. They do these things for the same large number of reasons that people have always hurt each other, such as revenge, greed, or sheer random vandalism. Successful attacks can be enormously damaging.

Attackers are willing to spend considerable time and effort in order to effect their exploits. Clever attackers may discover vulnerabilities and then widely publicize them to relatively ignorant "script kiddies" who can mount the attack without understanding the details. Clever attackers look for both "gaping hole" exploits (Code Red) and design attacks where many small vulnerabilities add up to one big one (ILOVEYOU).

Fortunately, there is something you can do, and you do not have to be a security expert either. Most security flaws have nothing to do with "security" code but rather are mistakes made in code that has nothing to do with the security system. By understanding the proper use of the tools provided by the .NET Runtime security system, you can design software that protects your users' data at a level commensurate with its importance. Good, secure designs force hostile attackers to defeat multiple defenses.

In the rest of this book, we will cover the usage of the .NET Runtime security system as a tool to help mitigate potential attacks against software written in VB.NET.

VB.NET
Code Security
Handbook
2

2

.NET and Security: An Overview

In this chapter, we will start with a discussion of the difference between role-based and code-based security systems, giving some examples of each with which you may already be familiar. Then, we will have a brief overview of some basic .NET concepts, which are relevant to the security system: stacks, assemblies, managed code and so on. Finally, we will dig into the .NET security namespaces and see how the various classes implement security concepts such as permissions and policies.

Role and Code Security

The .NET Runtime security system provides both **role**-based and **code**-based security. The distinction between the two is essentially this:

> **Role-based security systems grant or deny privileges based on data associated with the user running the code. Code-based security systems grant or deny privileges based on data associated with the code itself.**

Let's take a brief look at familiar examples of each: the **Windows security system** can be thought of as a primarily role-based security system whereas the **Internet Explorer security system** is primarily a code-based security system.

Note that this book does not intend to give a detailed description of either the Windows security system or the Internet Explorer security system. The Windows authentication and access control technology is quite complex, as are IE's specific mechanisms for ensuring secure web browsing. Rather, these are familiar examples to illustrate some of the features of role- and code-based security models.

After we look at these examples, we will discuss the organization of the .NET Framework security namespaces in general before digging into the specific classes used to implement code security in VB.NET programs. We will cover role-based security classes and advanced code security classes in the next chapter.

Security in Windows NT

Security for NT-based operating systems (Windows NT, Windows 2000, Windows XP, and .NET Server) is based upon the notion that the user logged on to the workstation is not necessarily the owner of the machine. The NT-based operating systems were designed for enterprise applications where there might be confidential files and where users ought not to be allowed to install whatever software they chose upon their boxes.

For example, if Alice the accountant logs on to a shared machine she will only be able to read those files and run those programs for which she has been granted the appropriate permissions. If she attempts to perform unauthorized actions (such as deleting protected files she does not own, installing new software, and so on), the Windows security system will prevent her from doing so. If Annette the administrator logs on to the same machine then she has full control over the entire contents of the machine and may configure it as she wishes.

This is a good example of a more general security principle: **the principle of least privilege**. We will come back to this general principle several times in this book.

> **Secure software grants enough rights for users to do what they need to do and no more.**

Not granting Alice the same administrative rights as Annette mitigates two general classes of security vulnerabilities. First, suppose Alice becomes a disgruntled employee. She will be unable to mount any attack that requires full administrative rights. She will be unable to lock other users out of the system, delete all their files, and so on. Second, suppose Alice remains benign but somehow a hostile program runs while she is logged in. (Perhaps she is infected with a virus that got past her virus checker, or perhaps she downloaded a hostile program from the Internet.) Since the hostile code runs with Alice's security token it too is unable to do anything that requires more rights than Alice has.

The Windows security model allows rights to be configured both for individual users and for groups of users. For example, an administrator could create an Excel file, which could be read by all users in the "full time employees" group but only modifiable by members of the "accountants" group.

When you log on to a Windows machine, the operating system first **authenticates** you. To verify that you really are who you say you are the machine may simply ask you for a password. More hard-core administrators might configure their machines to require authentication through additional hardware: a "smart card" reader or a biometric device that scans your thumbprint for instance.

Regardless of the technique used behind the scenes, somehow the operating system determines if the person logging in has supplied *sufficient* **evidence** of really being the owner of the given user name. Determining who you are is obviously a necessary first step in determining whether you are **authorized** to perform certain tasks.

The operating system then produces a **security token**. A security token is a data structure that contains two things. First, it contains **security identifiers** that describe who you are and your user group membership. Second, it contains a list of **privileges** you have been granted by the operating system.

The list of privileges is used to determine what tasks **in general** you are allowed to perform: are you allowed to log on? Run a backup program that reads other people's files? Debug another user's program? These are all privileges. You are granted the privileges associated with all the groups to which you belong.

The security identifiers for you and your groups are used to determine which **specific** objects (files, registry keys, and so on) you are allowed to access. Each file, registry key, and so on has an Access Control List (ACL), which determines which users and groups are allowed to, say, read it or delete it.

You can see the ACL of a file or folder by right-clicking on it to view the property page and selecting the Security tag. (Provided you possess permission to read the ACL, of course!)

Here, for example, you can see that one group (Administrators), one user, and the special operating system account (discussed below) are on the Access Control List for my "My Documents" folder. You can also see that the administrators group has been granted full rights. Anyone not on this list and not in a group on this list is granted no rights to the folder.

Suppose that you're logged in and authenticated on a Windows machine and decide to open a file using Excel. However what happens if you, or any of the groups you belong to, do not have read access privileges for that file? **You** should be denied read access, but how does the security system know that **Excel** should be prevented from accessing the file?

Essentially Windows assumes that any program that you started is running on your behalf; while those programs are running they can do anything you can do, and nothing you cannot. Every process running on the machine (and every thread in every process) has a copy of the security token of the account that started the process.

You might be wondering what security token is associated with code that runs while no user is logged in. For example, the various services such as web servers, e-mail servers and so on usually run constantly no matter who is logged in. Furthermore, it makes little sense to have the permissions and rights associated with long-running services change as users log in and out of the server!

Fortunately, the operating system also has security tokens that represent special "non human" accounts, such as the operating system itself and services such as the web server. The SYSTEM account used by the operating system is the most highly privileged account; any process running with a SYSTEM security token has full rights to do anything to the machine.

Code Security in Windows

The Windows security system is quite complex and we will not delve into it very deeply here. Though we have emphasized the role-based security aspects of Windows there are many other parts of the whole security story. For example, the new Software Restriction Policies system in Windows XP is a good example of a code-based security system integrated into Windows. This feature allows administrators to set policies that can prevent particular pieces of code from executing on any machine in a particular domain. It is particularly useful for halting the spread of viruses but can also be used to stop people running software that prevents a security threat.

Security in Windows 95/98/ME

The "down-level" Windows platforms (95, 98, and ME) were designed primarily for consumer use. While these operating systems do have an optional user-logon system, this is not a security system. Rather, it is simply a way to allow different machine users to have their own custom settings applied when they use the machine. There is no strong authentication, there are no ACLs on files, and there are no users with fewer rights than every other user. Effectively every user is a machine administrator and has full access to every feature of the operating system.

The Home edition of Windows XP is similar in that though it can be configured to have full NT user security, the out-of-the-box default is for all users to be machine administrators. This is for backwards compatibility with the down-level Windows platforms.

Security in Internet Explorer

The Windows NT security system is designed to restrict the rights of users by authenticating those users, determining what they are authorized to do, and ensuring that all programs that run on their behalf are given the same rights as the user. Suppose that you log in and start up Internet Explorer, then browse to a random web page on the Internet that contains some script:

```
<script language="vbscript">
Set FSO = CreateObject("Scripting.FileSystemObject")
FSO.DeleteFile "C:\Blah.txt", True
</script>
```

It should be obvious that this script would attempt to delete a (possibly vital) file from your file system. The script runs in Internet Explorer, which like any other process you start has your security token. If you have the right to delete that file then when the page renders IE could delete the file on your behalf. That might not be what you wanted to happen; perhaps you just wanted to surf the web unmolested by people trying to interfere with your file system.

Clearly, it is undesirable to offer all your privileges to anyone who happens to put up a hostile web page. Equally, to prevent all web page script code from running would make the web a dull place. After all, most pages with script are harmless and use the script for benign purposes. This is yet another instance of the aforementioned **principle of least privilege**. We can state it slightly differently in the context of a code-based security system:

> **Secure software grants just enough rights to a chunk of code so that it can do what the user wants.**

IE solves this problem by implementing its own security system independent of the underlying Windows security model. In IE's code-based security model the "server address" portion of the URL of every page is noted. All the scripts and objects created by a page are tagged with the server address of the page.

IE assigns each page into a certain **zone** based on the origin of the page. IE has five zones: Internet, Intranet, Trusted, Restricted, and a special implicit zone Local Machine, which is used for code run from the users own machine. You can put sites for which you wish to allow less stringent security checks into the Trusted zone; and similarly, put web sites that you suspect may be hostile into the Restricted zone.

When IE runs a script, it determines what restrictions should be placed upon the script by checking the zone of the page. For instance, a page loaded from a Trusted site might be granted the right to create potentially dangerous objects (such as the File System Object). That same page might produce a warning dialog when run from the Internet Sites zone and an error when run from the Restricted zone. (The actual behavior is configurable in the Security tab of the IE options dialog.)

You might wonder why IE does not simply use the Windows security system to solve the problem of web sites doing unwanted things. For instance, IE could modify its own security token, removing privileges that hostile pages need to do dangerous things. Perhaps it could create a security token with no rights to read the disk or do other harmful things, and then run the browser in a thread with this token rather than the user's token.

Unfortunately, that solution would not completely solve all the security problems associated with web browsing. Consider this scenario:

Imagine a page with a navigation bar frame on the left and a browsing frame beside it. If the user navigates the browsing frame to a different web site then the script running from the navigation bar frame must not be able to access any information about the browsing frame. If it could then hostile web page authors could create a page with an invisible "navigation bar" frame in order to read information about all the web sites you visit and post that private information back to the invisible frame's host. That would lead to potentially huge vulnerabilities; if you type a password into the browser then you assume that only the site to which you posted the password can actually receive it.

The problem essentially is that pages from disparate sites must be able to render in the same browser without accessing any information about each other. This problem cannot easily be solved with Windows user-based security. The Windows security system was designed to restrict the rights of users, not pages in framesets. IE's security system needs to be more granular and flexible.

Thus, the Internet Explorer implementers had to develop their own security system, which tracks the origins of all pages in the frameset, and prevents pages from one site from accessing any information about pages from a different site. Once a system for tracking the origin of every page is in place then it is relatively easy to categorize those pages into zones and restrict their rights accordingly.

One can think about the behavior of the IE security system quite independently of the Windows security system. However, even though IE's security system is conceptually independent of the Windows security system, both are in effect while IE is running! Suppose, for example, you browse to a page in the Intranet zone. Suppose further that the IE security system grants the page the right to load information from a particular file stored in a shared directory somewhere on your intranet. Since IE is running with your security token, the attempt to read the file will still fail if your account does not have permission to do so. The Windows security system is always on, even when other security systems such as the IE or .NET Runtime security systems are on as well.

IE's security mechanism is complex and highly configurable; we have barely scratched the surface. The details of any one aspect alone, such as how exactly objects are downloaded and created would take us far afield. The point we wish to get across is this:

> **Windows restricts the rights of users by authenticating their identities and granting them rights accordingly. IE's security system by contrast restricts the rights of individual chunks of code (on web pages) based on evidence describing the origins of the pages. It also restricts the ways in which these chunks of code may interact.**

The .NET security system needs to solve the same basic three problems: to restrict the rights of programs based on who is running them, to restrict the rights of chunks of code based on where they came from, and to restrict the ways in which code from disparate locations interacts.

.NET Security Concepts

Now that we have a basic idea of what we mean by role-based and code-based security, we can take a detailed look at how the .NET Runtime implements these concepts. The remainder of this chapter will mostly concentrate on code-based security. The next chapter will explore role-based security and some more advanced features of the code-based security system.

However, before we get into the details of the Framework's security namespaces we should clearly define some jargon associated with the .NET Runtime. What exactly do we mean by "managed code"? What is the "managed stack"? What is an "assembly"? What is an "appdomain"? What are the security implications of these things?

Managed Code

You have probably heard that one of the principle features of the .NET Runtime is that it is a system for executing **managed code**. What exactly does this mean? Essentially two things: first, the .NET Runtime provides useful services (such as a garbage-collecting memory manager) to all managed code. Providing these services in the runtime makes it easier for developers to write solid code. Second, it provides an implementation of abstract "virtual" machine that can be choosy about what code gets to run. The latter feature has interesting security implications; for instance, the .NET Runtime restricts certain malformed (and potentially hostile) kinds of code from running. In particular, the .NET Runtime checks code for **type safety**.

As Visual Basic programmers, you are already used to programming in a managed environment. The VB6 Runtime provides many of the same features as the .NET Runtime such as automatic garbage collection and type safety. However:

> While many languages, such as VB6, Java, VBScript, JScript, and so on execute in "managed" runtimes, henceforth we will reserve the word "managed" to specifically mean "managed by the .NET Runtime". All code not managed by .NET will be referred to as "unmanaged" code even if it is running in a type-safe virtual machine such as the Java VM, the VB6 Runtime or the Windows Scripting engines.

The Managed Intermediate Language

When you compile a Visual Basic .NET executable the compiler does not actually generate the machine code for your processor and write it into an executable file. Rather, it generates code in the .NET Intermediate Language (IL) and writes that into the executable assembly. When the .NET Runtime loads the assembly, it translates it into machine language "on the fly". This translation process is called "Just-In-Time (JIT) compilation" or more concisely, "jitting". The IL is translated to machine language "just in time" for it to run.

You can see the IL in any assembly (as well as other internal details) with the handy ILDASM tool that comes with the .NET Runtime SDK.

Type Safety

Perhaps the best way to understand what we mean by type safety is to look at some languages that are not type safe. Type-unsafe unmanaged languages such as C and C++ allow badly written programs like this fragment:

```
// C++
struct Rectangle
{
   short height;
   short width;
};
// ...
long myinteger = 123;
Rectangle myrectangle = { 10, 20 };
void * pointer = &myrectangle; // void* may refer to anything.
myinteger = *((int *)pointer);
```

If you do not speak C++ fluently, essentially this program takes the memory associated with a `Rectangle` object and treats it as though that memory actually stored an integer. This program is not type safe; only things that really are long integers should be stored in variables of type `long`. However, this program fragment would actually compile and run; but the results at run time would vary with implementation!

The equivalent program in any version of Visual Basic would compile but a type mismatch error would be generated when it was run. (If you compile this for VB.NET using the /optionstrict flag this error will even be caught at compile time):

```
' VB.NET

Module Module1

    Public Structure Rectangle
        Dim Height As Short
        Dim Width As Short
    End Structure

    Sub Main()
        Dim MyInteger As Long
        MyInteger = 123
        Dim MyRectangle As Rectangle
        MyRectangle.Height = 10
        MyRectangle.Width = 20
        Dim Ob As Object
        Ob = MyRectangle
        MyInteger = Ob ' Type mismatch: Rectangle cannot be cast to Long
    End Sub

End Module
```

It is clearly beneficial to disallow such badly written programs; languages like C are famous for allowing careless programmers to compile badly broken but hard-to-debug code. Type-safe languages bring these sorts of errors to the fore early so that developers can find and fix these problems as soon as possible.

It certainly seems odd that C++ allows you to stuff an instance of one data type into a variable of a completely different type. However, that fact alone does not lead to an obvious security problem. A slightly different example indicates why the managed .NET Runtime checks for type safety as part of the security system:

```
// C++
class MyThing
{
public:
    int id;
private:
    int secret_passcode;
// ...
};

// Hostile code wishes to determine secret passcode.
int ExtractSecrets(MyThing * thing)
{
    int * array = &thing->id;
    return array[1];
}
```

This function violates the type contract of MyThing. According to the class declaration, the contents of secret_passcode are only accessible from the methods of the MyThing class, but this function outside the class has managed to get the information out. It does so by taking advantage of the fact that id and secret_passcode are **likely** to be stored one after the other in memory, just as if in an array of integers. The hostile code violates the type system by treating the contents of the class as an array rather than an instance of MyThing. A similar program could be used to change the contents of private memory.

The Verifier

The .NET Runtime does not allow such chicanery. In managed code, any attempt to defeat type safety will result in some kind of error. In some cases, the error may be produced before the code even runs. The .NET security system runs a type-safety verification program over assemblies before they are executed, which catches obvious violations of the type-safety rules, and may prevent unverifiable code from running at all.

A command-line version of this program comes with the .NET Runtime SDK; you can use the peverify.exe utility to check any .NET assembly for type safety, should you ever need to. The verifier primarily looks for situations where type safety could be violated but also checks for potential problems such as misuse of the managed stack (see below).

In some cases such as the Rectangle example above the violation cannot be caught until run time. In this case, the verifier sees an assignment from Rectangle to Object (which **is** legal) and from Object to Long (which **might** be legal because the object might actually be a number). The verifier is not clever enough to determine that this particular program will always fail so it passes it, but the .NET Runtime will detect the violation at run time.

The Managed Stack

Suppose you write a short VB.NET program (in this case a simple console application), compile it, and then execute it:

```
' StackExample.vb

Imports System

Public Module StackExample

  Private Sub SayHello()
    Console.WriteLine("Hello")
  End Sub

  Private Sub SayGoodbye()
    Console.WriteLine("Goodbye")
  End Sub

  Public Sub Main()
```

```
      SayHello()
      SayGoodbye()
   End Sub

End Module
```

While the program is running the .NET Runtime internally maintains a data structure known as the **call stack**. There is one call stack per thread. The call stack consists of a list of **stack frames**, one per procedure call. When the runtime begins executing a new sub or function it creates a new stack frame describing the procedure (and information associated with it, such as the values of the arguments and local variables) and sticks the frame at the head of the list. When the current procedure (which is the one at the start of the list) returns then the stack frame is removed from the start of the list and destroyed.

In this example the call stack starts with just one entry: [Main]:

❏   Main() calls SayHello() and the call stack becomes [SayHello, Main]

❏   SayHello() calls WriteLine() and the call stack becomes [WriteLine, SayHello, Main]

❏   Writeline() eventually returns. The call stack becomes [SayHello, Main] again.

❏   SayHello() eventually returns. The call stack becomes [Main] again.

❏   Main calls SayGoodbye() and the call stack becomes [SayGoodbye, Main].

❏   And so on.

You see how this goes I'm sure. Eventually Main() returns and the program ends. The point is that the .NET Runtime must maintain a careful list so that when a function returns, the Runtime knows to what point execution is returning.

The .NET Runtime uses the managed stack for other purposes as well, including some that are of considerable importance to the security system. As we will see later in this chapter and throughout the rest of this book, **the .NET Runtime annotates the managed call stack with security information about the procedures on the stack**.

"A Stack" Versus "The Stack"

Note that a stack is **any** data structure that behaves like a "last in, first out" (LIFO) list. LIFO lists are extremely useful data structures and are used in many algorithms, not just for tracking the current execution state. If you need a data structure like this to implement some algorithm, you can use the convenient System.Collections.Stack object provided by the .NET Framework.

> **For the remainder of this book we will use the word "stack" to refer specifically to the managed call stack, not to LIFO lists in general.**

Examining the Managed Call Stack Yourself

The .NET Framework provides a class that allows you to write diagnostic programs that inspect the current state of the call stack:

```vb
' StackTrace.vb

Imports System
Imports System.Diagnostics

Public Module StackExample

  Private Sub ShowStack()
    Dim Trace As New StackTrace()
    Dim Frame As StackFrame
    Dim FrameNum As Integer
    Dim StackList As String = "[ "
    ' Iterate through the Stack extracting the methods names found
    For FrameNum = 0 To Trace.FrameCount - 1
      Frame = Trace.GetFrame(FrameNum)
      StackList = StackList & Frame.GetMethod().Name & " "
    Next
      Console.WriteLine(StackList & "]")
  End Sub

  Private Sub SayHello()
    Console.WriteLine("Hello")
    ShowStack()
  End Sub

  Private Sub SayGoodbye()
    Console.WriteLine("Goodbye")
    ShowStack()
  End Sub

  Public Sub Main()
    ShowStack()
    SayHello()
    SayGoodbye()
  End Sub

End Module
```

Compile the program with debug information (so that the stack trace can determine the names of all the methods) and you'll see that the complete call stack (except for the call to the StackTrace constructor itself) is captured by the trace.

```
> vbc /debug:full StackTrace.vb
> StackTrace.exe
[ ShowStack Main ]
Hello
[ ShowStack SayHello Main ]
Goodbye
[ ShowStack SayGoodbye Main ]
```

This is a useful diagnostic technique, particularly since you can extract stack trace information from caught exceptions to determine the source of the exception.

Assemblies

We have encountered the word "assembly" a few times already without clearly defining it. Probably the simplest way to think about assemblies is that they are containers for executable code. Some assemblies contain code that is to be used like an application; these have the EXE suffix like any other application. Some contain code that is used as a class library or a custom control; these have the DLL suffix.

> *It is worth noting that is also possible to create assemblies consisting of multiple files using the .NET assembly linker tool,* al.exe. *This can be useful for several reasons; for instance, you can link together modules written in different languages, or enhance performance by not loading the whole assembly in one go.*

If assemblies are merely executables and libraries, why introduce new jargon? Because .NET assemblies provide additional features, many of which have security implications. For example, assemblies provide a "strong naming" facility that ensures that when your assembly loads a library assembly it is loading the right one. We will discuss the strong naming facility in brief below and in detail in Chapter 6. Assemblies also provide a visibility rule: we discuss the Friend visibility modifier in Chapter 5. Finally, assemblies expose attributes that define their security requirements. We will discuss assembly security attributes below.

Application Domains

All code running on a Windows system is contained with in a process that controls physically isolated resources such as memory needed by the executing code. Processes are also an important security concept and inter-process communication is controlled by the Windows security system. This greatly enhances security but complicates inter-process communication. .NET introduces a further level of abstraction, the **appdomain**, which is a logical subdivision of a process. All managed code runs in a specific appdomain and many appdomains may run in a single process.

The .NET Runtime provides appdomains in part because they have many of the security advantages of process isolation but are not as resource-intensive as spinning up a new process. Appdomains have the security semantics mentioned in our discussion of the IE security model: code in different appdomains may be easily prevented from accessing code in other appdomains in the same process.

Security Namespaces in the .NET Framework

The .NET Runtime was designed to be a foundation for developers to easily create powerful and secure software solutions. The .NET Runtime has many features that enable it to lock down on the rights granted to code, both based on evidence about the user running the code (that is, role-based security) and evidence about the code itself (that is, code-based security).

Developers like to write programs that manipulate objects. Objects are a convenient way to aggregate functionality into one place. They provide a level of abstraction that permits the developer to treat the object as a "black box" that performs some task, freeing the developer from the burden of understanding the object's implementation details. The .NET Framework was specifically designed so that the .NET Runtime's security concepts would be available to developers in the form of objects. That way you, the developer, can write programs that use the security system as easily as you would use any other object model.

There are six namespaces used to organize the classes that represent and implement these security concepts. They are:

- `System.Security`
- `System.Web.Security`
- `System.Security.Cryptography`
- `System.Security.Principal`
- `System.Security.Policy`
- `System.Security.Permissions`

In this section, we will provide a brief overview of the namespaces that contain classes used to represent security concepts and briefly define those concepts. Later in this chapter, we will cover the interactions of **Policy** and **Permissions** in more detail, and in the following chapter, we will explore **Principals** in more detail as well as some of the more advanced code security features.

The Security Namespace

Ironically, the `System.Security` namespace is the least interesting of the five. It contains:

- Classes that represent sets of permissions. We will discuss the `PermissionSet/NamedPermissionSet` classes further when we discuss permissions.

- A `SecurityException`, which is thrown when any security error occurs, and `VerificationException`, which is thrown when the .NET Runtime's attempt to verify an assembly fails. Since the primary cause of a `SecurityException` is a failed attempt to obtain permission to do something, we shall discuss it in more detail when we discuss permissions.

❑   The `SecurityManager` class, which has useful functions for working with policies, so we will discuss it further when we discuss policies.

❑   Security attributes `SuppressUnmanagedCodeSecurityAttribute` and `UnverifiableCodeAttribute`. `SuppressUnmanagedCodeSecurityAttribute` is used to improve performance of managed code that must frequently call unmanaged code; we shall discuss its recommended usage in more detail in Chapter 4. `UnverifiableCodeAttribute` is a module-level attribute that is only of use to compiler writers and hence will not be covered further.

❑   `SecurityElement`, is a class used to help the CLR encode security information in XML format. We will not discuss security persistence further in this text; very few applications need to define custom security objects and persist them in XML format.

The Web Security Namespace

This namespace contains the classes used to manage the aspects of security specific to web servers. They are designed to make it easy to implement Passport authentication on web servers, handle security issues involving web page redirection and other server-specific tasks.

Though we will cover some coding design flaws that frequently lead to security vulnerabilities on servers we will not cover the use of the classes in this namespace in this text.

The Cryptography Namespace

The `System.Security.Cryptography` namespace contains classes that you can use to encrypt and decrypt data for secure storage and transmission, as well as related tasks such as generating unguessable random numbers, hashing documents, and so on.

Cryptography is a complex subject worthy of an entire book of its own. Cryptography and security are often mistaken for each other, but it is important to remember two things. First, many security vulnerabilities have nothing whatsoever to do with cryptography. Second, for the class of problems where cryptography is useful the correct choice of cryptographic algorithms, key management strategies, and so on is vital. One size most assuredly does not fit all in the world of crypto algorithms.

Describing the correct usage of the many classes in the `System.Security.Cryptography` namespace could fill the whole of this book. However, we will discuss poor cryptography practices in Chapter 5 and the use of the random number generator in Chapter 7.

The Principal Namespace

The `System.Security.Principal` namespace contains the classes used to manage role-based security in the .NET Runtime. As we know, role-based security is the notion of restricting the rights of code based on the identity of the current user and the roles that the authenticated user may play.

For example, you might develop an e-mail application where there are regular users and administrators. If the current user is not an administrator then your program could refuse to allow the user to change the e-mail server used by the application.

The .NET Runtime's security system is based upon the notion of **identity** and **principal** objects.

> **An identity object represents a specific entity, such as a user. A principal object contains an identity object, knows which roles that identity may perform, and may be used to act as the identity.**

If we compare this with the Windows security system example (which we discussed above) the user is equivalent to an identity object; and the security tokens act as principals. A token represents a specific user and knows the groups to which the user belongs. A token may be associated with processes that must run with the same rights as the user.

Note that the .NET Runtime's role-based security system is both integrated with and more general than the underlying Windows security system. Though you certainly may use Windows to authenticate users and restrict privileges based on Windows principals, you may also implement your own specific identities, principals, and roles.

The namespace contains five classes:

- ❑ `GenericIdentity` and `GenericPrincipal` allow you to define your own identities and roles for use with the security system.

- ❑ `WindowsIdentity` and `WindowsPrincipal` represent Windows-authenticated users and their principals.

- ❑ `WindowsImpersonationContext` is the class used to revert to the original user after temporarily impersonating another user.

We shall go into more details on the use of identities and principals in Chapter 3, and will cover some potential vulnerabilities introduced by careless use of impersonation in Chapter 5.

The Policy and Permissions Namespaces

The `System.Security.Policy` and `System.Security.Permissions` namespaces contain the classes that represent the .NET Runtime's code-based security system. We shall spend the rest of this chapter exploring the contents of these namespaces and describing the functions the classes play in implementing a code-based security system.

Code Security (From Ten Thousand Feet)

First let's describe how the .NET Runtime code security system works at a high level, and then we will more precisely define all the terms throughout the rest of the chapter. Essentially the code security system works like this:

When an **appdomain** loads an **assembly,** the **policy** system compares the **evidence collection** of the assembly to the **membership rules** of every **code group**, then determines to which code groups it belongs.

For example, suppose your machine is configured to recognize three code groups: the "All Code" group, the "Internet" code group, and the "Microsoft" code group. If the available evidence indicates that the assembly was downloaded from the Internet but was not implemented by Microsoft then the assembly would belong to the "All Code" and "Internet" code groups but not the "Microsoft" code group.

Each code group is associated with a particular **permission set**. A permission set consists of a list of **permissions**, which are objects that represent rights to perform various tasks (such as accessing the file system, creating user interface elements, changing security policy and so on).

The policy system logically combines the permission sets together to determine the **grant set** for the assembly. If when the .NET Runtime runs the code in the assembly it attempts an action controlled by a permission (say, it tries to create a window) then the security system does a **stack walk** to see if the assembly and its callers were granted the appropriate permission. If not then it prevents the "dangerous" operation from succeeding by throwing a **security exception**.

The Evidence Collection

Code security begins with evidence; evidence is the basic information that ultimately determines the rights and restrictions placed upon an assembly by the .NET Runtime policy evaluator.

Evidence is represented in the .NET Runtime by the `Evidence` object in the `System.Security.Policy` namespace. The `Evidence` object is a collection object, though slightly unusual in that it actually is two collections: a collection of **host evidence** and a collection of **assembly evidence**.

We need two collections, as it is extremely important that not all the evidence comes from the assembly itself. For example, the policy system usually grants *every* permission to any assembly that has the "I came from the local machine" evidence object. If evidence only came from the assembly itself then a hostile developer could put an assembly with this evidence up on the Internet and when you ran it, the policy system would grant full rights!

To prevent this problem, objects representing evidence known by the code loading the assembly go into the host evidence collection. Objects representing evidence specifically associated with the assembly go in the assembly collection.

Both collections can contain objects of any type. There are no restrictions on what objects may be used as evidence because the policy system is designed to be extensible. If you need to, you should be able to define your own custom objects to be used as evidence by the policy evaluator; in fact, we shall do so at the end of this chapter.

There are, however, some standard objects used as evidence. The items of evidence that usually actually travel with an assembly are the **publisher signature** and **strong name**, which indicate who wrote the assembly and its integrity in a cryptographically strong manner and the **hash**. The other kinds of evidence (**zone**, **URL**, and **site**) are determined by the .NET Runtime and describe where the assembly came from.

> **By default, when loading an assembly the .NET Runtime determines the evidence for you. If, however, your program explicitly loads another assembly then you may pass an evidence object in to the loader set up with whatever custom evidence you like.**

The Hash

A hash (sometimes called a digest) is fundamentally a hundred-or-so-bit number that uniquely identifies an assembly. It is generated by passing the assembly through a hash function. Cryptographically strong hashes are often referred to as digital signatures.

You might immediately wonder how a hash of any small, fixed length can **uniquely** identify an assembly. After all, a typical assembly is likely to be several *million* bits long. Obviously, the number of possible assemblies outnumbers the number of possible hashes by a mind-numbingly large factor.

The trick is that a hash is only statistically unique. Notice that with 128 bits there are an immense number of possible hashes. The number of assemblies that will ever actually be produced is a vanishing small fraction of the number of hashes available. Therefore, there are more than enough numbers available to uniquely identify every assembly.

A short, unique identifier for every assembly is useful evidence because an administrator could obtain the hashes of known-to-be-hostile assemblies (viruses, for instance) and create policies preventing execution of those assemblies. An extremely paranoid administrator could get the hashes of a few dozen assemblies and allow *only* assemblies with those hashes to run.

Let's consider that last scenario a bit more. Suppose the hypothetical paranoid administrator really has configured your machine to run only assemblies that have certain hash numbers. If a hash is just a number, what prevents attackers from creating a hostile assembly that has the same hash as a trusted assembly? That would fool the policy engine into granting execution rights to the hostile code.

The key is that the hash algorithm was specially designed by cryptologists to have some very interesting properties. One of the most important properties of a cryptographic hash function is that it is for all practical purposes impossible to find two different programs that have the same hash. You are guaranteed that any two assemblies that differ by even a single bit, have completely different hashes.

Note that a hash says nothing about where the assembly came from, who wrote it, or anything else. A hash is simply a convenient way to uniquely identify an assembly cheaply; that is, without having to specify every byte of the assembly, just the hundred-odd bits in the hash. Note also that it is impossible to "go backwards" and generate the assembly from the hash.

A hash is represented in the assembly evidence collection by the `System.Security.Policy.Hash` object. Later on in this section, we'll write some code that extracts all the evidence (including the hash) from an assembly.

The Strong Name

We normally think of the "name" of a file as the name used by the filesystem: `mscorlib.dll`, for instance, is the file containing many of the .NET Framework classes. The problem is that the ordinary name of a file really tells you nothing about the trustworthiness of the file. It would be foolish to write code that, say, granted full rights to any file named "`mscorlib.dll`". Attackers would simply name their hostile file after that or some other fully trusted file.

As anyone can give any file any name they want, the file name is not good quality evidence. A strong name on the other hand is a name that is guaranteed to be unique to a particular version of a particular assembly produced by a particular entity. If you load assemblies based on their strong names then you know that you are loading exactly the assemblies you intended to load, not hostile assemblies with the same name but actually implemented by attackers.

A strong name is represented in the assembly evidence collection by the `System.Security.Policy.StrongName` class. A strong name contains the assembly's name, version number, hash, and a public key. Later on, we'll write some code that extracts the strong name of an assembly.

We will describe the essentials of the cryptographic algorithms and the tools used to produce and consume strong-named assemblies in detail in Appendix A.

The Publisher Signature

An Authenticode publisher signature is conceptually similar to a strong name: a cryptographically strong encoded hash that identifies the author of a piece of code. A strong name essentially tells you nothing about a particular assembly other than that it was produced by an entity possessing a particular private key. However, a publisher signature contains more: a digital certificate that indicates that some third party vouches for the trustworthiness of that entity, in this case the publisher.

Such a third party is called a **certifying authority**. Rather than configuring your security system to trust strong names from dozens or hundreds of individual companies you can simply say "trust everyone who is trusted by Verisign", or "trust everyone who was issued a certificate by my company's certificate server".

A publisher signature is represented in the assembly evidence collection by the System.Security.Policy.Publisher class. See below for sample code that extracts publisher information from an evidence object.

We shall cover the interactions between publisher signatures and strong names in more detail in Chapter 6.

Host Evidence: The Zone, URL, and Site

The remaining standard evidence objects are not included with the assembly. Rather, the .NET Runtime determines them based on its knowledge of where the object came from.

Zones in .NET work much the same as they do in Internet Explorer: the five built-in zones are (in order from most to least trusted): My Computer, Intranet Site, Trusted Internet Site, Internet Site, and Untrusted Internet Site.

Zones are a very useful way to quickly specify the level of trust you wish to grant an assembly. The .NET Runtime's default security policy has many rules that use the zone evidence to determine the grant set. See below for a detailed discussion of the out-of-the-box policy. A zone is represented in the host evidence collection by the System.Security.Policy.Zone class.

The URL is just what it sounds like: the URL that the assembly came from. (Assemblies from the My Computer or Intranet zone will probably be "file" URLs rather than "http" URLs of course.) Assemblies that did not come from a "file" URL are also given an evidence object that specifies the server portion of the URL. The policy engine allows you to specify partial URLs to define code groups, so that administrators can declare policies such as "treat all assemblies in the temporary directory as though they came from the Internet".

The URL is represented in the host evidence collection by the
System.Security.Policy.Url class and the site is represented by the
System.Security.Policy.Site class.

> **If you copy an assembly from one location to another then
> you may be changing the zone that the .NET Runtime will
> infer when it loads the assembly. For example, if you copy
> an assembly from a local Intranet share to your local
> machine then you are effectively changing its zone from the
> less trusted Intranet zone to the more trusted My Computer
> zone. Remember, the .NET Runtime only knows where a
> program currently is, not where it was copied from.**

Summarizing Evidence

Essentially, there are two kinds of evidence: that which tells you facts about the actual
bits of the assembly (such as who implemented it) and that which tells you facts about
its location. The policy system is highly extensible; any object can be used as evidence.
However, for most practical purposes the evidence used is described by Hash,
StrongName, Publisher, Zone, Url and Site objects.

Here is a handy program that tells you what evidence the .NET Runtime generates
when it loads an assembly:

```
' EvidenceExtractor.vb

Imports System
Imports System.Reflection
Imports System.Security
Imports System.Security.Policy
Imports Microsoft.VisualBasic

Public Module EvidenceExtractor

  Public Sub Main()
    Console.Writeline("Enter Assembly Name:")
    Dim AssemblyName = Console.Readline()
    PrintEvidence(AssemblyName)
    ' Must be in current directory, or use full path
  End Sub

  Private Sub PrintEvidence(AsmPath As String)
    Dim Asmb As [Assembly]
```

Assembly is a VB.NET keyword, so either bracket it, as we have done here, or write
System.Reflection.Assembly.

```
Dim Ev As Object
Dim Hash As Hash
Dim StrongName As StrongName
Dim Publisher As Publisher
Dim Zone As Zone
Dim URL As Url
Dim Site As Site

Asmb = [Assembly].LoadFrom(AsmPath)
For Each Ev In Asmb.Evidence
   Console.WriteLine(Ev.GetType().ToString() & ":")
   Select Case Ev.GetType().ToString()
     Case "System.Security.Policy.Hash"
       Hash = CType(Ev, Hash)
       Console.WriteLine("    MD5: " & BytesToString(Hash.MD5))
       Console.WriteLine("    SHA1:" & BytesToString(Hash.SHA1))
```

The .NET Runtime actually uses two industry-standard hash algorithms: the 128-bit RSA MD5 algorithm and the 160-bit SHA1 hash algorithm. To get the hash value in string form we've created a BytesToString() method.

```
     Case "System.Security.Policy.StrongName"
       StrongName = CType(Ev, StrongName)
       Console.WriteLine("    Name: " & StrongName.Name)
     Case "System.Security.Policy.Publisher"
       Publisher = CType(Ev, Publisher)
       Console.WriteLine("    Issued By: " & _
       Publisher.Certificate.GetIssuerName())
       Console.WriteLine("    Name:     " & _
       Publisher.Certificate.GetName())
     Case "System.Security.Policy.Zone"
       Zone = CType(Ev, Zone)
       Console.WriteLine("    Zone: " & _
       Zone.SecurityZone.ToString())
     Case "System.Security.Policy.Url"
       URL = CType(Ev, Url)
       Console.WriteLine("    URL: " & Url.Value)
     Case "System.Security.Policy.Site"
       Site = CType(Ev, Site)
       Console.WriteLine("    Site: " & Site.Name)
     Case Else
       Console.WriteLine(Ev.ToString())
   End Select
  Next
End Sub

Private Function BytesToString(Bytes As Byte()) As String
   Dim B As Byte
   For Each B In Bytes
     BytesToString = BytesToString & Right("0" & Hex(CInt(B)),2)
   Next
End Function

End Module
```

If you compile this and run it in the Framework directory you'll see what evidence the .NET Runtime determines when it loads the VB.NET runtime library:

```
> EvidenceExtractor.exe
Enter Assembly Name: Microsoft.VisualBasic.dll
System.Security.Policy.Zone:
    Zone: MyComputer
System.Security.Policy.Url:
    URL: file://C:/WINDOWS/Microsoft.NET/Framework/v1.0.3705/
Microsoft.VisualBasic.DLL
System.Security.Policy.StrongName:
    Name: Microsoft.VisualBasic
System.Security.Policy.Hash:
    MD5: 18049D17840A0F6540F49D869DCCDCF4
    SHA1:C076842CB37C41AC874D77BF2FB0A777C1E730C6
```

Policy and Permissions

Now we have an overall view of how the code security system works, it is time to look at the heart, to the system, policy, and permission objects, in detail. First, however, let's recap on what we have already learned about them:

The policy system compares the evidence collection of the assembly to the membership rules of every code group to determine to which code groups it belongs. Each code group is associated with a particular permission that consists of a list of permissions. The policy system logically combines the permission sets together to determine the grant set for the assembly.

In this section, we shall look at:

❑   What built-in permission objects are available

❑   How they are combined into permission sets

❑   How enterprise-wide, machine-wide, user-specific, and application-specific policy levels interact

❑   How code groups are defined

❑   What the default policy is when the .NET Runtime is installed

In the following section, we will see how these objects all work together to actually detect attempted security violations in order to prevent them.

Permission Objects

A **permission object** is an object usually used to represent access to some particular dangerous operation. The .NET Framework has many permission classes, each of which typically may represent several different individual rights. An instance of the class represents a particular permission: for instance, an instance of the EnvironmentPermission class might represent "the right to read the TEMP environment variable but not to write it".

Most of the permission objects are in the `System.Security.Permissions` namespace. A few very domain-specific permissions are found in other namespaces. A few of the more commonly used permission objects are:

- `System.Drawing.Printing.PrintingPermission` – represents the right to use printers

- `System.Security.Permissions.EnvironmentPermission` – represents the right to read and write environment variables

- `System.Security.Permissions.FileDialogPermission` – represents the right to create file dialogs

- `System.Security.Permissions.FileIOPermission` – represents the right to access the file system

- `System.Security.Permissions.IsolatedStoragePermission` – represents the right to access strictly isolated portions of the file system

- `System.Security.Permissions.ReflectionPermission` – represents the right to override visibility constraints (such as `Private`) on members of objects

- `System.Security.Permissions.RegistryPermission` – represents the right to access the registry

- `System.Security.Permissions.SecurityPermission` – represents the right to manipulate the security system itself

- `System.Security.Permissions.UIPermission` – represents the right to create user interface elements

As you can probably see, all of these operations could be misused by hostile code. The policy system allows administrators to decide which rights they would like to give to certain code and which should be restricted. For example, even quite untrusted code can be granted an `IsolatedStoragePermission` object with a small quota size; the worst that hostile code could do with that is waste a few kilobytes of your disk. However, only extremely highly trusted code should be granted the `SecurityPermission` that allows code to modify security policy.

Certain permissions do not grant the right to perform some potentially dangerous action. It is convenient for the developer to be able to express notions such as "does the evidence indicate that this code is from the Internet?" in the same way that we express "does the evidence indicate that this code may access the file system?"

Therefore, the `System.Security.Permissions` namespace also includes permission classes such as `SiteIdentityPermission`, `PublisherIdentityPermission`, `StrongNameIdentityPermission`, `UrlIdentityPermission`, and `ZoneIdentityPermission` to represent that an assembly possesses evidence indicating that the code is from the specified URL/site/zone/publisher or has the specified strong name.

In a similar vein, the .NET Runtime's role-based security system also uses permission objects to represent predicates such as "is the current user in the role of Accountant?". We shall cover the use of the `PrincipalPermission` class in Chapter 3.

Later in this chapter, we shall see exactly how the code access security objects are used. For now, we shall continue with an overview of the policy system.

Permission Set Objects

Zero or more permission objects may be grouped into a **permission set object**. Though there are only a small number of permission classes, the number of configurations of each class is potentially infinite. (For example, you could (in theory) have a different instance of `FileIOPermission` for every possible filename.) Therefore, the number of possible permission sets is also practically infinite.

A permission set is represented in the `System.Security` namespace by the `PermissionSet` class and by its derived class, `NamedPermissionSet`. The only difference between the two is that a named permission set has a name and description associated with it.

A few sets are used all the time by the .NET Framework; these commonly used sets have specific names; we shall discuss the contents of these default permission sets below. An example showing the construction of a new named permission set may be found at the end of this chapter.

Policy Levels

The entire set of rules that govern the determination of the grant set from the evidence is called the **policy**. Policy is divided into four **policy levels**: **Enterprise**, **Machine**, **User**, and **AppDomain**. These represent the security rules that apply to the entire enterprise network, all users on a specific machine, a specific user, and a specific appdomain.

These four policy levels allow network administrators to set policy for every machine on the network, machine administrators to set policy for individual machines, you to set policy for yourself, and programs to set their own policies per application domain.

As an example of the last one, you might write a program that performs some mathematical calculation using a third-party library. You could set a policy in your appdomain stating that any third-party calculation library assembly should be granted no permissions to do anything except execute – no UI, no printing, no file system access, just the math.

The policy evaluator ensures that all restrictions of each policy level are applied. For instance, if the machine administrator sets policy saying that no code from the Internet may run and the user sets policy saying that Internet code can run then the machine policy level, being more restrictive, wins. An attempt to run code from the Internet will fail.

Note that if the situation were reversed (that is, if the user policy level were the more restrictive policy) then the attempt would still fail. If two policy levels disagree then the more restrictive one is always chosen; or, put another way:

> **In order for a permission to be in the final grant set, it must be in the grant sets of all four policy levels.**

A policy level is represented by the `System.Security.Policy.PolicyLevel` class. Should you need to programmatically examine the four policy levels, the easiest way to do so is via the `System.Security.SecurityManager` object's `PolicyHierarchy` collection. If you need to create an appdomain policy level, see the end of the chapter for an example.

Code Groups

Each policy level consists of what is essentially a hierarchy of nested **code groups**. Code groups use **membership conditions** for categorizing assemblies based on evidence. For example, the "LocalIntranet_Zone" code group's membership condition is, unsurprisingly, "The assembly evidence must contain a `Zone` object with its `SecurityZone` property set to `Intranet.`"

Each code group has a **policy statement** that indicates which **permission set** is associated with it. For example, the "My_Computer_Zone" code group's permission set contains all permissions. Any assembly loaded from your machine is therefore automatically "fully trusted". The "Restricted_Zone" code group's permission set contains no permissions, not even the permission to execute! Most other code groups have permission sets containing some set of reasonably restrictive permissions.

As you have probably guessed from their names, most of the default code groups use `Zone` objects for their membership conditions. Some also use `StrongName` objects, and some have no evidence requirements whatsoever; all code belongs to the "All_Code" code group no matter what evidence it has. We shall describe the default code groups in more detail below.

The policy level's hierarchy of code groups also contains information on how to handle the situations where an assembly belongs to multiple code groups. There are two typical behaviors, one for nested code groups, and one for sibling code groups. If code groups are nested then the permission set of the inner group is only granted if the code also belongs to the outer group. For siblings, both permission sets are usually granted.

For example, the "Microsoft_Strong_Name" code group is a subgroup of the "My_Computer" code group. The permissions granted by the "Microsoft_Strong_Name" code group are only granted if the assembly has both the right strong name evidence and the right zone evidence.

Conversely, if they were siblings then the "Microsoft_Strong_Name" code group's permission set would be granted to any assembly with the strong name evidence regardless of its zone.

The default behavior out-of-the-box is to take the conjunction of all the permissions in each group's permission set, though other custom rules are possible (as we will see.) This makes sense; if the assembly evidence shows that it is a member of both the "Internet_Zone" code group and the "Signed by someone I trust" code group then it should gain *all* the rights for each group.

For convenience, the .NET Runtime also uses code groups to represent a few things that are not code groups per se. As we will see below, the .NET Runtime also allows you to have "pseudo" code groups that represent concepts such as "code in this group may connect to the web site it came from". These are convenient to represent as code groups because they can be inserted as subgroups.

Code groups, their policy statements, and their membership conditions are represented in the `System.Security.Policy` namespace by the `CodeGroup`, `PolicyStatement`, and `MembershipCondition` classes. For an example of using these to set custom policy, see the end of the chapter.

Viewing Your Policy

You can view and manipulate your .NET security settings with the .NET configuration tool installed with the .NET SDK (or with the `CASPOL.EXE` command-line program if you prefer to look at the underlying XML configuration files directly). Here you can see the code group hierarchy and built-in permission sets. You can also edit membership conditions and create new policy.

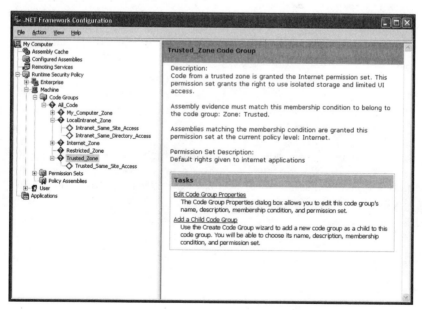

By default the only policy level with anything interesting in it, out-of-the-box, is the Machine level. As you can see, the policy level is a hierarchy of code groups. Each group has a descriptive pane that indicates what evidence is required by the membership condition and what permission set is indicated by the policy statement. If you click on Edit Code Group Properties you can see how the policy rules for resolving nesting and sibling relationships are set as well.

Notice also the three special code groups used to indicate that code from the Internet and Intranet has the right to connect back to where it came from.

> **It goes without saying, but we will say it regardless: do not edit your own security settings carelessly!**

Out-of-the-Box Permission Sets

The "out of the box" policy is the default policy configured when you install the .NET Runtime. The enterprise, user, and appdomain policy levels by default grant full trust to everything. Since we know that the .NET Runtime will grant permissions only if they are found in all policy levels this does not make the security policy any weaker than the machine policy.

The machine policy consists of seven named permission sets and a hierarchy of eight code groups. Note that not every out-of-the-box permission set is used by an out-of-the-box code group. Here we shall discuss the contents of each permission set and give the names of the code groups that grant them, if any.

Note also that these are just the built-in permission sets. Though it is not possible to edit the contents of the built-in sets it is certainly possible to define your own permission sets containing any mix of permissions you like. We shall give an example of writing custom permission sets latter.

Nothing

The Nothing permission set is empty: an assembly that is granted only this permission set will not even execute.

Since the Nothing permission set is associated with the "All_Code" root code group, every assembly is granted the Nothing permission set. Of course, some assemblies are granted other permission sets as well. Note also that code from the "Restricted_Zone" group is granted only the Nothing permission set by default.

> **If you have the Service Pack One release of the .NET Framework then the "Internet_Zone" code group is treated the same as the "Restricted_Zone" code group. This differs from the initial release in which it was treated like the "Trusted_Zone" code group. After conferring with customers and security experts, Microsoft decided that the ability to run managed code off normal Internet sites should be an "opt in" feature, at least for now. The default policy for the "Internet_Zone" code group may change again in future releases.**

Execution

The Execution permission set grants the right to execute, no more, no less. Code with only this permission may not access the disk, create user interface elements, access the network, and so on. This is the most restrictive permission set there is without preventing execution altogether. By default, no code groups have just this permission set.

Internet

The Internet permission set grants a few highly restrictive rights to programs in the "Trusted_Zone" code group. It grants the right to:

❏ Execute

❏ Open file dialog boxes

❏ Read and write ten kilobytes of isolated disk storage. The assembly may not access data associated with other web sites or other users

❏ Create top-level user interface elements such as message boxes

❏ Have limited access to the clipboard

❏ Create a printer dialog box

❏ Access the web site that it came from

This permission set is by default always granted to code in the "Trusted_Zone" code group. See the note above regarding when this permission set is granted to code from the "Internet_Zone" group.

Local Intranet

The permission set granted to code run from your local intranet is designed to let most applications do everything they need to do without allowing them full access to your resources. (This is the Principle of Least Privilege in action: grant enough rights to get work done, but no more.)

It is much more powerful than the Internet permission set. Assemblies in the "LocalIntranet_Zone" code group are granted a permission set containing permission to:

- ❏ Execute (obviously).

- ❏ Discover your user name.

- ❏ Produce and manipulate file dialog boxes.

- ❏ Read and write an unlimited amount of data stored on certain isolated portions of your disk. Full disk access is not granted. (The assembly may not access files associated with users other than the current user or assemblies other than itself.)

- ❏ Read files from the directory from which it was executed (if executed from a share).

- ❏ Access the Intranet web site from which it was executed (if executed from a web page).

- ❏ Emit new code (though this code obviously must be no more privileged than its creator).

- ❏ Create user interface elements without restriction..

- ❏ Contact your Domain Name Server without restriction..

- ❏ Use your default printer without restriction and create a printer dialog for other printers.

- ❏ Read and write your event log, including creating new event sources and new logs but not including deleting event sources and logs or listening to events.

- ❏ Override the security restrictions of its caller. We will discuss this feature in detail when we discuss luring attacks and stack walks below.

Skip Verification

As we mentioned earlier, when the .NET Runtime loads an assembly it does a quick check of all the code in the assembly to ensure that the code is well formed and type safe. Though the number of situations in which you would want to skip verification before running code is quite small, there is a permission set containing only the permission to skip verification just in case you need it.

> **VB.NET developers should never need to skip verification; this feature was really added for Managed C++ and other non-type safe languages.**

By default no code group grants this permission set explicitly. This permission set should only be granted to highly trusted code, if ever.

Note that since the .NET Runtime grants the right to skip verification to assemblies granted this or the following permission sets, if the .NET Runtime determines that an assembly has the right to skip verification then it does not run the verifier. There is no point in running the verifier if any error it produces will simply be ignored.

Full Trust and Everything

The first two named permission sets, "Full Trust" and "Everything" grant all rights. This point bears repeating: fully trusted code can do everything that you can do. It can read and write your disk, change your security policy, and so on, as though it were you doing it.

The difference between "Full Trust" and "Everything" is subtle. "Everything" grants full rights on every permission object that comes built-in to the .NET Framework. The .NET Framework allows you to create your own custom permission objects should you for some reason need to, so "Full Trust" grants any permission whether it is built in or custom. In most situations, this makes no difference and generally, you should give fully trusted code the "Full Trust" permission set.

Obviously not every assembly should be fully trusted. By default, full trust is granted only to code installed on your local machine and code with a Microsoft or ECMA strong name – ECMA is the European Computer Manufacturer's Association, the standards body under which some aspects of the .NET Runtime are standardized.

An Oddity

You might have noticed something odd about the preceding statement. Since the Microsoft_Strong_Name and ECMA_Strong_Name code groups are subgroups of the My_Computer code group, and since all grant full trust, why have three code groups at all? It is rather like saying to someone "I'll fully trust you if you live with me, or if you live with me and are named Bob, or if you live with me and are named Bill". The latter two clauses seem redundant.

There is actually a method to this seeming madness, however, which may be enlightening to understand. There are two reasons for this; first, there are separate groups so that administrators may easily modify their default policies. The implementers of the .NET Runtime realized that a common policy might be "grant code in the My_Computer_Zone code group permission set X, grant code in the Microsoft_Strong_Name and ECMA_Strong_Name code groups full trust". Permission set X might not be the "Full Trust" permission set. That explains why there are separate code groups; so that each can easily be given a permission set. However, that does not explain why they are nested.

Consider the following unpleasant scenario: tomorrow a major security hole is found in a Microsoft strong-named assembly that has shipped to customers. Perhaps the security hole allows code in the Internet_Zone code group to do some operation normally forbidden to such code.

Next, Microsoft issues a new version of the assembly that fixes the problem and distributes it to customers. Millions of customers download the fixed version; wipe the broken version off their machines, and everything is fine. The broken assembly is gone and the users are safe, right?

However, suppose the default policy is that any Microsoft strong-named assembly is granted full trust, no matter what its location. If that was the default policy then an attacker could write a program that takes advantage of the security hole and put their program and the old, broken version of the Microsoft strong-named assembly on a web site. If you could be tricked into loading the attacking assembly then it could load the broken assembly from the Internet. That would mean that the attacking assembly could load a fully trusted assembly with a known security hole.

In other words: such a policy would make it impossible to fix a strong-named assembly with a security hole and be sure users are actually protected from the exploit! The default policy is therefore to ensure that a fully trusted Microsoft/ECMA strong-named assemblies are only fully trusted if they come from the local machine. In that case, the only way an attacker can use the exploit on a machine with the fixed version is to somehow cause you to install the broken version again.

A Quick Review

That is rather a lot of complicated material at once. We now have enough of an overview of both the concepts of code-based security and the specific classes in the security namespaces to see how exactly the classes are used in practical code. Before we do so, let's sum up the story so far:

The primary purpose of the security system is to prevent **hostile** code from successfully **stealing data**, **modifying data**, or **denying services** while still allowing **benign** code to work. It does this by applying a **policy**: taking **evidence** about an **assembly** to determine its **code groups membership** then **granting** it a set of **permissions** determined by the code groups' associated **permission sets**.

The evidence normally consists of: evidence about the assembly **itself** (such as its **hash**), evidence about the **author** of the assembly (such as its **strong name** and/or **publisher**), and evidence about the **location** of the assembly (such as its **zone** and **URL**).

The stronger the evidence is that the assembly is not hostile, the more rights are granted. By default code from the Internet gets few permissions (if any), code on your intranet gets some useful permissions and code on your own machine gets full permissions to do anything.

The .NET Runtime policy evaluator determines the rights granted to individual assemblies. This security system is in addition to the underlying Windows user security system that determines what the rights and privileges of users are.

.NET Code Security in Practice

Now that we've looked at the theory behind the code security system and the classes that represent those theoretical concepts, we can look at how security is actually enforced practically.

A First Attempt at a Security Violation

Consider a simple case first: you run an executable from a network share on your intranet. The security system will check the evidence, run the policy algorithm, and grant a set of permissions to the assembly. The evidence in this case will indicate that the assembly comes from the local intranet.

One of the granted permissions is the right to read and write to an "isolated storage" of unlimited size. You can think of an isolated storage as a special directory associated with a particular user who is using a particular application. Being able to read and write to a local isolated storage allows the intranet application to store files on your machine but does not grant the right to read or write an arbitrary file on your machine. Applications run from the intranet are assumed to need to save and load information about themselves but not necessarily to access information about other users or applications.

For example, here's a short program that creates a per-user, per-domain, per-assembly isolated storage, creates a file stream in that storage and creates a text file. Such a program would run from a local intranet site. If the total storage size did not exceed a few KB then it would also run if loaded from a trusted Internet site.

```vb
' IsolatedStorage.vb

Imports System
Imports System.IO
Imports System.IO.IsolatedStorage

Public Module IsoExample

  Public Sub Main()
    Dim FileName As String = "Temp.txt"
    Dim IsoStore As IsolatedStorageFile
    IsoStore = IsolatedStorageFile.GetStore(IsolatedStorageScope. _
      User Or IsolatedStorageScope.Domain Or _
      IsolatedStorageScope.Assembly, Nothing, Nothing)
    Dim IsoStream As New IsolatedStorageFileStream(FileName, _
      FileMode.OpenOrCreate, IsoStore)
    Dim Writer As New StreamWriter(IsoStream)
    Writer.WriteLine("This is isolated")
    Writer.Close()
    IsoStore.Close()
  End Sub

End Module
```

Compile this console application (with the Visual Studio .NET IDE or the VBC.EXE command-line compiler) and copy the executable out to a shared intranet folder. (If you do not have an intranet connection handy then you can share out a directory on your own machine and connect to it locally as though it were a remote machine! From the .NET Runtime security system's point of view that is an intranet share.) Sure enough when you run it from the share it executes just fine. Somewhere deep under your <user>\Local Settings\Application Data\IsolatedStorage folder the .NET Runtime has created an isolated storage directory, opened a file, and written one line of text into it.

Now try doing the same with a very similar program that does not use isolated storage:

```
' NormalStorage.vb

Imports System
Imports System.IO

Public Module FileExample

  Public Sub Main()
    Dim FileName As String = "Temp.txt"
    Dim FStream As New FileStream(FileName, FileMode.OpenOrCreate, _
        FileAccess.Write)
    Dim Writer As New StreamWriter(FStream)
    Writer.WriteLine("This is not isolated")
    Writer.Close()
    FStream.Close()
  End Sub

End Module
```

If as before you copy it out to a share and run it then you will get a debugger exception. If you let the exception go so that it writes the call stack out to the command prompt, you will see something like this: (some details removed for clarity)

Unhandled Exception: System.Security.SecurityException: Request for the permission of type System.Security.Permissions.FileIOPermission, mscorlib, Version=1.0.3300.0, Culture=neutral, PublicKeyToken=b77a5c561934e089 failed.
...
The state of the failed permission was:
<IPermission class="System.Security.Permissions.FileIOPermission, mscorlib,
         Version=1.0.3300.0, Culture=neutral, PublicKeyToken=b77a5c561934e089"
         version="1"
         Write="H:\Temp.txt"/>

What has happened here? When the .NET Runtime attempts to create the file stream it **demands** the right to write a file. This demand is done automatically by the file stream class provided by the .NET Framework. However, the evidence indicates that the calling executable is in the LocalIntranet_Zone code group. It has therefore not been granted the right to read an arbitrary file. Since the calling executable was not **granted** this right the demand fails and throws a **security exception**. The dangerous file system code never runs.

If you now attempt to run this code from a directory on your local machine it should run just fine. The assembly on the local machine is granted full trust based on its evidence.

The Stack Walk

Something may have struck you as a bit odd about that last example. The code that actually accesses the file system (that is, the `FileStream` object) is part of the .NET Framework. This code is from an assembly that has a Microsoft strong name and is stored on your local machine's hard disk. In other words, it is actually a *fully trusted* assembly that ultimately attempts to open the file. Why does the attempt not succeed?

Recall that above we discussed the managed call stack: the data structure inside the .NET Runtime that tracks every method that has begun and not yet ended. In this particular case, the managed stack has two entries at the point of failure: the file stream constructor and the `Main` function. The .NET Runtime is aware that these two procedures are on the stack and furthermore, that they are from different assemblies. In this example, we have less privileged intranet code calling fully privileged local machine code. A key feature of the .NET security system is this:

> **To do any operation controlled by permission then every assembly on the current call stack must be granted that permission.**

(There are exceptions to this rule, which we will get into shortly.)

In our example, the .NET Framework library that contains the file stream constructor certainly has permission to open files! However, not every assembly on the call stack has this right so the demand fails. This process of checking the grant set of every assembly on the managed call stack is called a **stack walk**.

> **A demand for a permission causes a stack walk. The .NET Runtime traverses the call stack verifying that every caller on it has a grant set containing the permission. If any does not then it throws an exception immediately.**

The Luring Attack

Unsurprisingly, this pattern of trying to lure high-trust code into doing the dirty work for low-trust code is extremely common. The so-called **luring attack** is one of the most basic attack patterns. For example, if you had highly trusted code used to transfer money from one bank account to another then clearly any caller of that code should also be highly trusted. Attackers could attempt to design clever programs that lure the more trusted code into transferring money into their bank accounts.

Obviously the more highly trusted your code is, the more dangerous a luring attack becomes. This is a corollary of the principle of least privilege; the fewer permissions your code is granted the less likely it is that anyone can lure your code into doing harm. The difficulty in writing secure code is finding the balance where your code has few enough permissions to prevent serious harm, enough permissions to get its job done, and enough safeguards to ensure that attempts to misuse the granted permissions are likely to fail.

> **Stack walks are an example of such a safeguard. They are an excellent basis upon which to build secure applications. However, do not think that, just because the runtime will take care of some luring attacks for you, you can write sloppy code. Stack walks are one tool in your toolbox, not a panacea.**

In the rest of this book, we will cover how to prevent flaws that lead to vulnerability to luring attacks as well as many other non-luring attacks.

Luring Attacks, Partial Trust, and the "APTC" Attribute

A major source of potential vulnerabilities is buggy fully trusted code written by developers who do not understand all the potential attacks. This is both common and understandable; most developers are not accustomed to thinking like attackers. All good developers test their programs to ensure that they operate correctly when used correctly. Unfortunately, the idea of testing a program to see if it can be exploited when used maliciously does not occur to many developers until it is too late.

No security system in the world can protect users from buggy highly-trusted code, so it is the duty of developers to design and implement their assemblies carefully. In Chapter 5, we shall look at several common design patterns that lead to such flaws.

Note that successful luring attacks by definition deal with hostile partially trusted code calling benign but flawed highly trusted code. Luring attacks never involve hostile fully trusted code for the obvious reason that hostile fully trusted code is already fully trusted; it has no need to trick any other assembly into doing its work for it because there is nothing stopping it from doing the deed itself.

The designers of the .NET Runtime realized that a very common luring attack pattern would probably therefore be as follows: some benign developers produce a strong-named assembly intended to be fully trusted and distribute it to customers. However, the developers have not adequately vetted their code for security flaws, leaving a possible luring attack. If then, the customers are tricked into running a hostile, low-trust assembly (say, from the Internet), which lures the strong-named benign code into doing something that hurts the user.

The .NET Runtime implementers therefore insist that all strong named assemblies be stamped with an attribute that states, "We, the developers of this assembly, aver that we have looked for potential luring attacks in this code." Any strong-named assembly not possessing this attribute may not be called by a partially trusted assembly; the attempt to run the partially trusted code will fail before calling into the strong-named assembly.

This attribute is not set by default, obviously! That would defeat its purpose. To mark an assembly with this attribute and thereby state that it is safe to be called from partially trusted code, just add this line to the start of your program:

```
<assembly:System.Security.AllowPartiallyTrustedCallersAttribute()>
```

Henceforth we shall refer to this rather long name by the abbreviation "APTCA".

> **APTCA is only required for strong-named code. Strong-named code is globally accessible because it is usually put in the Global Assembly Cache and therefore is callable by any untrusted assembly. If you intend to strong-name your assembly then it will not be callable by partially trusted code unless you explicitly mark it as safe. APTCA is your statement that you have exercised due diligence in looking for and eliminating vulnerabilities, so do not apply it lightly!**

Note that unlike a normal stack walk the check for the attribute only considers the immediate caller and called assemblies. For example, suppose Zulu is a fully trusted strong-named APTCA assembly. If partially trusted assembly Alpha calls Zulu then the call will succeed. If that then causes Zulu to call non-APTCA strong-named assembly Bravo then the call will succeed even though partially-trusted Alpha is on the call stack. Zulu has stated that it is always safe to be called from partially trusted code, which **implies that Zulu cannot be lured into misusing Bravo.**

Figure 1

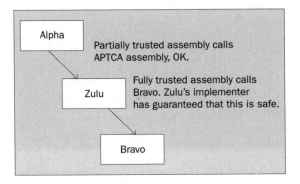

The demand for full trust made by strong named assemblies that lack APTCA is an example of a **link demand.** A link demand is a weaker, faster flavor of demand that only checks the previous caller and only checks once. We will cover link demands extensively in Chapter 3.

Forcing a Stack Walk with "Demand"

Recall our example of a local intranet program trying (and failing) to open a file on the local machine without using isolated storage. When the .NET Runtime did the stack walk how exactly did it know what permission to look for? The file stream constructor simply demanded the appropriate permission. How?

Recall that permissions are represented by objects in the .NET Framework. To demand a particular permission all you need to do is call the Demand() method of the appropriate permission object. Here's an example: a program that determines whether the code possesses permission to write to a particular file:

```
' DemandExample.vb

Imports System
Imports System.Security
Imports System.Security.Permissions
Imports System.Windows.Forms

Public Module DemandExample

  Private Function CheckFilePerm(FileName As String) As Boolean
    Dim FilePerm As New FileIOPermission( _
      FileIOPermissionAccess.Write, FileName)
    CheckFilePerm = False
    Try
      FilePerm.Demand()
      CheckFilePerm = True
    Catch
    End Try
  End Function

  Public Sub Main()
    Dim FileName As String = "D:\Temp.txt"
    If CheckFilePerm(FileName) Then
      MessageBox.Show("You have permission to write " & FileName)
    Else
      MessageBox.Show("You do not have permission to write " _
                      & FileName)
    End If
  End Sub

End Module
```

If you compile and run the assembly on a local machine you will find that the assembly has access, but again if you copy the executable to an intranet share and run it from there, it does not.

> **Notice that this check is to see whether the code has permission. The demand does not check to see if the ACL for the file permits the current user to write to the file. In order for an actual write to succeed the .NET Runtime security system must allow the code to write to the file and the Windows security system must allow the current user to write to the file. This code only checks the former.**

Why Would You Ever Force a Stack Walk?

We have already seen that attempting to access a file demands the appropriate permission. If the runtime libraries always demand the appropriate permissions before they do anything dangerous then why would you, the VB.NET developer, ever need to do a demand?

There are actually many times when you need to force an appropriate demand. We will look at most of these later on but for now here are several reasons why you might want to do a demand yourself: performance, good error handling, or avoiding security problems created by caching.

Performance

If you know that in a few minutes you are going to require a certain permission then you might as well ask for it immediately rather than wasting any time. For example:

```
Sub SaveSortedArray()
    ' ...
    SortHugeArray()
    SaveArrayToDisk()
    ' ...
End Sub
```

What if the caller lacks file IO permission? Then all the time spent sorting the array is for naught. Instead, you can demand the permission up front and save on the cost of sorting the array.

```
Sub SaveSortedArray(Filename As String)
    ' ...
    Dim FilePerm As New FileIOPermission( _
        FileIOPermissionAccess.Write, FileName)
    FilePerm.Demand()
    SortHugeArray()
    SaveArrayToDisk(FileName)
    ' ...
End Sub
```

> **Do not, however, fall into the common trap of "armchair
> performance analysis". Since this will, do two stack walks (one
> up front, one in the subroutine that saves to disk) instead of
> just one it would be a mistake to do so if the stack walk was
> actually more expensive than the array sort. Measure carefully
> when making decisions based on performance.**

Design for Graceful Failure

Another good reason to do your own demands is to implement programs that enable
more features when they are run with more trust. For example, you might design a
notification system that falls back to a more basic mode when run with
Internet permissions.

Internet programs are allowed to create simple message boxes but restricted from full
access to all user interface features. (Without this restriction a hostile assembly from the
Internet could create a dialog box that looked exactly like a standard Windows "enter
your password" dialog box and trick unwitting users into typing passwords into dialogs
controlled by hostile code.)

```
Dim UIPerm As New UIPermission(PermissionState.Unrestricted)
Try
    UIPerm.Demand()
    ShowFancyMessageBox()
Catch
    ShowSimpleMessageBox()
End Try
```

Again, it is not *necessary* to put the demand up front. After all, the attempt to show the
message box will throw an error. However, this pattern makes the security semantics –
that is, the meaningful security behavior intended by the developer – very clear. It is
always wise to have clear security semantics.

Cache Data Correctly

Here is an example where doing your own demand is not just a good idea but in fact
required. Consider this extremely common design pattern: to avoid calling the same
method repeatedly, a method caches the result of one call in some handy location.
Caches are often used to improve performance; in this case, we avoid multiple calls to
the environment variable code when the result is unlikely to ever change.

```
Private SystemDir As String = ""
Public Function SysDir() As String
    If SystemDir = "" Then
        SystemDir = _
            System.Environment.ExpandEnvironmentVariables("%WINDIR%")
    End If
    SysDir = SystemDir
End Function
```

This looks fine but actually, it has a very serious security bug. Suppose this method is in a fully trusted assembly but the very first caller to this function is in an assembly from the Internet. Perhaps the call stack looks like this:

Figure 2

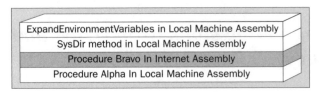

In other words, a method `Alpha` in a fully trusted assembly calls a method `Bravo` in a partially trusted assembly, which calls the method above in a fully trusted assembly, which calls the .NET Framework method that expands an environment variable.

The Internet_Zone code group does not grant permission to access this environment variable. `ExpandEnvironmentVariables` will demand this permission. The stack walk will therefore fail and throw an exception (which presumably someone catches). So far, everything is fine.

Next, all the procedures on the stack return control to `Alpha`, which calls `Charlie`:

Figure 3

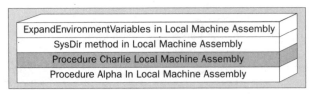

`SystemDir` is still an empty string because the first call to `ExpandEnvironmentVariables()` failed. Now the entire call stack is fully trusted, so the call succeeds and `SystemDir` is filled in.

Here's the problem: after that, every call succeeds whether the call stack is fully trusted or not! Since `SystemDir` is now filled in, a future call to `Bravo` will succeed where the previous one failed. This method could leak privileged information to code that should not possess it.

If you cache data that was obtained through some privileged operation then you probably want to ensure that access to the cached data is also protected. In this case, you would demand the `EnvironmentPermission`.

```
Public Function SysDir() As String
    Dim EnvPerm As New EnvironmentPermission( _
        EnvironmentPermissionAccess.Read, "WINDIR")
    EnvPerm.Demand()
    If SystemDir = "" Then
```

```
        SystemDir = _
            System.Environment.ExpandEnvironmentVariables("%WINDIR%")
        End If
        SysDir = SystemDir
    End Function
```

Restricting Permissions with "Deny" and "PermitOnly"

Suppose you are developing a program that needs to be highly trusted; perhaps because it has to modify the file system. Usually, a program that can modify the file system might as well be fully trusted and is therefore granted every permission. Now suppose that the program wishes to call a method in a less-trusted assembly; perhaps there is some sort of third-party add-in/customization that the user trusts less than your code.

What would be helpful in this situation is if you could say "Yes, I am granted permissions X, Y, and Z but I know that the following call will never demand permissions Y and Z unless somehow we are calling hostile code, so do not let a demand for anything but X to succeed."

We know that a permission object has a `Demand()` method to force a stack walk. All code permission objects also have `Deny()` and `PermitOnly()` methods that will cause a stack walk to fail immediately.

Consider this code, which calls the third-party customization:

```
    Public Sub MySub()
        Dim UIPerm As New UIPermission(PermissionState.Unrestricted)
        UIPerm.PermitOnly()
        CallUICustomization()
    End Sub
```

Now suppose that somehow an attacker manages to get a hostile customization library on the user's machine. If the attack causes a demand for any permission other than user interface creation permission the stack walk will automatically fail when it reaches `MySub()`. Once `MySub()` returns the `PermitOnly` mark is removed from the stack.

(Note that later we will see that sufficiently privileged called code could override the `PermitOnly`. We shall discuss this further in the sections below on asserting and on reducing grant sets. We shall discuss limiting the rights of customizable software in more detail at the end of this chapter.)

You might be wondering how it is that any code can run at all, since the permission to execute is not represented by the `UIPermission` object. (The right to execute code is represented by a `SecurityPermission` object.) Unlike most permissions, the right to execute is only checked when an assembly is loaded, not every time it executes!

You might also wonder what happens when two PermitOnly decorations are placed on the same stack frame. Does that combine them into a "permit either"? Or a "permit neither?" In fact it is not possible to use two PermitOnly decorations on the same stack frame and doing so will result in a security exception. The correct way to "permit either" is to use a custom permission set.

The complement to PermitOnly() is Deny(), which as you probably have guessed, marks only particular permissions as denied.

```
Public Sub MyOtherSub()
    Dim UIPerm As New UIPermission(PermissionState.Unrestricted)
    UIPerm.Deny()
    CallOtherCustomization()
End Sub
```

In this example, the MyOtherSub() stack frame is annotated with a denial of all user interface permissions. If the code it calls demands any user interface permission then the request will be denied no matter what the present assembly's grant set contains.

Generally, Deny() is less useful than PermitOnly(). A good guideline to follow when designing secure code is:

> **Write code which makes "what is allowed" (PermitOnly)
> explicit rather than attempting to enumerate "what is not
> allowed" (Deny).**

Note also that Deny() and PermitOnly() only affect stack walks. The actual grant set of the assembly is not changed by a Deny or a PermitOnly(). The Deny() or PermitOnly() disappears when the frame that created them is removed from the stack.

Custom Permission Sets

If you need to PermitOnly() or Deny() some group of permissions then use a PermissionSet object. In the code example below, we create a new PermissionSet object and a couple of Permission objects. The Permission objects are added to the PermissionSet using its AddPermission() method. Then, rather than trying to call PermitOnly() on multiple Permision objects (which we know won't work) we can call it on the PermSet.

```
Dim PermSet as New PermissionSet(PermissionState.None)
Dim UIPerm As New UIPermission(PermissionState.Unrestricted)
Dim FilePerm As New FileIOPermission(PermissionState.Unrestricted)
PermSet.AddPermission(UIPerm)
PermSet.AddPermission(FilePerm)
PermSet.PermitOnly()' Permits only UI and File IO
```

Of course you may also call Demand() on an entire PermissionSet if you need to.

Reverting Restrictions

In some rare cases, you may need to turn your stack frame restrictions on and off dynamically. For instance, suppose you wanted to change the set of permissions permitted within a stack frame halfway through. The CodeAccessPermission class (which is the base class of all the permission classes) has shared methods to do this:

```
Dim PermSet as New PermissionSet(PermissionState.None)
Dim UIPerm As New UIPermission(PermissionState.Unrestricted)
Dim FilePerm As New FileIOPermission(PermissionState.Unrestricted)
PermSet.AddPermission(UIPerm)
PermSet.AddPermission(FilePerm)
PermSet.PermitOnly()
DoDangerousThing()
CodeAccessPermission.RevertPermitOnly()
FilePerm.PermitOnly()
DoOtherDangerousThing()
```

However, code like this gets hard to read, analyze, and understand. Security code should be as easy to understand as possible so that future maintainers do not accidentally introduce bugs. In a case like the one above, it might be clearer to break it up into several helper functions each with its own appropriate stack restrictions.

> Note that RevertPermitOnly() only reverts PermitOnly() restrictions, not Deny restrictions. Use RevertDeny() for them. Note also that there is no way to revert individual restrictions from a permission set in a particular stack frame.

An Oddity

This example illustrates an interesting fact about the .NET security system's stack walking behavior. What do you suppose this code does when run from a fully trusted zone?

```
' DenyDemand.vb
Imports System.Security.Permissions

Module DenyDemand

  Sub MySub()
    Dim FilePerm As New FileIOPermission(PermissionState.Unrestricted)
    FilePerm.Deny()
    FilePerm.Demand()
  End Sub

  Sub Main()
    MySub()
  End Sub

End Module
```

Obviously, an exception is thrown at `FilePerm.Demand()` because the permission has just been denied, right?

Wrong; this actually succeeds. Remember that a stack walk verifies that all the **callers** have a particular permission. The demand checks the caller of `MySub()`, its caller and so on up the call stack, but it never checks `MySub()` itself. If `MySub()` goes on to call something that in its turn demands the file I/O permission then the stack walk will find the right denied on `MySub()` of course.

This is more of an oddity than a possible vulnerability; this pattern of denying a permission and then immediately demanding it is not usually found in practice.

Overriding Stack Walks with Assert

The point of the stack walk is to mitigate possible luring attacks: attacks where a less trusted hostile caller uses more trusted benign code to do its dirty work. However, there is certainly such a thing as going too far. Suppose you write a program that must be callable by a partially trusted caller but needs to do something that requires a high level of trust. For instance: a fully trusted program that needs to read a data file off your hard disk, by default this cannot be called from code running from the Intranet zone. The stack walk caused by the attempt to access the file system will fail when it gets to the Intranet zone assembly.

Suppose though that you have carefully gone through your highly trusted file-accessing code and determined that even when called from an Intranet zone assembly, there is no harm that it could do. Suppose further that you had some good reason for the code to be called by a less-trusted assembly. How would you enable this?

The first thought might be "grant full trust to the code in the Intranet zone". That would be a bad idea; then hostile assemblies in the Intranet zone would not need to lure fully trusted assemblies into doing bad things; they already would be fully trusted assemblies!

What you really want is a way to say "Yes, I know that my caller does not have the right to access this file, but I guarantee that there is no luring attack here so let me access it." The method that implements this concept is called `Assert()`.

> **Do not confuse the permission object's `Assert()` method with the `Debug.Assert()` method. They are completely different; this is just an unfortunate name collision. `Debug.Assert()` is a diagnostic tool that tells you when a program invariant has been violated. The `Assert()` method of a permission object allows that permission to be granted even if callers higher on the call stack were not granted the necessary permission.**

Assert() is the opposite of Deny(). When you Deny() a permission then the permission is never granted even if it otherwise would be. When you Assert() a permission then the permission is granted even if the caller lacks the demanded permission.

Consider this code for example:

```
Public Sub MySub()
  Dim EnvPerm As New _
    EnvironmentPermission(PermissionState.Unrestricted)
  EnvPerm.Assert()
  DoTheWork()
End Sub
```

Now suppose that the caller of MySub() lacks the right to read environment variables but MySub() and DoTheWork() are granted this right. If DoTheWork() calls a method that demands this permission then the stack walk will terminate successfully when it finds the assert annotation on the MySub stack frame. MySub's less-privileged caller is never checked. When MySub() returns the assert disappears off the call stack.

The right to assert permissions is restricted to intranet zone and fully trusted assemblies by default. Note that obviously an assembly may not assert a permission that it was not granted in the first place! An assembly from the local intranet can assert the right to create arbitrary UI, for example, but not the right to read the entire file system. Furthermore, it should be clear why asserting does not itself cause a stack walk to look for the permission to assert. The whole point of asserting is to prevent a full stack walk that looks for an ungranted permission; in such a scenario the caller probably does not itself have the right to assert, otherwise the called code would not need to.

> **Asserting is essentially deliberately turning off the stack walking mechanism for a particular permission or permission set. This mechanism is designed to mitigate luring attacks and therefore must be turned off only when you are absolutely sure that you have eliminated potential luring attacks. Use Assert() sparingly and with caution.**

Much like RevertPermitOnly() and RevertDeny(), you may revert your asserts with CodeAccessPermission.RevertAssert(). Also, the RevertAll() method reverts all three types of stack walk modifiers.

Using Asserts and Demands Together

A common design pattern when writing secure VB.NET code is to assert a permission after demanding a weaker permission, this is usually done when fully trusted code calls into unmanaged code.

Recall that by "unmanaged" code we mean any code not under the direct control of the .NET Runtime. At some point, you may need to call into an underlying operating system API not directly available in the .NET Framework or perhaps you need to call some pre-.NET custom control.

The runtime has no way of telling whether the unmanaged code in the control is type safe. Nor does it have any way to enforce security policy on that code. Unmanaged code is not likely to demand stack walks either.

> **Unmanaged code can do anything that the operating system allows the user to do. Unmanaged code is not restricted by the .NET security system at all.**

Calling Unmanaged Code Securely

If you need to call into unmanaged code to make some operating system call then first of all, be aware that your assembly will have to be granted the right to call unmanaged code. Since unmanaged code can do anything, by default only fully trusted code is granted this right. Second, if your trusted assembly is going to be called by a partially trusted caller then the trusted assembly will have to assert the right to call unmanaged code. A partially trusted caller will not be granted this right.

There may well be cases where the call into unmanaged code is perfectly safe. For example, you might be calling an unmanaged method that fetches the current time, or does some other harmless thing. In such a case you can simply assert the right to call unmanaged code, do the interop call and return. Since your code cannot be lured into doing something dangerous with its assertion, it requires no corresponding demand before calling the unmanaged code.

However, most calls into unmanaged code will do something dangerous. If you want to be called by callers who lack the right to call unmanaged code then you have to ensure that they cannot use the functionality exposed without the appropriate permissions.

Let's consider an example. Suppose you decided that you absolutely, positively had to have your fully trusted library provide a method that made multiple beep-beep noises. Furthermore, you've decided that the only way to really do it right is to call into the operating system's "MessageBeep" API.

First, you'd need to make a private method that calls the API via the managed/unmanaged interop layer. Then the fully trusted managed wrapper method would have to assert the right to call unmanaged code so that the demand is not passed on to the partially trusted callers.

However, should just any old code be allowed to make beep-beep noises? That seems like a potentially obnoxious thing to do. You might decide that this was obnoxious enough that only code that could already do other obnoxious things, such as create pop-up message boxes, should be allowed to do this.

This implies that you must demand the right to produce user interface elements and assert the right to call unmanaged code. This pairing of an assertion of a high privilege with a demand for a lower privilege is a common design pattern.

> **Any time you assert powerful permissions such as the right to call unmanaged code you must ensure that that there is no way in which hostile partially trusted code can use the asserted permission to harm the user. A good way to do that is to demand an appropriate permission, ensuring that the partially trusted caller is sufficiently trusted.**

Here's an example that creates a class library containing a method that calls the unmanaged `MessageBeep` API after demanding permission to produce UI elements.

```
'Beep.vb
Imports System
Imports System.Security
Imports System.Security.Permissions
Imports System.Runtime.InteropServices

Public Class MyBeeper
```

After the usual imports and so on we need to make the unmanaged and non COM based `MessageBeep` function available to our .NET code. We can do this by declaring a `DllImport` attribute pointing to the relevant DLL (`user32.dll`), and setting the `EntryPoint` to point to the required function.

```
    <DllImport("user32.dll", CharSet := CharSet.Unicode, _
      EntryPoint := "MessageBeep")> _
    Private Shared Function MessageBeep(ByVal uType As Integer) _
      As Integer
    End Function

    Public Shared Sub Beep(ByVal BeepType As Integer)
      If BeepType < 0 Or BeepType > 4 Then
        Throw New ArgumentException()
      End If

      Dim UIPerm As New UIPermission(UIPermissionWindow.SafeSubWindows)
      Dim UnmanagedCodePerm As New _
        SecurityPermission(SecurityPermissionFlag.UnmanagedCode)
      Try
        UIPerm.Demand()
      Catch
        Exit Sub
      End Try
      UnmanagedCodePerm.Assert()
      MessageBeep(BeepType * 16)
    End Sub

End Class
```

If you want to test the `MyBeeper` class, simply add the following code:

```
Module TestBeep
  Sub Main()
    MyBeeper.Beep(1)
  End Sub
End Module
```

When it is run, you should hear one of the windows system sounds – unless you've turned them off for some reason.

There are a few interesting features in the `MyBeeper` class. First, note that if the caller passes a bad argument then the code immediately throws an exception right back. This is not merely a good idea: it is vital that you validate your arguments, particularly when passing them on to unmanaged code.

Suppose there were a flaw in `MessageBeep()` that caused a buffer overrun or other vulnerability when passed some huge integer? Again, this is part of our strategy of multiple, layered defenses. We shall return to this theme of writing code that vets parameters in Chapter 5.

> **If you aggressively validate the data passed to you by untrusted callers then those callers cannot take advantage of vulnerabilities caused by your passing bad data on to less secure or buggy code.**

Second, note that if the argument is correct but the stack walk discovers that the caller lacks UI permission then the resulting security exception is not passed back to the caller. Whether you should just (in this case, literally) "fail silently" or pass the security exception on depends entirely on what the right thing to do is for the particular example.

In this case, it seems reasonable not to honor the request and make noise without an exception. In some applications, you might want to explicitly tell the caller that the call failed for security reasons. We shall discuss common problems with exception handling and security further in Chapter 5.

Note that this is in fact only slightly different from how `Interaction.Beep` is actually implemented in the Visual Basic .NET runtime library. The main two differences are first that the runtime's version demands that the caller support either `SafeSubWindows` or `SafeTopLevelWindows`. Second, it can only make one kind of noise.

Declarative Security

So far the demands, asserts, and so on that we have added to functions have all been in the form of method calls on permission objects. This technique is called **imperative security**. The .NET Framework also supports **declarative security**.

Practically speaking, the difference between imperative and declarative security is simply a matter of notation. In most programming languages, there are some statements that do things and some statements that "describe the program". The statement:

```
Private Sub Foo(Bar As Integer)
```

does not "do" anything. This is not an imperative command that does something interesting at run time. Rather it is a declaration to the VB.NET compiler that you want to create a method with particular visibility and type constraints. Contrast that with statements such as:

```
Console.WriteLine("Hello, world!")
```

Clearly, this does something. It is an imperative, a command to the .NET Runtime that it should write some text to the console.

We have seen so far only examples of imperative security programming. We are issuing methods on objects to deny or assert permissions. VB.NET also provides a declarative syntax for security operations, and in fact, some features only have declarative forms, as we shall see.

Why Use Declarative Security?

Suppose you have to put a particular demand on every method in a class: not only is that a lot of duplicated code, but you also run the risk of adding a new method and forgetting to add the security code, creating a vulnerability.

Visual Basic .NET uses attribute syntax to enable you to declare the security semantics of methods, classes, and assemblies. For example, these two code fragments are essentially the same as far as their security semantics are concerned:

```
Public Sub DoIt()
  Dim UnmanagedCodePerm As New _
    SecurityPermission(SecurityPermissionFlag.UnmanagedCode)
  UnmanagedCodePerm.Demand()
    ' ...
End Sub
```

```
<SecurityPermissionAttribute(SecurityAction.Demand, Flags := _
 SecurityPermissionFlag.UnmanagedCode)> _
Public Sub DoIt()
    ' ...
End Sub
```

Every permission object has a corresponding attribute object. By choosing the appropriate attribute object and passing the correct arguments you can annotate methods with declarative demands that are then actually executed whenever the method is called.

You may also add declarative security attributes to classes, which is the same as adding the attribute to all members of the class:

```
' DeclarativeSecurity.vb

Imports System.Security.Permissions

<SecurityPermissionAttribute(SecurityAction.Demand, Flags := _
SecurityPermissionFlag.UnmanagedCode)> _
Public Class Unmanaged

    Public Sub MySub()
        ' ...
    End Sub

    Public Sub MySub2()
        ' ...
    End Sub

End Class
```

Here MySub() and all the other methods of MyClass() automatically get the attribute. However, there is one important "gotcha" to be wary of:

> **Declarative security attributes on methods replace the declarative security attributes (of the same action: assert, deny, and so on) of their classes. They do not combine together.**

So for instance in this example MySubAlpha() demands the right to call unmanaged code but MySubBravo() does not; it only demands the right to read environment variables:

```
' ClassDeclaration.vb

Imports System.Security.Permissions

<SecurityPermissionAttribute(SecurityAction.Demand, Flags := _
SecurityPermissionFlag.UnmanagedCode)> _
Public Class  MethodDeclartaion

    Public Sub MySubAlpha() ' Demands UMC permission
    End Sub
```

```
<EnvironmentPermissionAttribute(SecurityAction.Demand, _
Unrestricted := True)> _
Public Sub MySubBravo() ' Demands Env permission, not UMC.
End Sub

End Class
```

This replacement only happens when the attributes use the same action. If instead we asserted a permission in the method attribute then the method would get both the assert and demand attributes applied to it.

```
' MethodDeclaration.vb

Imports System.Security.Permissions

<SecurityPermissionAttribute(SecurityAction.Demand, Flags := _
SecurityPermissionFlag.UnmanagedCode)> _
Public Class MethodDeclartaion

  Public Sub MySubAlpha() ' Demands UMC permission
  End Sub

  <EnvironmentPermissionAttribute(SecurityAction.Assert, _
  Unrestricted := True)> _
  Public Sub MySubBravo() ' Asserts Env permission, Demands UMC.
  End Sub

End Class
```

This distinction can be rather confusing in complex code. It is probably best to avoid mixing class security attributes with method security attributes. Use good judgment to write maintainable, understandable code.

Reducing the Grant Set

We know that the policy system grants a set of permissions to an assembly based on evidence. We have just seen how programs can manipulate that grant set at run time. Programs can check to see if every assembly on the call stack has a particular permission with Demand(). They can cause a stack walk looking for a particular permission to succeed with Assert() or fail with Deny() and PermitOnly().

It is important to note, however, that Deny() and PermitOnly() do not actually change the set of permissions granted to an assembly. All they do is temporarily change the behavior of stack walks at run time by telling the security system "even if every assembly is granted this permission, deny it." When the stack frame annotated with the Deny is no longer on the stack, the permission can again be successfully demanded.

Note also that denying a permission does not prevent it from being asserted. An assembly granted the right to assert could assert any permission it was originally granted regardless of the current annotations on the call stack.

We know that one of the best techniques for writing secure code is to require as few privileges as possible. An attacker is unlikely to be able to use your code to take advantage of a permission that your code was never granted! You also do not want to be in the converse situation: if you know ahead of time that you will always require a particular permission to be granted, then you should document that fact and prevent your program from running if it cannot be granted.

Remember, you do not know ahead of time what permissions your code will be granted because you do not know what the policy is going to be on your customers' machines. If you use declarative security to carefully, document exactly which permissions you need and do not need then your program is more likely to be used safely.

Refusing Specific Permissions

If you deny a permission then any demand for that specific permission lower down the call stack will fail when the stack walk reaches the deny. The analog of Deny() for a grant set is RequestRefuse.

```
Imports System
Imports System.Security
Imports System.Security.Permissions
Imports System.IO
<Assembly: FileIOPermission(SecurityAction.RequestRefuse, _
  Unrestricted := True)>
```

If you added this code to your application then the assembly would never be granted any file I/O permissions, even if it was run from the local machine and had full trust. This greatly reduces the risk that some vulnerability in your assembly could be exploited to gain access to the file system.

Note that this attribute may only be used on assemblies. You cannot put a RequestRefuse on a class or method. Only assemblies are granted permissions by policy; the classes and methods in that assembly get their permissions from its grant set.

Requiring Permissions

If you know ahead of time that your program will not work properly without certain permissions in the grant set then it is a very good idea to document that fact with a RequestMinimum security attribute. Consider what can happen if you do not; suppose you have written an application that takes input from the user and writes it to disk. If the user's policy does not grant your application the right to write to disk then the user will enter their data, but they will be unable to save it and will thereby wasting time. It is far better to simply fail to start the application altogether.

Furthermore, if you use a declarative security attribute to document what your requirements are then policy administrators can use tools (such as `permview.exe`) to determine what policy they need to set in order for their users to run your program effectively. Do not make your customers have to guess what kind of policy you require! There are only three possibilities. They might grant too few permissions, leading to exceptions, frustrated users, and lost data. They might grant too many permissions, possibly exacerbating any vulnerabilities in your code. Alternatively, they might guess completely correctly, but that seems unlikely!

The syntax for a `RequestMinimum` attribute is straightforward. For example, this requires that your assembly be granted full access to the file system. If it is not granted that right then it will not load at all:

```
<assembly: FileIOPermission(SecurityAction.RequestMinimum, _
  Unrestricted := True)>
```

A `RequestMinimum` does not restrict the granted permission set in any way.

Requesting Optional Permissions

If a `RequestRefuse` is like a `Deny` then a `RequestOptional` is like a `PermitOnly`. A `RequestOptional` attribute essentially lists the permissions, which you would like to have granted but can live without. For example, your program might have a "print" option. You could do a `RequestOptional` for permission to access the printer and then check to see if it was granted when the program runs.

This way you can let the .NET policy administrators know that your program will function correctly without the optional permissions but that more features may be enabled if they are granted. The administrators can then make informed decisions when setting policy.

If `RequestOptional` and `RequestMinimum` are used together to limit the grant set of an assembly (rather than `RequestRefuse`) the security system will not grant any permission that is not in the lists of optional and required permissions.

The syntax for a `RequestOptional` attribute is no surprise:

```
<assembly: FileIOPermission(SecurityAction.RequestOptional, _
  Unrestricted := True)>
```

If you have no `RequestOptional` attribute then the security system will assume that you want every permission as an optional permission and will grant the largest possible permission set. If you would like to restrict the grant set to only the minimum required permissions and have no optional permissions then use this syntax:

```
<assembly: PermissionSet(SecurityAction.RequestOptional, _
  Unrestricted := False)>
```

78

This essentially makes the optional permission set empty, so only the minimum required permissions will be granted.

Declarative Security with Permission Sets

Occasionally you might want to express "I require as a minimum all the permissions in the `LocalIntranet` code group" or some other code group. You can apply declarative security to code groups as well as individual permissions. For example:

```
<assembly: PermissionSetAttribute(SecurityAction.RequestMinimum, _
  Name := "LocalIntranet")>
```

The legal values for the `Name` argument are the names of the built-in code groups: `Nothing`, `Execution`, `Internet`, `LocalIntranet`, `FullTrust`, and `SkipVerification`. You may not use the `Everything` permission set or a custom permission set in a declarative security attribute as the contents of these permission sets are not known until after the assembly is loaded.

Note also that this syntax for applying some security action to every permission in a named permission set is also legal for all the other security actions. For example, you could have a declarative "demand for every permission in the `FullTrust` permission set" attribute on a method or a class.

Assembly Attributes Overview

The foregoing discussion of assembly attributes might be somewhat confusing. Let's sum up what happens when an assembly is loaded:

❑ First, the policy evaluator determines the grant set based on evidence.

❑ Second, it checks to see if there are minimum requirements, which are not met. If so, then the assembly load fails.

❑ Third, it checks to see if there are refused permissions that were granted. If so, it removes them from the grant set.

❑ Fourth, it checks to see if there are optional requests. Unlike the previous two steps, if there are no optional permissions requested then it assumes that every permission has been requested as an optional permission. Any permission granted that is not in the minimum and/or optional sets is removed from the grant set.

Summary

We have covered the basic "control surfaces" of the entire security system. We have seen practical examples of the use of permission objects to make demands upon callers, restrict called code, and override those restrictions when necessary.

Our description of the tools at your disposal is almost over. In the next chapter, we will cover the remaining features of the security system such as link demands and inheritance demands. We will then start describing the sorts of common flaws programmers accidentally write into their programs, and how these flaws lead to security vulnerabilities. We will discuss how to think like a hacker, play a few rounds of "spot the defect", and give some best practices for what to do when you find a security issue, both before and after it ships to your customers.

VB.NET

Code Security

Handbook

3

3

Advanced .NET Security

In the previous chapter, we discussed the basics of the .NET security system; that is certainly enough for an understanding of the security system's mechanics. However, to really understand all the possible uses and abuses of the security system we will have to look at some more advanced topics:

❑ **Link demands** – first, we will concentrate on the potential pitfalls of the link demand; there are a large number of potentially security-impacting mistakes involving this type of demand.

❑ **Inheritance demands** – while you can control inheritance using access modifiers such a `Friend` and `Protected`, these are quite coarse distinctions. Inheritance demands allow you to let only code with specific privileges extend your public classes.

❑ **Code security and reflection** – .NET's Reflection layer contains many security features built in to prevent people abusing it. Here we explain how these interact with the standard code security system.

❑ **Role-based security** – sometimes it is necessary to directly interact with the Windows security system, usually to get a permission that not available to the current user. Here we look at how to get information from the Windows security systems and how to impersonate other users.

The Link Demand

The link demand is one of the most commonly misunderstood, and therefore misused, features of the .NET security system. Link demands are made when code is JIT compiled, so, before we define exactly what a link demand is, we first need to delve a little into how the JIT compiler works.

Compiling Just In Time

As we discussed in the previous chapter, when you compile a Visual Basic .NET executable the compiler does not actually generate machine code. Rather, it generates code in the .NET Intermediate Language (IL) and writes that into the executable. When the .NET runtime loads the assembly it runs the policy engine to determine the grant set, runs the IL type-safety verifier on partially trusted assemblies and then translates it into machine language on the fly, one method at a time. This translation process is called "Just-In-Time (JIT) compilation" or more concisely, "jitting"; as the IL is translated to machine language "just in time" for it to run. The machine language version of the method is then used every time the method is executed; methods are jitted only once. However, the machine language state is (usually) discarded when the application domain running the program is destroyed,

There are several reasons why Microsoft designed the .NET Runtime in this manner. First, assemblies containing IL have sufficient "metadata" – data about the contents of the assembly – to be self-describing. IL is sufficiently "high level" that the verifier can determine that the managed code does not violate type safety rules, misalign the stack, perform dangerous pointer arithmetic, or do other dangerous operations that would make the code crash-prone or insecure.

Second, IL is portable. A .NET executable will run on any processor architecture for which there is an implementation of the runtime. It is worth noting that the JIT compiler can optimize the generated machine language specifically for its processor architecture.

Third, jitted code is much faster than interpreted IL would be and is almost as fast as native-compiled code, although, there is clearly some overhead associated with both the JIT compilation and with the automatic error checking inserted into the native code.

> *There could be situations in which JIT compiling is faster: IL tends to be smaller than machine code as the JITer can take into account information not available at static compile time. Smaller size means that less time is needed to read it off disk. In some cases, it is faster to read the smaller code and JIT compile it than to read the corresponding machine code and skip the JIT compilation.*

Fourth, it is easier to write a compiler that compiles to IL than to machine language. The System.Reflection.Emit namespace provides tools that make it easy to implement language compilers that target the .NET runtime.

> *System.Reflection.Emit has a set of classes that can dynamically emit IL code from run-time code, or even create complete PE (standard windows executable) files on disk. Therefore, it is not just compiler writers who benefit; the ability to easily emit new code assemblies dynamically using Reflection permits all kinds of innovative solutions.*

Making Demands at "Link Time"

We already know how a demand works; some chunk of code creates a permission object and calls the Demand() method on it. This triggers a stack walk which proceeds to examine the stack frame of every caller until either a frame lacking the given permission is found (in which case the demand fails and the runtime throws an exception), an assertion for the permission is found, or the walk runs out of frames to examine. If the stack walk terminates with an assertion or by verifying that every assembly on the stack was granted the permission then the demand succeeds. All this happens at run time; a link demand is a special kind of demand that does not require a stack walk at run time. There are many differences between a link demand and a regular demand:

- ❑ A regular demand happens every time the demanding code runs. A link demand happens only once, when the code is jitted.

- ❑ A regular demand may be either a "declarative" attribute or an "imperative" call on a permission object. A link demand is always represented by a declarative attribute on a method, class, or assembly – this follows from the first point: the code is not running yet when it is jitted, so it makes no sense to do a link demand dynamically.

- ❑ A regular demand walks the stack. A link demand happens before the code runs, so there is no call stack. A link demand checks only to see that the calling assembly has the required permission in its grant set.

- ❑ Since a link demand does no stack walk and only runs once, link demands are on average much faster than regular demands.

From the above list, one thing should be clear:

> **Though faster, a link demand is a far weaker approach for determining authorization than a regular demand.**

Creating a Link Demand

Actually creating a link demand is very easy, should you actually need to do so. Link demands can only be declarative security demands. This should make sense: imperative demands cannot happen until code runs, but declarative demands are known by the compiler ahead of time.

A declarative link demand is exactly like a regular demand except that the security action is changed from SecurityAction.Demand to SecurityAction.LinkDemand:

```
'LinkDemand.vb

Imports System.Security.Permissions

Public Class SomeClass

  <SecurityPermissionAttribute( _
  SecurityAction.LinkDemand, Unrestricted:=True)> _
  Public Sub DoTheThing()
     ' ...
  End Sub

End Class
```

A link demand can also be placed on classes and interfaces. Like other declarative security attributes, remember that if you have link demands on methods then they replace any link demands on the class.

An Example

To understand the difference between a link demand and a regular demand a little better, consider this rather complicated scenario. We have five assemblies: `Alpha.dll`, `Bravo.dll`, `Charlie.dll`, `Delta.dll`, and `Echo.dll`. Now suppose we have a permission that controls all aspects of the security system, assemblies with that permission can be considered fully trusted. Further, suppose that every assembly except `Charlie.dll` has been granted this permission.

Alpha calls methods in Bravo and Charlie:

```
' From Alpha.DLL, granted full trust
Public Class AClass
  Public Shared Sub ASub()
    BClass.BSub()
    CClass.CSub()
  End Sub
End Class
```

Bravo calls a method in Delta:

```
' From Bravo.DLL, granted full trust
Public Class BClass
  Public Shared Sub BSub()
    DClass.DSub()
  End Sub
End Class
```

Charlie also calls a method in Delta but this assembly unlike the others is not fully trusted:

```
' From Charlie.DLL, NOT granted full trust
Public Class CClass
  Public Shared Sub CSub()
    DClass.DSub()
  End Sub
End Class
```

Delta calls a method in Echo:

```
' From Delta.DLL, granted full trust
Public Class DClass
  Public Shared Sub DSub()
    EClass.ESub()
  End Sub
End Class
```

The method in Echo ESub() is decorated with the demand:

```
' From Echo.DLL, granted full trust
Imports System.Security.Permissions

Public Class EClass
  <SecurityPermissionAttribute( _
  SecurityAction.Demand, Unrestricted:=True)> _
  Public Shared Sub ESub()
  End Sub
End Class
```

Suppose (as shown in Figure 1) you call ASub(), which calls BSub(), which calls DSub(), which calls ESub(), which demands a permission. The stack walk determines that Alpha, Bravo, and Delta have all been granted the permission, so the demand succeeds.

Figure 1

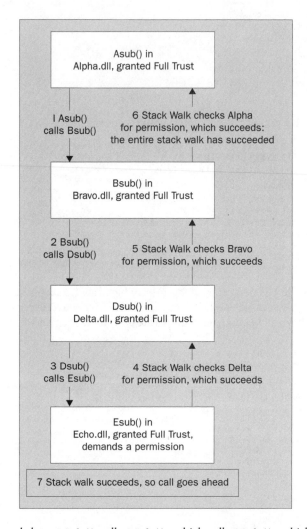

A few microseconds later ASub() calls CSub(), which calls DSub(), which calls ESub(). ESub() cares not a bit that it just finished demanding this permission previously. It demands it again and this time the stack walk determines that Charlie was not granted the demanded permission. The demand fails and ESub() throws an exception.

Figure 2

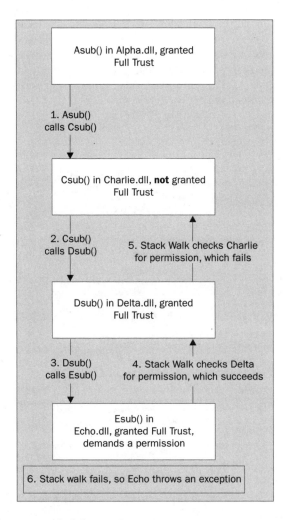

Now let's modify ESub() slightly:

```
' From Echo.DLL, granted full trust
Public Class EClass
  <SecurityPermissionAttribute( _
  SecurityAction.LinkDemand, Unrestricted:=True)> _
  Public Shared Sub ESub()
    ' ...
  End Sub
End Class
```

Things are now considerably different:

Suppose ASub() calls BSub(), which *for the first time* calls DSub(). (That is, this is the first call made to DSub() in this appdomain period, not merely the first call to DSub() from BSub().) On the first call to DSub() it will be translated from IL to machine language. As it is translated the jitter will notice that there is a call to ESub() in there. The jitter knows that ESub() has a link demand so at that point it verifies that Delta.dll was granted the permission. Delta was granted full trust, so the jitter finishes translating DSub(), which runs and calls ESub() as expected. No stack walk occurs; only Delta's grant set is checked.

Figure 3

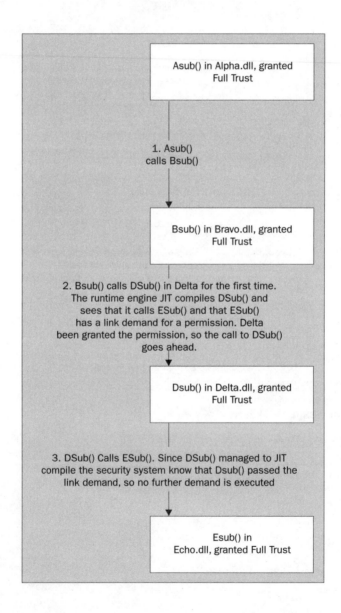

A few microseconds after that, ASub() calls CSub(), which calls DSub(). DSub() has already been jitted once and therefore will not be jitted again. The runtime does no stack walk whatsoever. *Even though Charlie lacks the permission the call to* ESub() it *succeeds.*

Figure 4

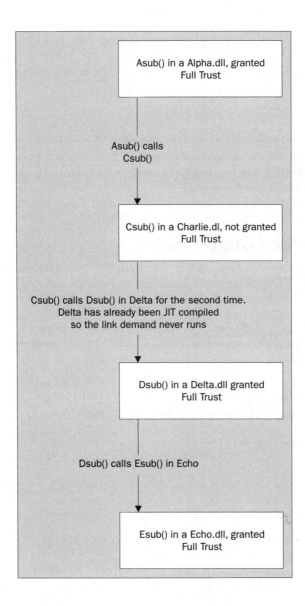

Responsibilities of the Caller

The scenario sketched out above should indicate to you that any time you call a method with a link demand you are taking on certain responsibilities. Essentially the method with the link demand is saying:

"All my immediate callers must have certain permissions to use me. I promise to not constantly bother you with demands every time you call me. I promise that I will only ask one time per immediate caller and I promise that I will not even ask their callers for permission. In return, all immediate callers must make sure that every single time you call me you are not allowing any kind of luring attack or other misuse by any untrusted caller."

In other words:

> **A method, class, or assembly with a link demand consigns responsibility for its secure use onto its callers in exchange for improved performance.**

When to Use Link Demands

Ideally, you should avoid ever using link demands. The .NET Framework classes do use link demands extensively (presently on several hundred methods), for certain time-critical methods. The designers of the framework's classes considered the risk entailed by skipping full stack walks and consigning responsibility to avoiding luring attacks to be worth the gain in performance. The decision to take that risk for the sake of squeezing out more performance is a complex one, not to be made lightly. Err on the side of caution, not raw speed.

However, there may be some cases where you need to make a link demand. If you are writing some code that must be secured, is extremely performance-sensitive, and much less expensive than a stack walk then it might be tempting to use a link demand.

Note that it only makes sense to do this if the "cost" of the link-demand-protected method is much, much smaller than the cost of walking the stack. If the protected method already takes ten times longer than a stack walk then removing the stack walk will only speed up the method by around 10%. If on the other hand the protected method takes one-tenth the amount of time the stack walk takes then removing the stack walk will speed up the method considerably.

The actual amount of time required to do a successful stack walk depends on factors such as the height of the stack, whether there are asserts on the stack, and so on. Generally, you can expect that a full stack walk will take several hundred to several thousand, machine cycles – around a microsecond. Think very carefully before weakening your security to save microseconds. There are few applications where every microsecond counts.

We will look in detail at the security vulnerabilities that you can introduce by incorrectly adding link demands in Chapter 5.

Calling Methods that have Link Demands

As we have already said, when you call a method that makes a link demand you take the responsibility for security. Let's look at a concrete example to see what that actually means. Suppose you have written a fully-trusted component that for some reason needs to get at the underlying handle to a bitmap object. Perhaps you need to call some unmanaged legacy C++ code that modifies the bitmap, for instance:

```
' Bitmap.vb
Imports System
Imports System.Drawing
Class SomeClass
    ' ...
    Public MyBitmap As Bitmap()
    ' ...
    Public Sub DoTheThing
```

For security reasons, the handle is stored as local variable HBitmap only available within the method.

```
    Dim HBitmap As IntPtr
    HBitmap = MyBitmap.GetHBitmap()
    ' Call some unmanaged code that takes HBitmap
    End Sub

End class
```

The GetHBitmap() method is one of the .NET Framework methods that uses link demands, in this case for permission to call unmanaged code. This method needs to be protected as it exposes information about the underlying state of the operating system. One of the pillars of the .NET security model is that all details about memory, kernel object handles and so on should remain unavailable to untrusted managed code.

GetHBitmap() does a link demand rather than a full demand because the implementers of the method assumed that highly performance-sensitive code might be fetching a lot of handles. Fetching the handle is extremely inexpensive; doing a full stack walk every time the handle is fetched could increase the required time enormously. The price the author of the performance-sensitive code pays for this optimization, however, is that the code must never pass the results out to the outside world. That bitmap handle must never be stored in a public member variable, for example. That would enable untrusted code to lure you into leaking secret information.

Discovering Link Demands

We have seen that you should take special precautions when calling methods that make link demands. Clearly, you have to be able to discover that the method you are calling makes such a demand. Unfortunately, there is currently no easy way to determine if you are inadvertently calling a framework (or third party) method, class, or assembly with a link demand on it. One seemingly obvious solution would be to use reflection to examine a method's attributes. Unfortunately, security attributes work differently from all other attributes; it is possible to determine that a security attribute has been set, but not what type it is!

The implementers of the .NET security system are aware of this shortcoming and hopefully they will address it in a future release of the framework, by providing tools that check your assemblies for accidental use of methods that make link demands.

Link Demands and APTCA

Something we mentioned in the previous chapter probably makes more sense now that you understand link demands. Recall that we said "If a partially-trusted assembly (call it Alpha) calls a strong-named assembly (Bravo) then the call will fail unless Bravo was compiled with an `AllowPartiallyTrustedCallerAttribute` (APTCA). Note that unlike a security demand's stack walk, the check for the attribute only considers the immediate caller and called assemblies."

When Alpha is JIT compiled, the jitter notes that it makes a call to a method from a strong-named assembly. If that assembly lacks APTCA, it does a link demand for the full trust permission set.

This fact has interesting ramifications. For example, suppose your strong-named assembly `Foxtrot.dll` does not have APTCA and it contains a public interface definition (`IWhatever`). Then suppose further that the fully-trusted assembly `Golf.dll` contains a class that implements `IWhatever`, which is called from the partially-trusted assembly `Hotel.dll`:

```
' From Foxtrot.DLL: Strong named, no APTCA
Public Interface IWhatever
  Sub DoTheThing()
End Interface
```

```
' From Golf.DLL: Fully trusted:
Public Class GClass
Implements IWhatever
  Public Sub DoTheThing() _
  Implements IWhatever.DoTheThing
  ' ...
  End Sub
End Class
```

```
' From Hotel.DLL: Partially trusted
Public Class HClass
  Public Sub HSub()
    Dim IW As IWhatever
    IW = New GClass()
    IW.DoTheThing()
  End Sub
End Class
```

If HSub() calls via the IWhatever interface then the call will fail. Remember, the jitter is working on the types described in the IL and knows nothing about the run-time implementation of those types. IWhatever is a type from an assembly that does a link demand for full trust. The fact that the actual implementation is from assembly Golf.dll is unknown to the JIT compiler. Had the code read:

```
' From Hotel.DLL: Partially trusted
Public Class HClass

Sub HSub()
  Dim G As GClass
  G = New GClass()
  G.DoTheThing()
  End Sub
End Class
```

then there would be no problem.

> **Link demands are always determined from the compile-time type of the expression used to make the call, not the run-time type.**

Suppressing Unmanaged Code Demands

While we are on the subject of dangerous ways to improve performance by skipping stack walks, there is an even more dangerous kind of link demand induced by the SuppressUnmanagedCodeSecurityAttribute attribute.

Suppose you have a method that must do many, many small, short, inexpensive calls into unmanaged code. Perhaps you are doing some high-performance graphics and need to call the operating system directly, for instance. Even if you assert the right to call unmanaged code, every call will do a stack walk. The stack walk will terminate as soon as it hits the Assert, of course. However, even a one-function-deep stack walk imposes a cost that may be high compared to the cost of the unmanaged call.

To mitigate this performance problem you can decorate a method with the SuppressUnmanagedCodeSecurityAttribute attribute. This attribute is equivalent to adding a link demand for the right to call unmanaged code to the method. In addition to doing a link demand, it also turns off the .NET unmanaged code interop layer's demands for unmanaged code permissions.

Making a link demand for unmanaged code is already dangerous, since you are essentially giving the responsibility for calling the method safely to the callers. Suppressing demands is clearly not something to be done lightly. As with any link demand, do not use this attribute unless you have an extremely compelling reason.

Link Demands Summary

Link demands are usually more trouble than they are worth. Though they give you a considerable performance boost in a small number of scenarios, they add two risks. First, there is the risk that you implement the link demand incorrectly – accidentally leaving a hole whereby an untrusted caller can bypass the link demand. Second, by eliminating the full stack walk you add risk to any third parties who use your code without understanding how to use your methods securely.

The Inheritance Demand

There is one more kind of demand that we have not considered yet, the **inheritance demand**. We will get into the ways you could use inheritance demands to mitigate vulnerabilities in the next couple of chapters. Like link demands, inheritance demands may only be expressed declaratively; there is no imperative form of the inheritance demand.

An inheritance demand allows you to ensure that only sufficiently privileged third parties may extend your public classes. For example, you could insist that only fully trusted callers be allowed to extend your class:

```
Imports System.Security.Permissions

<PermissionSetAttribute(SecurityAction.InheritanceDemand, _
Name := "FullTrust")> _
Public Class Animal
'  ...
End Class
```

Inheritance demands are transitive; if class Animal has an inheritance demand then a derived class Mammal must be in an assembly that is granted the demanded permission (full trust in this example). If class Primate extends Mammal then Primate must also be granted the permission demanded by class Animal's implementer regardless of whether Mammal duplicates that inheritance demand.

Generally, inheritance demands are put on entire classes. However, it is possible to put an inheritance demand on individual methods. If a method in a base class has an inheritance demand but the class as a whole does not, then any assembly may extend the base class. However, only those assemblies that are granted the desired privilege may override the protected method.

```
Imports System.Security.Permissions

Public Class Animal

<PermissionSetAttribute(SecurityAction.InheritanceDemand, _
Name := "FullTrust")> _
    Public Overridable Sub DoSomething()
        ' ...
    End Sub

End Class
```

Here any assembly may override `SomeBaseClass` but only fully trusted assemblies may override `DoTheThing()`.

We will give some practical uses for the inheritance demand in the following chapters.

Security and Reflection

One of the more powerful features of the .NET Framework is the self-describing nature of assemblies, classes, and methods. The ability to take an assembly and enumerate its types at run time, create an instance of an arbitrary type, and invoke a method on the instance is implemented using the Reflection classes contained in the `System.Reflection` namespace.

This ability to create objects of various types by invoking type objects at run time is powerful and useful. However, it also eliminates compile-time type information about the methods called via reflection and introduces a "proxy" layer between the caller and the called code. Both have security implications.

Reflection and Link Demands

At this point, you might be wondering about something. We know that link demands only check the previous caller. We also know that if the previous caller is fully trusted then the link demand will succeed. However, the Reflection classes are in a fully trusted assembly, since the entire .NET Framework is fully trusted. Furthermore, a partially trusted assembly may use Reflection to call any public method in any assembly. So what happens when an untrusted assembly calls a method with a link demand via Reflection? This appears to be a security hole.

Figure 5

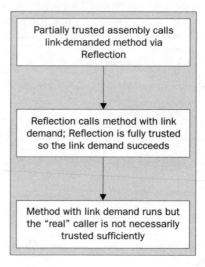

Fortunately, this potential vulnerability is mitigated by the implementation of the Reflection layer. The Reflection classes detect when they are calling a method that requires a link demand and convert it into the equivalent full demand. This full demand then happens every time the method is called via Reflection, not just the first time.

Why does Reflection do a full stack walk rather than just passing the link demand on to its caller? There are two reasons. First, any possible performance gain has already been lost; calling a method through Reflection is much more expensive than calling it directly. Therefore, there is no performance reason not to do the full stack walk.

Second, why would you be calling through Reflection in the first place? The purpose of the Reflection layer is to let you make calls to methods at run time without having to know details of the method implementation at compile time. However, if that is the case then presumably your program does not know that the method you are calling has a link demand!

Link demands effectively put the onus of security upon their caller but in this case, the caller is almost certainly not aware that the method called does a link demand. It is therefore safer to turn the link demand into a full demand every time the method is called through Reflection.

Reflection and Assert

The right to assert a permission is itself controlled by a permission. When an assembly attempts to assert a permission the security system does two things. First, it checks to see if the current assembly has been granted the `SecurityPermissionFlag.Assertion` right. That check does not do a stack walk! That would obviously defeat the point of the assertion, which is to override the stack walking behavior. Only the assembly attempting to assert is checked for the right to assert.

Second, it checks to ensure that the permission asserted is one granted to the assembly; you cannot assert more rights than you were granted in the first place!

You might therefore be wondering what happens when a partially trusted caller asserts a permission by calling the Assert() method via Reflection. At the point of the assertion the caller of the assert method will be the fully trusted Reflection layer. The security system will check to see that the caller has the permission to assert and the permission asserted, which will succeed because Reflection is in a fully trusted assembly. Again, this appears to be a security hole.

Appearances can be deceiving. Can you see why this is **not** a vulnerability? Do you see why it still does not do what you might expect?

```
' Reflection.vb

Imports System
Imports System.Reflection
Imports System.Security.Permissions

Public Module Reflection

  Public Sub Main()
    Dim Perm As New _
      SecurityPermission(SecurityPermissionFlag.UnmanagedCode)
    Dim PermType As Type
    Dim AssertMethod As MethodInfo
    PermType = Perm.GetType()
    AssertMethod = PermType.GetMethod("Assert")
    AssertMethod.Invoke(Perm, Nothing)
  End Sub

End Module
```

Figure 6

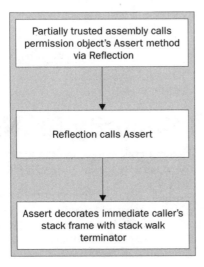

Partially trusted assembly calls permission object's Assert method via Reflection

Reflection calls Assert

Assert decorates immediate caller's stack frame with stack walk terminator

The assert annotates the caller's stack frame with the asserted permission object so that any stack walk caused by a demand for that permission terminates successfully. In this case, Reflection's stack frame is decorated. When the call to Reflection returns the decoration disappears along with the Reflection stack frame. It is as if the assert was never performed.

While this is not a vulnerability, it is certainly misleading. Anyone who calls Assert() on a permission object via Reflection would not actually assert anything because the decorated stack frame, Reflection's stack frame, would be immediately destroyed. For this reason, the Reflection layer simply refuses to call Assert on a permission object.

> **Any attempt to assert a permission via Reflection causes an exception.**

Specifically, the program above produces:

```
System.ArgumentException: Security method may not be called
through reflection.
```

Reflection and Deny/PermitOnly

Given what you now know about calling Assert() via Reflection it should be clear that calling Deny() through Reflection would cause a security vulnerability. If you could successfully deny a permission by calling via Reflection then again, Reflection's stack frame would be annotated and promptly disappear. When the caller goes on to call something else, the deny would no longer be in effect and the called code could successfully demand the permission.

To mitigate this vulnerability the reflection layer does the same thing as it does for Assert: throws the above exception if you attempt to Deny() (or PermitOnly()) a permission or permission set via Reflection.

We shall cover some more ways in which Reflection can be misused to cause security holes in Chapter 5.

Role-Based Security in .NET

Though this book is primarily about code-based security it could not hurt to have a brief overview of how role-based security works in the .NET Runtime.

Recall that role-based security grants permissions based on the identity of the user running the code, as opposed to code-based security, which grants permissions based on evidence about the code. You already know that the .NET Framework represents code-based security concepts such as "policy" and "evidence" with .NET objects. Unsurprisingly, objects are also used to represent role-based security concepts.

The two most important classes are Identity objects, which represent individuals (for instance, users on a network) and Principal objects, which represent the combination of an identity and its roles (for instance, Administrator, Power User, Backup Operator, and so on).

Identity Objects

An identity object represents information about an individual user, such as the user name and the security provider used to authenticate that user. For example, an identity object could represent the anonymous requester of some web page, or it could represent a user logged into a particular domain authenticated with the Kerberos security provider.

Windows Identity Objects

The .NET Framework notion of identity is extremely generic. It is possible to define your own classes that represent particular sorts of identities. The most common use for role-based security is to determine if a particular Windows user has permission to access some resource. The framework provides the WindowsIdentity class to encapsulate the information about an authenticated Windows user.

As we noted in the last chapter, every process and every thread in each process has a particular security token associated with it. This is how the operating system determines what rights and privileges any given process possesses. You can see this security information by fetching the current WindowsIdentity object:

```vb
'WindowsIdentity.vb

Imports System
Imports System.Security.Principal

Module WindowsIdentityExample
  Public Sub Main()
    Dim CurIdentity As WindowsIdentity
    CurIdentity = WindowsIdentity.GetCurrent()
    Console.WriteLine("Name:              " & CurIdentity.Name)
    Console.WriteLine("Authenticated?: " & _
                   CurIdentity.IsAuthenticated)
    Console.WriteLine("Authentication: " & _
                   CurIdentity.AuthenticationType)
    Console.WriteLine("Anonymous?:      " & CurIdentity.IsAnonymous)
    Console.WriteLine("Guest?:          " & CurIdentity.IsGuest)
    Console.WriteLine("System?:         " & CurIdentity.IsSystem)
  End Sub
End Module
```

When this is executed, it produces output similar to this:

```
Name:              SALES\Bruce Campbell
Authenticated?:    True
Authentication:    NTLM
Anonymous?:        False
Guest?:            False
System?:           False
```

Now you can use the various properties of the CurIdentity object to see who the current user is. The properties of the object are AuthenticationType, IsAnonymous, IsAuthenticated, IsGuest, IsSystem, Name, and Token. The authentication type identifies what security provider was used to authenticate the user. For instance, the standard NTLM login or the Kerberos systems are common security providers. The four Boolean properties are straightforward, identifying whether the user is anonymous, authenticated, a guest, or the account representing the operating system itself. The Name property contains the current user name. The Token property contains a pointer to the actual underlying operating system token representing this identity, should you need it to make a call into an unmanaged API that takes a security token.

Accessing this information is a highly privileged operation. Only highly trusted code is able to discover security-sensitive information such as the user name and authentication method. Getting a valid user name and knowing what authentication mechanism must be circumvented are the first things any attacker would like to know.

> **For obvious security reasons, the specific "credential" information used to validate an identity is not stored with the Identity object. An Identity object may represent a user authenticated with a valid password but the password itself is not stored in the object.**

Custom Identity Objects

Your application may have the notion of multiple identities without requiring all the overhead of the secure Windows authentication mechanisms. For instance, you might be writing a multi-player game where you need to keep track of information about player identities. Or perhaps your application grants rights to different kinds of users (developers vs. users, or accountants vs. salespeople, and so on) that have no corresponding Windows user groups.

In this case, you can create simple identity objects with the GenericIdentity class or create your own identity objects by writing a class that implements the IIdentity interface.

In these cases, the onus for correctly authenticating the users is entirely yours. Designing a robust, secure custom authentication system is difficult and well beyond the scope of this book. There are many issues, such as how to securely determine identity, how to store credential information safely, how to deal with compromised passwords and so on.

If you need to create custom identity objects then think carefully about the security ramifications of creating your own identity objects when you design your application. Remember that the more privileged an identity is, the more carefully you must authenticate any user or code claiming to have that identity.

The .NET Framework also provides some special-purpose identity objects: FormsIdentity and PassportIdentity that are used by webform-based ASP.NET applications and for Microsoft Passport authentication, respectively. A detailed discussion of ASP.NET authentication would take us rather far afield, so we will not discuss it further in this text. The Wrox book *ASP.NET Security* (ISBN: 1-86100-620-9) provides extensive coverage of ASP.NET security issues, including authentication.

Principal Objects

A principal object contains an identity object and it also determines if the user identified by the identity object is authorized to "play a given role". In Windows, roles are the same as user groups, such as "Administrators" or "Power Users". You can also define your own roles such as "Lecturer", "Student", "Accountant", "Lawyer", "Evil Wizard", and so on depending on what kind of multi-user program you are designing.

Principal Policy

We know that from the operating system's point of view each thread has a security token that uniquely specifies the identity, group membership, and privileges of the thread. From the .NET Runtime's point of view, each thread has a principal associated with it that determines the identity of that thread and the roles it supports. However, since the .NET Runtime supports the abstract notion of generic custom identities and principals, the principal object associated with a thread may be different from the security token used by the underlying operating system.

> **The principal associated with a thread is usually not the WindowsPrincipal object corresponding to the actual underlying security token. By default, the .NET Runtime assigns a generic principal object to each thread.**

There is a good reason for this; again, it comes back to our model of multiple defenses that reveal as little information to attackers as possible. If the .NET Runtime automatically associated a WindowsPrincipal object representing you, every time you ran a VB.NET program then any (even untrusted) code could determine your identity and roles by demanding the appropriate permissions. Remember that untrusted code is not allowed to *set* the principal of a thread but it is allowed to *read* it.

The decision whether to use the `WindowsPrincipal` object corresponding to the current security token or an anonymous, generic principal is controlled by principal policy. Principal policy may be set on a per-AppDomain basis using the `SetPrincipalPolicy` method. You have two choices:

```
AppDomain.CurrentDomain.SetPrincipalPolicy( _
    PrincipalPolicy.UnauthenticatedPrincipal)
```

The above is the default behavior. Your other choice is:

```
AppDomain.CurrentDomain.SetPrincipalPolicy( _
    PrincipalPolicy.WindowsPrincipal)
```

Note that the principal of a given thread is generated lazily. This means that the principal object is not actually created until the first time it is read. If you change the policy before you read a thread's principal for the first time then the policy change will be reflected in the principal object. If you change the policy after reading the principal object for a given thread then the principal does not change unless you explicitly reset it.

> **The ability to change an appdomain's principal policy or a thread's principal is usually restricted to fully trusted code. However, all code has the right to read the current thread principal regardless of its level of trust.**

Checking Roles

Suppose you are writing an application and wish to restrict particular functionality to only users in a particular role. Let's suppose for instance that you are writing a backup utility and want to check to see that the user is a member of the Backup Operators group. There are several different ways to do this.

Checking for a Group by Name

The most direct way to check to see if a principal represents a user in a particular group is to just check the name of the group. First, we shall set the principal policy so that the current user's principal is associated with the thread instead of the generic principal. Second, we shall fetch the principal from the current thread and see if it is in a particular role. In this example, we shall see if the current user is a member of the backup operators group.

```
' Backup1.vb

Imports System
Imports System.Threading
Imports System.Security.Principal
```

```
Module CheckBackup
  Sub Main()
    AppDomain.CurrentDomain.SetPrincipalPolicy( _
      PrincipalPolicy.WindowsPrincipal)
    Console.WriteLine(Thread.CurrentPrincipal.IsInRole( _
      "BUILTIN\Backup Operators"))
    ' IsInRole returns a Boolean
  End Sub
End Module
```

Note that the string you pass to `IsInRole()` must be the exact, fully qualified name of the user group. Here are some common group names:

```
LOCAL
BUILTIN\Backup Operators
BUILTIN\Users
BUILTIN\Administrators
[YourMachineNameHere]\Debugger Users
Everyone
```

Using the Built-in Enumeration

If you are looking for one of the standard groups then you can use a special version of the `IsInRole()` method that takes an enumerated value:

```
'Backup2.vb

Imports System
Imports System.Threading
Imports System.Security.Principal

Module CheckBackup
  Sub Main()
    AppDomain.CurrentDomain.SetPrincipalPolicy( _
      PrincipalPolicy.WindowsPrincipal)
    Dim WP As WindowsPrincipal
    WP = Thread.CurrentPrincipal
    Console.WriteLine(WP.IsInRole(WindowsBuiltInRole.BackupOperator))
  End Sub
End Module
```

The legal arguments to this version of `IsInRole` are:

```
WindowsBuiltInRole.AccountOperator
WindowsBuiltInRole.Administrator
WindowsBuiltInRole.BackupOperator
WindowsBuiltInRole.Guest
WindowsBuiltInRole.PowerUser
WindowsBuiltInRole.PrintOperator
WindowsBuiltInRole.Replicator
WindowsBuiltInRole.SystemOperator
WindowsBuiltInRole.User
```

These are equivalent to using "BUILTIN\AccountOperators",
"BUILTIN\Administrators", and so on.

You might be wondering why we stuck the current principal into a variable first, unlike
the previous example. Watch out for this common error:

```
f = _
    Thread.CurrentPrincipal.IsInRole(WindowsBuiltInRole.BackupOperator)
```

The WindowsPrincipal object has an overloaded IsInRole() method which takes
a WindowsBuiltInRole value. The IPrincipal interface's IsInRole() method
takes a string and has no overloads. The fragment above gives the compiler no hint
that the object returned is really a WindowsPrincipal object and so the VB.NET
compiler cannot choose to use the correct overload. Instead, it converts the
enumerated value to a string. This is effectively the same as

```
Thread.CurrentPrincipal.IsInRole("WindowsBuiltInRole.BackupOperator")
```

Which is clearly false (unless you happen to be a member of a group called
"WindowsBuiltInRole.BackupOperator").

> **Always give the compiler enough information to pick the
> right overloaded method.**

Demanding the Identity and Group with Imperative Security

Another way to check for a particular role is to demand it using a permission object.
The PrincipalPermission constructor takes three arguments: an identity string, a
role string, and a Boolean indicating whether you care if the identity was authenticated
or not. Here for example we demand that the principal object is for any authenticated
backup operator.

```
'Backup3.vb

Imports System
Imports System.Threading
Imports System.Security.Principal
Imports System.Security.Permissions

Module CheckBackup
  Sub Main()
    AppDomain.CurrentDomain.SetPrincipalPolicy( _
      PrincipalPolicy.WindowsPrincipal)
    Dim Perm As New PrincipalPermission( _
      Nothing, "BUILTIN\Backup Operators", True)
    Perm.Demand()
  End Sub
End Module
```

Like any other demand, this throws a security exception if the permission cannot be obtained. Note, however, that this demand does not do a stack walk. Stack walks are part of the code security system, not the role security system. When doing role security checks the demand simply verifies that the principal object associated with the current thread represents the given identity in the given role.

To clarify further, the right to, say, set principal policy, or change the principal of a given thread is protected by code security. These operations will do demands that walk the stack to ensure that the code is authorized to change the principal. These operations are typically restricted to only fully trusted code. The demand for a particular identity or role is simply a check on the current principal object, not a check for any properties of the code on the call stack. A `PrincipalPermission` object does not support the `Assert()`, `PermitOnly()`, or `Deny()` methods; these make no sense on a permission that does not affect the code security stack walk mechanism.

When using the imperative permission form to check role security you can check for any combination of identity and role. In the example above, we passed `Nothing` for the identity and a string for the role. You could also check just for an identity if you wanted to ensure that only a specific user could access some code:

```
Dim Perm As New PrincipalPermission( _
    "MYDOMAIN\LeahJones", Nothing, True)
```

Alternatively, for that matter, you could just check for "any authenticated identity":

```
Dim Perm As New PrincipalPermission( _
    Nothing, Nothing, True)
```

The permission object:

```
Dim Perm As New PrincipalPermission( _
    Nothing, Nothing, False)
```

represents "any identity, any role, the identity need not be authenticated". However, checking for the permission object is essentially meaningless, as it can never throw an exception when demanded.

Demand the Identity and Group with Declarative Security

Finally, you can use a declarative form of the permission as well:

```
' Backup4.vb

Imports System
Imports System.Threading
Imports System.Security.Principal
Imports System.Security.Permissions
Module CheckBackup
<PrincipalPermissionAttribute(SecurityAction.Demand, _
    Role := "BUILTIN\Backup Operators")> _
```

```
    Sub DoBackup()
       ' ...
    End Sub
    Sub Main()
       AppDomain.CurrentDomain.SetPrincipalPolicy( _
          PrincipalPolicy.WindowsPrincipal)
       DoBackup()
    End Sub
 End Module
```

The declarative form of the permission is similar to the imperative form. You can specify or omit the identity, role, and authentication status. For example, you could restrict the method to only a specific, authenticated backup operator:

```
    <PrincipalPermissionAttribute(SecurityAction.Demand, _
       Name := "MYDOMAIN\LeahJones", _
       Role := "BUILTIN\Backup Operators",_
       Authenticated := True)> _
    Sub DoBackup()
```

Instead of setting the fields you do not care about to Nothing just omit the arguments from the attribute.

The only legal action for the declarative principal permission attribute is SecurityAction.Demand. As we mentioned above, it makes no sense to Assert, PermitOnly or Deny a permission that has nothing to do with the state of the stack. It also makes no sense to LinkDemand or InheritanceDemand a principal permission; these demands are only performed the first time the code is called from a particular context. Since there is nothing stopping fully trusted code from changing the principal between calls we must check every single time the method is called to ensure that the demand is still met. An attempt to do any action other than Demand on a PrincipalPermissionAttribute will cause a compilation error.

Finally, note that combining declarative role security attributes works like any other declarative security attribute. If you have declarative demands on both a method and its enclosing class then the method demand replaces the class demand rather than doing both demands.

So Which Should I Use?

From a security perspective, none of the methods above is any better or worse than another. The differences are entirely a matter of how you want success and failure information communicated to you. Whether you prefer to check a return code or trap an exception is a matter of style and program design. Use whatever techniques fit in well with your programming style.

Impersonation with WindowsIdentity Objects

As we mentioned above, the underlying Windows role-based security system is based on the notion of associating a token with each thread. The token represents the identity, rights, privileges, and group membership of the user. A thread then acts on behalf of that user and can do anything that that user is authorized to do.

It is occasionally convenient to **impersonate** another user temporarily. Impersonation is rather like putting on a disguise; underneath it is still you, but to the world, it looks like you are someone else. For example, suppose that you have two accounts on a particular machine: a regular user account and an administrator account. Being a security-conscious administrator, you only use the administrator account when you absolutely have to. If you habitually use your administrator account, stop now! If you fall prey to a virus or other attack then the attacker will have administrator privileges.

The reason most administrators habitually use their administrator account is because it is convenient. If you have to reconfigure the machine or read some file ACL'd to the administrator account it is a pain to log off, log in to the administrator account, make the change, log off and log back on again as a regular user.

If you are designing an application that has a "user" mode and an "administrator" mode then you should try to make it easy for administrators to run as users. Consider temporarily impersonating the administrator account when you need to rather than forcing the administrator to run your application in the administrator account.

Unfortunately, there is at this time no .NET Framework method to create an authenticated `WindowsIdentity` object directly, so here we'll create some simple code to do that.

What we are going to do here is call the unmanaged `LogonUser` Win32 API to obtain the security token for a given authenticated user. We can then use that token to construct the appropriate `WindowsIdentity` object and impersonate the user.

```
' Impersonate.vb

Imports System
Imports System.Security.Principal
Imports System.Security.Permissions
Imports System.Runtime.InteropServices

Public Module ImpersonationExample
```

First, we shall just make some declarations so that we can do the unmanaged call.

```
<DllImport("advapi32.dll")> _
Private Function LogonUser(lpszUsername As String, _
lpszDomain As String, lpszPassword As String, _
dwLogonType As Integer, dwLogonProvider As Integer, _
ByRef phToken As Integer) As Boolean
End Function
```

```
<DllImport("Kernel32.dll")> _
Private Function GetLastError() As Integer
End Function

Private Enum Logon
   Interactive       = 2
   Network           = 3
   Batch             = 4
   Service           = 5
   Unlock            = 7
   NetworkCleartext  = 8
   NewCredentials    = 9
End Enum

Private Enum Provider
   UseDefault   = 0
   WindowsNT35  = 1
   WindowsNT40  = 2
   Windows2000  = 3
End Enum
```

The GetWindowsIdentity() method takes in the necessary strings, calls the unmanaged API, and if successful, constructs an identity object.

```
<SecurityPermissionAttribute(SecurityAction.Demand, _
ControlPrincipal := True, UnmanagedCode := True)> _
Private Function GetWindowsIdentity(UserName As String, _
Domain As String, Password As String) As WindowsIdentity
   Dim SecurityToken As Integer
   Dim Success As Boolean
   Success = LogonUser(UserName, Domain, Password, _
     Logon.Network, Provider.UseDefault, SecurityToken)
   If Not Success Then
     Throw New System.Exception("Logon Failed. Error: " & _
       GetLastError())
   End If
   GetWindowsIdentity = new WindowsIdentity(new _
                                    IntPtr(SecurityToken))
End Function
```

Now we can use this method to temporarily make the operating system think a different user is associated with this thread.

```
Public Sub Main()
    Dim NewIdentity As WindowsIdentity
    Dim CurIdentity As WindowsIdentity
    Dim NewContext As WindowsImpersonationContext
    Dim UserName, Domain, Password As String
```

First, we need to get the details of the account to impersonate.

```
Console.WriteLine("Enter Domain")
Domain = Console.ReadLine()
Console.WriteLine("Enter User Name")
UserName = Console.ReadLine()
```

For simplicity, we will let the password be visible on the console, but this is obviously a bad thing to do in any real situation. Unfortunately, the System.Console class does not contain many of the features you actually need to control the console, such as a function that controls echoing. To control this you would need to access the API using interop.

```
Console.WriteLine("Enter Password")
Password  = Console.ReadLine()

NewIdentity = GetWindowsIdentity(UserName, Domain, Password)
NewContext = NewIdentity.Impersonate()
```

After we create a new identity objects we call the Impersonate() method and the thread now behaves as though the authenticated user identified by NewIdentity started it.

```
CurIdentity = WindowsIdentity.GetCurrent()
Console.WriteLine("Impersonating: " & CurIdentity.Name)
```

We'll print the current identity out to the console just to check.

```
NewContext.Undo()
```

Calling the Undo() method reverts the thread to the identity of its creator

```
CurIdentity = WindowsIdentity.GetCurrent()
Console.WriteLine("Actually:      " & CurIdentity.Name)
    End Sub
End Module
```

Before we go on, let's take this opportunity to do a quick security review of this short program. It has some good features: only those things that need to be public are public, for example. The "magic" constants passed to the unmanaged code are encapsulated by self-documenting enumerations. The error message is not overly informative. The error handling is aggressive, causing an exception no matter what the error condition was.

It also has some shortcomings. For instance, it does not check to see if the caller attempted to pass a ten-million-character domain name, or that the domain name contains only valid characters and so on. The more rigorously you can validate data the less likely it is that a hostile caller will get hostile data into unmanaged code where it could cause a buffer overrun.

Impersonation can be tricky and dangerous; you should design and review any use of impersonation carefully. We shall cover a number of ways you can introduce security vulnerabilities by using impersonation in Chapters 4 and 5.

Summary

The .NET Runtime's security system is complex and powerful. It implements both code-based concepts (such as link demands and inheritance demands) and role-based concepts (such as principals and identities).

The code-based security system provides heuristics (such as stack walks) to help reduce vulnerabilities, but those features come at a price. Should you absolutely need to write dangerous, high performance code you can do so, but at the cost of pushing the responsibility for correct use of the code onto your trusted callers.

The role-based security system is an abstract superset of the Windows security system with its users and groups. You can use Windows-based identities and principals to ensure that only authorized users may use your programs. You can use impersonation to temporarily change the rights associated with a particular thread or appdomain. You can also create your own custom identities and roles (though you take on the burden of implementing appropriate authentication if you do so).

We've compared the process of writing secure software to building bank vaults several times in this book. Security-conscious people who know how to correctly use tools and materials to construct secure buildings build good vaults. They know how to spot vulnerabilities and mitigate them. They think like attackers every step of the way.

If you have made it this far then you have a good overview of a quite complex security system. However, there is one area we've not yet looked at in detail, creating custom policies and evidence. We'll look at these techniques while considering how you might secure an application that can be customized with third-party modules.

VB.NET

Code Security

Handbook

4

4

Security and Customizable Applications

This chapter deals with programmatic manipulation of the evidence and policy, which enables you to precisely control the permissions granted to other code. Not every application needs the flexibility and power of custom policy, but examining these issues will also give you an insight in to how policies work at a low level.

One of the most challenging tasks for code-based security is an application that can be customized using third-party modules. This is exactly the sort of situation where we need to use advanced techniques like custom policies. Therefore, we'll examine custom policies by looking at the security challenges that arise while implementing such a customizable application.

What are the Security Challenges?

Suppose that you wanted to create an ecosystem simulator that lets users write custom assemblies representing predators and prey, such as the Terrarium game at http://www.GotDotNet.com/. Alternatively, perhaps you want to write a program that does financial calculations and you want to allow third parties to write custom assemblies that perform unusual tax calculations. Internet Explorer is an excellent example of a program that can be customized, both with scripts and with third-party controls. In fact, when you start looking you'll find all sorts customizable programs.

Now consider the security implications of writing such a program. We can probably assume that your "host" program will require full trust from the user in order to run. However, it would be very nice indeed to not require that all third-party customizations are also fully trusted. After all, why should the user have to grant a customization that just does tax calculations, full rights? It is also worth remembering that if the customization creates an opening for an attacker, customers may quite rightly consider the creators of the main application to be just as much at fault as who ever wrote the customization.

It comes back to running with the least privilege again. If the customization is run with the fewest possible permissions then the risk of damage due to a hostile customization is greatly reduced. The risk of hostile code taking advantage of security flaws in the customization is also greatly reduced.

If it's Broke then Fix It

Let's come up with a couple of naïve, broken implementations that show how not to secure a customizable application. We shall analyze why they are insecure and figure out ways to mitigate those insecurities. Then later on we'll suggest some better solutions to this problem.

First, we shall need some infrastructure though. The host and the customization will communicate over this interface:

```
' TaxInt.vb
Public Interface ITaxCustomization
    Function ComputeTaxes(ByVal Amount As Decimal) As Decimal
End Interface
```

Here's a typical benign customization implementation that for demonstration purposes just does some very simple calculation:

```
' TaxPlugin.vb
Public Class TaxPlugin
    Implements ITaxCustomization
    Public Function ComputeTaxes(ByVal Amount As Decimal) As Decimal _
    Implements ITaxCustomization.ComputeTaxes
        ComputeTaxes = Amount * 0.087
    End Function
End Class
```

Attempt One: Ask the User

Now let's come up with a seemingly correct host and see how things can go terribly wrong. We'll use Reflection to load the class out of the customized assembly, instantiate it, and call the method.

The `System.Reflection` *namespace contains classes that allow you to get information about assemblies such as their constituent: types, classes, and so on even if you have no prior knowledge about their contents.*

Why not just give the users the choice? Here we shall ask the users whether they want to load a potentially hostile customization or not. We begin by asking for permission to load the customization assembly, then load the assembly, find a class definition in it, invoke the constructor for the class, and call the class on the interface described above.

(Note that a realistic customizable host would allow the user to decide which customization to use, but for this illustrative example we will simply hard-code the path.)

```
' TaxBad1.vb

Imports Microsoft.VisualBasic
Imports System
Imports System.Reflection
Public Module TaxHost

    Public Sub Main()
        Dim Asm As Assembly
        Dim CustomType As Type
        Dim CustomCtor As ConstructorInfo
        Dim Types(-1) As Type
        Dim Args(-1) As Object
        Dim Custom As ITaxCustomization
        Dim Amount As Decimal = 12.34
        Dim Result As Decimal
```

Here we just import the necessary namespaces and declare the necessary types.

```
        Dim DoCust As MsgBoxResult
        DoCust = Interaction.MsgBox( _
            "Do you want to run a potentially dangerous customization?", _
            MsgBoxStyle.YesNo Or MsgBoxStyle.Question, "Security Warning")
        If DoCust = MsgBoxResult.No Then Exit Sub
```

Here is the code to generate the message box and exit the Sub if the user declines to load the assembly.

```
        Asm = Assembly.LoadFrom("custom\taxplugin.dll")
        CustomType = Asm.GetType("TaxPlugin")
        If CustomType Is Nothing Then Throw New Exception("Bad Type")
        CustomCtor = CustomType.GetConstructor(Types)
        If CustomCtor Is Nothing Then Throw New Exception("Bad Ctor")
        Custom = CustomCtor.Invoke(Args)
        Result = Custom.ComputeTaxes(Amount)
        Console.Writeline(Result)
    End Sub
End Module
```

Here we load the assembly containing the customization into a `System.Reflection.Assembly` object using Reflection. Then we call the `GetType()` method to get a reference to the `TaxPlugin` class or throw an exception if this fails. Next we get `TaxPlugin's` constructor and call `invoke()` on it to instantiate the `TaxPlugin` class. Finally we call the custom `ComputeTaxes()` method and print out the result.

> **This is absolutely the worst thing you can do. This is in fact even worse than doing nothing at all.**

Look at this from the user's point of view. There is Alice in Accounting using your nifty new customizable tax package; she downloads the latest tax customizations, goes to compute some taxes and is then faced with a security dialog. Alice now has an important choice to make and absolutely no data upon which to make a sensible choice. Furthermore, she is an accountant, not a computer security expert: even if she did have the data, she would not know what is the right thing to do anyway.

From the user's point of view the dialog box actually says

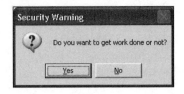

Alice will very quickly learn that pressing "No" stops her from do her job and pressing, "Yes" will allow her to get on with her work. This is a classic example of behavioral modification through positive reinforcement. Every time Alice clicks "Yes", something good happens, so she will get in the habit of always clicking "Yes" when faced with a security decision.

Obviously, that is a terrible habit to get into. Eventually Alice or someone like her will download a hostile customization, click "Yes", and allow some attacker to own the machine.

Lest you think that this is mere theory, think about the ILOVEYOU virus. **Every single person** of the millions who spread the infection to someone else clicked OK on a dialog box that clearly stated that the script they were about to run might be hostile. Most of them had clicked OK hundreds of times previously without spreading a virus. How were they to know that it would ever be any different?

The entire point of the policy system is to make security decisions ahead of time and then apply that policy consistently, rather than forcing the user to continually re-evaluate their opinions about the trustworthiness of code. Users make bad trust decisions, so do not even give them the choice. If they want to change their opinions about code then they can reconfigure their policy.

> When faced with a choice between security and productivity, users will choose productivity every time. You have to make it secure and productive without involving the user.

Attempt Two: Use PermitOnly

We know how to restrict the rights of code already, right? Just put a note on the stack saying that we should only permit execution and nothing else before calling the potentially hostile function.

Unfortunately, this does not work either:

```
' TaxBad2.vb

Imports System
Imports System.Reflection
Imports System.Security
Imports System.Security.Permissions

Public Module TaxHost
  Public Sub Main()
    Dim Asm As System.Reflection.Assembly
    Dim CustomType As Type
    Dim CustomCtor As ConstructorInfo
    Dim Types(-1) As Type
    Dim Args(-1) As Object
    Dim Custom As ITaxCustomization
    Dim Amount As Decimal = 12.34
    Dim Result As Decimal
```

Here we will again load the assembly off disk, get the type, the constructor, and so on. However, this time instead of asking the user whether to load it or not, we will just put a `PermitOnly` on the stack before the call. If the assembly is hostile then hopefully it will demand some permission when it attempts to do something hostile, but the stack walk will not succeed:

```
    Dim Execution As New _
        SecurityPermission(SecurityPermissionFlag.Execution)

    Asm = System.Reflection.Assembly.LoadFrom("custom\taxplugin.dll")
    CustomType = Asm.GetType("TaxPlugin")
    If CustomType Is Nothing Then Throw New Exception("Bad Type")
    CustomCtor = CustomType.GetConstructor(Types)
    If CustomCtor Is Nothing Then Throw New Exception("Bad Ctor")

    Custom = CustomCtor.Invoke(Args)
    Execution.PermitOnly()
    Result = Custom.ComputeTaxes(Amount)
    Console.Writeline(Result)

  End Sub
End Module
```

There are two big security problems with this solution. Do you see them?

The first problem is that the PermitOnly() is in the wrong place. This code runs the constructor of a potentially hostile object before it locks down the permissions on the stack! That PermitOnly() should go before the invocation, not after.

Second, the PermitOnly() does not protect you in the least. Since the assembly has been loaded from the local disk it is fully trusted. Fully trusted code may assert any right it chooses regardless of what is on the stack; the whole point of asserting is to override the limitations imposed by the caller.

Furthermore, even if there were some way to prevent these two serious problems, there are also some less crucial problems with this approach. For instance, suppose you have many code paths in which you call in to the untrusted assembly. You would have to make sure that you put the appropriate restrictions on every call. How likely are you to miss one and thereby introduce a vulnerability?

Attempt Three: Lock down the Directory

The fundamental problem with Attempt Two is that the potentially hostile assembly is on the local machine and therefore fully trusted. What if you modified the user policy level so that assemblies loaded out of the customization directory were put into the "execute only" code group?

This approach is far better than the previous attempt, but it has some problems of its own. First off, why modify the user policy level? You would have to modify the policy of every user on the machine. Better to modify the machine policy level. However, it is likely that only the machine administrator will be able to make changes to the machine policy level.

That means that you would have to ensure that your installation program is executable only by the administrator (which seems like a reasonable requirement) and that the administrator does not mind your program mucking with their policy (which seems less likely, but still not totally unreasonable).

This approach also has the drawback that customizations must be stored on the local machine. That eliminates desirable scenarios such as caches of customizations run from web sites or from machines on your intranet.

Aside from those drawbacks, this is actually a reasonable approach. It is somewhat similar to the approach ASP.NET uses to separate pages into different application domains by putting them in different virtual root directories.

Attempt Four: Say it is from the Internet

One of the overloads of the Assembly.LoadFrom() method takes an Evidence object as an argument. You can use this to override the evidence that the assembly loader will obtain from the load path. You could "trick" the policy evaluator into thinking that the assembly came from the Internet and therefore should be granted fewer rights.

It is too late to change the grant set after the assembly has been loaded. By that point, the evidence has already been used. Instead, you will have to create a new host evidence collection and tell the loader to use it rather than figuring out its own evidence based on the path.

We could modify the original code to create a new evidence collection, stick in host evidence indicating that this came from the Internet Zone, and load the assembly with our evidence rather than the default evidence:

```vb
' TaxBad4.vb
Imports System
Imports System.Reflection
Imports System.Security
Imports System.Security.Permissions
Imports System.Security.Policy

Public Module TaxHost
   Public Sub Main()
      Dim Asm As System.Reflection.Assembly
      Dim CustomType As Type
      Dim CustomCtor As ConstructorInfo
      Dim Types(-1) As Type
      Dim Args(-1) As Object
      Dim Custom As ITaxCustomization
      Dim Amount As Decimal = 12.34
      Dim Result As Decimal

      Dim MyEv as New Evidence()
      Dim InternetZone as new Zone(SecurityZone.Internet)
      MyEv.AddHost(InternetZone)
      Asm = System.Reflection.Assembly.LoadFrom(" _
         custom\taxplugin.dll", MyEv)
```

Note that the right to manipulate evidence when loading an assembly is in fact itself controlled by a permission. The code above will demand the right to manipulate evidence, a permission that is by default granted only to fully trusted code. For this reason, any application that must manipulate the security system by changing evidence or policy must be fully trusted. This should make sense: the ability to change how the security system works should only be granted to extremely trustworthy code!

```vb
      CustomType = Asm.GetType("TaxPlugin")
      If CustomType Is Nothing Then Throw New Exception("Bad Type")
      CustomCtor = CustomType.GetConstructor(Types)
      If CustomCtor Is Nothing Then Throw New Exception("Bad Ctor")

      Custom = CustomCtor.Invoke(Args)
      Result = Custom.ComputeTaxes(Amount)
      Console.Writeline(Result)

   End Sub
End Module
```

Why is Attempt Four a Bad Idea?

Depending on exactly what kind of customized application you wish to build, this may be exactly the right solution. If you believe that using customizations in your application is exactly as dangerous to the user as downloading code off the Internet, and if you believe that the user will never want to make a distinction between Internet code and customizations then yes, this is the right thing to do. It is quick, easy, and simple; it does what the user wants.

However, in this particular case this is probably not what you want. Remember that in the first service pack of the .NET Runtime the default grant set for the Internet zone is empty! Essentially, you are saying to your user "in order to customize this application you must enable running code from the Internet". That seems like a strange thing to tell your users. If they do not want to run code from the Internet then why should they have to turn it back on just to do their taxes?

Perhaps it would be better to use the trusted sites zone; that at least has some permissions in it. Ultimately pegging the rights of the customization to the rights associated with some zone is a bad idea because you do not control what those rights are. If your goal is to always allow only permission to execute and you never need to allow any other permissions then you will need some mechanism independent of the default permission sets associated with zones.

Attempt Five: Custom Policy

Essentially, you want the security system to treat customization assemblies used with your application as special. They are in a code group of their own that gets permission to execute and no more. This implies the following tasks:

- ❑ We must create a **custom evidence object** for our "special" **assembly** that is independent of the zone or path information.

- ❑ This evidence object needs to be associated with a **code group.** That entails writing a **custom membership condition** that maps the evidence to a particular code group.

- ❑ We will need to associate a **permission set** with that code group.

- ❑ Finally, we will create an **appdomain policy level** and add the code group to it.

Custom Evidence

Any serializable object can be used as evidence. The object must be serializable because evidence may be supplied for entire appdomains, not just assemblies. If the creator of a new appdomain supplies evidence then that evidence will have to be moved from the parent appdomain to the new one, which requires serialization. (We will not be moving evidence around between appdomains, but still, this is a requirement on custom evidence objects.)

We are going to put the customization "in a sandbox", so we shall call our custom evidence object SandboxEvidence. Declaring the evidence is the easy part. Just declare a new serializable class:

```
<Serializable()> Friend NotInheritable Class SandboxEvidence
End Class
```

The class needs no body if there is no further complexity to the evidence. The Url evidence object in contrast needs a constructor because a given piece of evidence can refer to a specific URL. We shall avoid that complexity in this example. All that matters about this sort of evidence is its type; it carries no other information with it.

Custom Membership Condition

The next thing we need to do is give the policy engine the ability to recognize that an Evidence collection contains a SandboxEvidence object. The policy engine uses **membership condition objects** to determine if a particular Evidence object contains a particular sort of evidence.

Policy is persisted in the operating system as an XML file describing the various membership conditions. If we were attempting to write new custom membership conditions for the user, machine, or enterprise policy levels rather than just a specific host's appdomain policy level then we would need to write code to persist the custom membership condition as XML.

Fortunately, we can skip this step for the custom appdomain policy case, as the custom policy will never be persisted. (The appdomain and the associated policy are going to go away when the program ends and are created again when we start it again, so there is nothing to persist.) When we put all the code together, you'll see the non-implemented methods that would do the XML persistence.

The membership condition simply checks all the evidence to see if the sandbox evidence is there. Here we have the only interesting method of our custom membership condition: the code that checks to see if a given evidence object meets our condition for group membership in the sandbox group. Since the only distinguishing property of the evidence object is its type that is all we check:

```
Imports Microsoft.VisualBasic
Imports System
Imports System.Reflection
Imports System.Security
Imports System.Security.Policy
Imports System.Security.Permissions

<Serializable()> Friend NotInheritable Class
SandboxMembershipCondition
    Implements IMembershipCondition
    Public Function Check(Ev As Evidence) As Boolean _
```

```
Implements IMembershipCondition.Check
   Dim EvOb As Object
   For Each EvOb In Ev
      If TypeOf EvOb Is SandboxEvidence Then
         Check = True
         Exit Function
      End If
   Next
   Check = False
End Function
```

The rest of this class contains the other methods that are required by the
IMembershipCondition interface.

```
Public Function Copy() As IMembershipCondition _
   Implements IMembershipCondition.Copy
   ' They are all the same
   Copy = New SandboxMembershipCondition()
End Function

Overrides Overloads Public Function Equals(Ob As Object) _
   As Boolean Implements IMembershipCondition.Equals
      Equals = Ob Is Me
End Function

Overrides Overloads Public Function ToString() As String _
 Implements IMembershipCondition.ToString
   ToString = "SandboxMembershipCondition"
End Function
```

We are not actually saving the policy. If you wanted to modify the enterprise, machine
or user policy levels then you would have to save and read the XML by providing
implementations for the methods below. As we mentioned earlier the
System.Security.SecurityElement class can be used for this.

```
Public Sub FromXml(e As SecurityElement) _
   Implements ISecurityEncodable.FromXml
      ' Omitted
End Sub

Public Function ToXml() As SecurityElement _
 Implements ISecurityEncodable.ToXml
      ' Omitted
End Function

Public Sub FromXml(e As SecurityElement, Level As PolicyLevel) _
   Implements ISecurityPolicyEncodable.FromXml
      ' Omitted
End Sub
```

```
Public Function ToXml(Level As PolicyLevel) As SecurityElement _
Implements ISecurityPolicyEncodable.ToXml
  ' Omitted
End Function
End Class
```

Custom Permission Set

So far, we have some custom evidence and a custom rule that defines a membership condition for a custom code group. Now we must create objects representing the set of permissions and the code group, and then glue them together.

First, we create the permission set. This will be an extremely restrictive permission set, which only allows code to execute. Of course, you can add whatever permissions you'd care to grant but this time we will just grant execution:

```
Public Module TaxHost

  Public Sub Main()
```

We wish to load a custom DLL to do this calculation. A realistic customizable host would provide some choice to the user, such as which country's tax laws they would like to use. How ever for our Illustrative purposes, hard-coding the name of the customization will do.

```
Dim Asm As System.Reflection.Assembly
Dim CustomType As Type
Dim CustomCtor As ConstructorInfo
Dim Types(-1) As Type
Dim Args(-1) As Object
Dim Custom As ITaxCustomization
Dim Amount As Decimal = 12.34
Dim Result As Decimal
Dim SandBoxPerms As New NamedPermissionSet("sandbox", _
  PermissionState.None) ' Create it empty
Dim Execution As New _
  SecurityPermission(SecurityPermissionFlag.Execution)
SandboxPerms.AddPermission(Execution)
```

Since the "execution only" permission set is one of the built-in permission sets, we could also use the GetNamedPermissionSet() method to fetch it. (We do not do this above because this example is intended to show how you can create your own permission sets. We will see shortly how to use GetNamedPermissionSet() as well.)

Custom Policy

Now we actually create the new custom appdomain policy object and tell it about our new permission set:

```
Dim PolLev As PolicyLevel
PolLev = PolicyLevel.CreateAppDomainLevel()
PolLev.AddNamedPermissionSet(SandBoxPerms)
```

We now have a reference to the fourth policy level, and the policy level knows about our permission set. Recall that a policy level consists of a tree of code groups. Each code group determines whether a given assembly belongs to it based on the evidence and grants a particular permission set as a result.

Each code group also determines how the permissions granted are combined with the permission sets granted in other code groups. Normally the rule is "Just combine them all together; if an assembly is in multiple code groups then it gets all the rights granted by each group." This should make sense: if the assembly evidence indicates that it is in the local machine, all code, and Microsoft strong-named code groups then it should get all permissions from the three groups.

There are other rules that code groups could define. For example, the rule might be "If the evidence indicates that the assembly is in group X then stop and just grant permissions associated with group X, otherwise continue to look for other groups". We shall see an example of both "union" and "first match" code groups below.

By default, the appdomain policy level is created with a single code group containing all code and granting full trust. Remember that the appdomain policy level will be combined with the enterprise, machine, and user policy levels in the most restrictive way. You cannot grant more rights to an assembly through a custom appdomain policy level than you could through any other policy level. It is therefore OK for the default appdomain policy to grant all rights.

The appdomain policy we want to express is this: "Check to see if the assembly has sandbox evidence. If it does then apply only the sandbox permission set, otherwise grant full trust (and let the other policy levels restrict it further if necessary).

To do this we will create a three-group hierarchy. The root group will contain the empty permission set and have the rule "Check the first subgroup. If there is a match use its permission set, otherwise use the second subgroup." The first subgroup will check for the sandbox evidence and (if it matches) apply only execution permission. The second subgroup will match all code and apply all permissions.

Figure 1

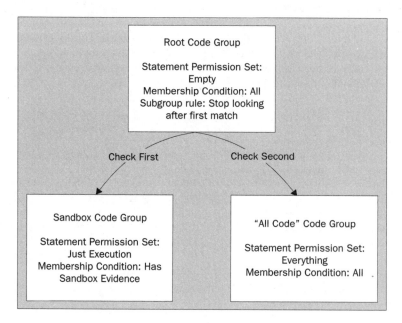

We need to create three code groups. Each code group contains a membership condition and a policy statement. Each policy statement contains a permission set. Once the code groups are created, we need to organize them in to the tree shown in Figure 1.

Let's look at the permission sets first. We have already created the sandbox code group's permission set above. We need permission sets for the other two. The permission sets for these are built into the policy system by default with the names "Nothing" and "Everything".

The policy system represents information about permission sets in code groups as "policy statement" objects, so we shall also create three of those, one for each code group.

```
Dim NoPerms As NamedPermissionSet
NoPerms = PolLev.GetNamedPermissionSet("Nothing")
Dim AllPerms As NamedPermissionSet
AllPerms = PolLev.GetNamedPermissionSet("Everything")
Dim NoStatement As New PolicyStatement(NoPerms)
Dim AllStatement As New PolicyStatement(AllPerms)
Dim SBStatement As New PolicyStatement(SandboxPerms)
```

We also need the membership conditions for each code group. Since two of them match all code we only need to create two membership conditions: our custom condition and the built-in "all code" condition, which matches everything:

```
Dim SBCondition As New SandboxMembershipCondition()
Dim AllCondition As New AllMembershipCondition()
```

Finally, we have everything we need to create the code groups. The root code group is a "first match" group. The other two code groups do not have any child subgroups, so the technique they use to combine the permission sets of their subgroups is not important; we'll make them the standard "union" code group.

```
Dim RootCodeGroup As New FirstMatchCodeGroup(AllCondition, _
                                             NoStatement)
' match all code, grant nothing
Dim SBCodeGroup As New UnionCodeGroup(SBCondition, SBStatement)
' match sandbox code, grant execute
Dim AllCodeGroup As New UnionCodeGroup(AllCondition, AllStatement)
' match all code, grant everything
```

Now all we need to do is give them the tree relationship and give the root of the tree to the policy level:

```
RootCodeGroup.AddChild(SBCodeGroup)
RootCodeGroup.AddChild(AllCodeGroup)
PolLev.RootCodeGroup = RootCodeGroup
```

We are almost done. We have created a policy but not actually applied it to the appdomain yet.

> **Note that you may change the appdomain policy of a given appdomain only once.**

```
AppDomain.CurrentDomain.SetAppDomainPolicy(PolLev)
```

Now, think back; why we were doing this in the first place? Because we wanted to have a custom policy associated with custom evidence when loading an assembly. Finally, we can add the sandbox evidence to the evidence:

```
Dim MyEv as New Evidence()
Dim CustEv As New SandboxEvidence()
MyEv.AddHost(CustEv)
Asm = System.Reflection.Assembly.LoadFrom( _
  "custom\taxplugin.dll", MyEv)

CustomType = Asm.GetType("TaxPlugin")
If CustomType Is Nothing Then Throw New Exception("Bad Type")
CustomCtor = CustomType.GetConstructor(Types)
If CustomCtor Is Nothing Then Throw New Exception("Bad Ctor")
```

```
    Custom = CustomCtor.Invoke(Args)
    Result = Custom.ComputeTaxes(Amount)
    Console.Writeline(Result)

  End Sub

End Module
```

If you try writing various customizations and loading them with and without the custom evidence you will soon find that the ones with the evidence cannot do anything except execute regular code. They cannot create user interface elements, access the file system, or perform any other privileged operation.

Pros and Cons of Custom Policies

The obvious benefit of custom policy is that you can set up the policy once and from that point onward, the customization assemblies are completely locked down as far as their grant set goes. You know exactly of what they are capable.

The obvious drawback is the considerable complexity! The policy model is extremely powerful and flexible. It lets you construct very intricate hierarchical policies if you need to. The vast majority of applications will not require anywhere near this level of sophisticated use of the policy system. However, as more and more applications become customizable and as code becomes more mobile, the ability to implement custom security policy becomes compelling.

Summary

It should now be clear that while protecting customizable applications is a challenging task it is well within the capabilities of the .NET code security system. We have also seen how to programmatically construct new evidence objects and new policies, and how to lock down assemblies.

In the next chapter, we will learn how to build secure software by exploring common and esoteric mistakes that can lead to vulnerabilities in your programs.

129

VB.NET

Code Security

Handbook

5

5

How to Write Insecure Code

In the previous chapters, we discussed the features of the .NET security system; you should now have a good working familiarity with all the security tools at your disposal. Now it is just a matter of using those tools correctly.

In this chapter, we will look at code security from the perspective of what bad practices can cause vulnerabilities in your VB.NET code. Software development is complicated and even code that works just fine when used normally often has unintended behaviors when used by hostile callers. In other words, we will be looking at some examples of "worst practices" in the areas of:

- ❑ Object-oriented code
- ❑ Link demands
- ❑ Exception handling
- ❑ Canonicalization
- ❑ Attempts to keep secrets
- ❑ Server-side code
- ❑ Threading code
- ❑ Serialization code
- ❑ Delegates

In the next chapter, we will look at security from the opposite perspective: what proactive things you can do to minimize the number of mistakes, and mitigate the vulnerabilities introduced by any that are made. We shall turn the worst practices below around and see what best practices they give us.

How to Write Insecure Object-Oriented Code

Visual Basic .NET has many powerful object-oriented features. An important aim of object-oriented programming techniques is to make it easier for large teams to manage the complexity of large software projects. Abstractions such as class hierarchies allow you to encapsulate information, reuse code, and hide implementation details.

One of the unfortunate downsides of these new object-oriented features is that they add complexity to the language. This means that there are some new opportunities to introduce flaws with security implications. In this section, we shall look at some of those flaws and discuss ways to mitigate the vulnerabilities they cause.

Worst Practice: Fail to Restrict Access

VB.NET has access modifiers which restrict untrusted code from seeing certain fields or calling certain methods on a class. These allow you to keep secrets and maintain logical internal consistency. Although as we will see below, it is not possible to prevent a **user** from discovering the secrets contained in your code, it is possible to prevent **untrusted code** from discovering them. (Fully trusted code may do anything a user can do, including running disassemblers, calling your private methods, and so on).

> **Getting the visibility modifiers correct in your code is a good idea not just for security reasons; it also makes writing robust, usable, maintainable code easier by clearly describing the public and private interfaces to your objects. In this text, however, we will mainly look at visibility modifiers from a security perspective.**

A Brief Refresher on Access Modifiers

VB.NET has five access modifiers: `Public`, `Protected`, `Friend`, `Protected Friend`, and `Private`. These modify the visibility of classes, structures, interfaces, functions, subroutines, properties, events, delegates, member variables, enumerations, and constants. Briefly, the access modifiers work as follows:

❑ `Public` elements are visible to all code; this is the least restrictive access modifier.

❑ `Protected` elements are visible to any code in the class same class or any of its subclasses, regardless of whether the subclass is in the same assembly as the class or not.

❑ `Friend` elements are visible to any other code in the same assembly.

❑ Protected Friend combines Protected and Friend in the least restrictive manner. That is, a Protected Friend element in a class is accessible from any code in the class, any code in the assembly, or any code in a derived class from another assembly. (VB.NET does not provide syntax to grant only the disjunction of Protected and Friend; there is no way to express "visible to any subclass in this assembly").

❑ Private elements are visible only to the other elements in its scope and below. For example, a private function in a class is visible to all other functions and subroutines in the class, as well as all functions and subroutines in any nested class, but not visible to members of another (non-nested) class in the same assembly. This is the most restrictive access modifier.

> **All of the rules above may be overridden by any code granted the MemberAccess permission of the ReflectionPermission object. (This permission is normally granted to only fully trusted code.) Sufficiently trusted code has the right to call any method in any class from any assembly regardless of its visibility.**

Worst Practice: Make too much Public

Keeping your public interface as simple and clean as possible will help you write robust, easily understood, maintainable code. From a security perspective the larger and more complex your public interface is, the more possible attack vectors you provide your attackers.

Since the default accessibility for functions and subroutines inside classes is Public, this is an easy mistake to make:

```
Public Class SomeClass
    <PermissionSetAttribute(SecurityPermissionFlag.Demand, _
    Name := "FullTrust" > _
    Public Shared Sub DoSomething()
        ' [omitted: do some setup code, then call a helper...]
        ReallyDoTheThing()
    End Sub

    Shared Sub ReallyDoTheThing()
        ' ...
    End Sub
```

Now any untrusted caller can come along and call ReallyDoTheThing(), bypassing the security check. ReallyDoTheThing() should be marked as Private.

> **Think hard about the visibility of your code elements. Make as much Private or Friend as possible. Only make things Public if they really need to be.**

Best Practice: Spell it Out

Without checking the documentation, what is the accessibility of this class?

```
Class MyClass
End Class
```

The default accessibility for classes in an assembly is Friend. The default for properties accessor functions and methods in a class is Public. The default for fields and constants in a class is Private. Do not get in the habit of relying on these defaults! An important attribute of maintainable, secure code is that its security semantics are immediately understandable without anyone having to go to the documentation.

Here's another way of looking at it. What's the difference between these two classes?

```
Public Class Foo
  Sub Bar()
  End Sub
End Class
```

```
Public Class Foo
  Public Sub Bar()
  End Sub
End Class
```

Is there a difference? The compiler will not think so. However, you are writing code for two audiences: the compiler and your coworkers (and for that matter, future versions of yourself!) Though *semantically* these code fragments say the same thing, there is more *information* conveyed by the latter fragment. The first fragment says:

"There are two possibilities. Perhaps the author of method Bar() intended Bar() to be public and simply neglected to put the access modifier on. Alternatively, perhaps the author has misremembered the default; Bar() was not intended to be public and this code contains a flaw that may impact our security."

The second says:

"The author of method Bar() clearly intended Bar() to be public. If there is a security flaw here it is due to bad design rather than simple forgetfulness."

Which would you rather read when doing a security review of all your code?

134

> **Make your intentions clear – spell out the visibility of all program elements.**

Worst Practice: Allow Subclassing by Untrusted Assemblies

As your programs get larger and more people work on them, you may end up constructing class hierarchies to manage the complexity. Class hierarchies are very useful; they allow you to treat objects polymorphically. For instance, a Manager object may be treated as a special kind of Employee object. They also allow you to share code (a Manager object and an Employee object may share the TakeSickLeave() method implementation) and they allow easy extensibility (a Manager object might have a GiveRaise() method not found on the Employee class.)

```
Public Class Employee

   Public Sub TakeSickLeave(Leave As Date)
      ' ...
   End Sub
   ' ...
End Class

Public Class Manager
Inherits Employee
   Public Overridable Sub GiveRaise(Report As Employee, _
                              Raise As Decimal)
      ' ...
   End Sub
   ' ...
End Class
```

The access modifiers clearly spell out the visibility of each class and method, but what about the right to create derived classes? If untrusted assemblies can subclass one of your classes then a number of potentially bad things could happen.

First, all Protected (or Protected Friend) elements of an instance of the class become visible to the untrusted assembly. If any of the data stored in protected fields is sensitive then it can be stolen. If changing the protected data or calling any of the protected methods could cause problems then you should either restrict who can extend your classes, or reconsider the decision to make them Protected rather than Private.

Second, even if you have no Protected elements, a hostile inheritor can replace your overridable methods with their own versions. The overridden method will have the grant set of the untrusted assembly of course, but if the method does not do what you intend it to do then it could cause logical errors in your program or produce unwanted side effects. For example, if a hostile assembly created a subclass of Manager called EvilManager then it could change the implementation of GiveRaise() to do something other than granting the given raise to the given employee. However, the object would be a perfectly good instance of Manager even though its methods might not do the right thing.

Friend Overridable Methods are Overridable by Unfriendly People

Be careful when implementing methods on inheritable classes marked as `Friend Overridable`. While it is impossible to do this in VB.NET, other .NET languages allow inheritors to override `Friend` methods. Here's an example: suppose you have a hierarchy of business objects where you have overridden some method, in this case, `CanMakePurchases()`. Perhaps the algorithm for determining whether an ordinary employee can make purchases is different from that for managers:

```
Public Class Employee
   Friend Overridable Function CanMakePurchases() As Boolean
      ' ...
   End Function
   ' ...
End Class

Public Class Manager
Inherits Employee
   Friend Overrides Function CanMakePurchases() As Boolean
      ' ...
   End Function
   ' ...
End Class
```

Here `Employee`'s `CanMakePurchases()` and `Manager`'s `CanMakePurchases()` are visible to only other elements in your assembly. It is not possible for code outside this assembly to call `CanMakePurchases()` on either of these objects.

Suppose further that your assembly has some code something like this:

```
Public Sub SubmitPurchaseOrder(Emp As Employee)
   ' ...
   If Emp.CanMakePurchases() Then
      ' ...
End Sub
```

A hostile assembly cannot call `CanMakePurchases()`, but that's not what the hostile assembly wants to do! It could subclass your public `Employee` class and implement its own `CanMakePurchases()` method that always returned `True`. It could then pass such an object to `SubmitPurchaseOrder()`

> **The fact that `Friend` methods are not visible does not actually stop them from being overridden.**

The reason behind this oddity is that the .NET Runtime was designed as a general runtime suitable for implementing many languages (object-oriented and otherwise.) There are popular object-oriented languages (such as C++) that allow overriding of non-visible members, so the ability to do so is built into the runtime. You cannot do this in VB.NET but an attacker could override a VB.NET class using another language that supports this concept, or could even write the IL directly.

Best Practice: Locking down your Classes

Much as you should get in the habit of making everything as private as possible, you should also get in the habit of sealing your classes. If there is no good reason, why a class, particularly a public class, should be extensible then just mark it `NotInheritable`.

If your class must be inheritable, then go through and mark all the methods that do not explicitly need to be overridden as `NotOverridable`. Though the default for public methods is `NotOverridable`, you might want to increase the readability and clarity of your code by specifying the attribute even when it is redundant.

If a class must be inheritable and a method must be overridable then consider using an inheritance demand to ensure that only sufficiently trusted assemblies could extend your class and override its methods. If for instance you want only fully trusted callers to be able to subclass one of your public extensible classes then you may express that through an inheritance demand. For example:

```
Imports System.Security.Permissions
<PermissionSetAttribute(SecurityAction.InheritanceDemand, _
Name := "FullTrust")> _
Public Class SomeBaseClass
' ...
End Class
```

Now any assembly that is not fully trusted but contains a class that attempts to subclass this class will not even load.

How to Write Bad Link Demands

As we said in the previous chapter, you really should not create link demands of your own at all, unless you have an extremely good reason. The most common reason for using a link demand instead of a regular demand is to improve performance. Always remember that performance is not a justification without measurements. Carefully measure the performance with regular demands and with link demands before you take the step of foisting security requirements upon your callers.

If you are set on using link demands, make sure that you use them correctly. There are a great many ways to use link demands incorrectly. Let's look at some of them.

Worst Practice: Inconsistent Link Demands in Class Hierarchies

What is wrong with the following code?

```
' BadLinkDemand.vb

Imports System
Imports System.Security
Imports System.Security.Permissions

Public Class Shape
  Overridable Public Sub DrawMe()
    Console.Writeline("Shape.DrawMe")
  End Sub
End Class

Public Class Square
Inherits Shape

  <SecurityPermissionAttribute(SecurityAction.LinkDemand, _
  Unrestricted:=True)> _
  Overrides Public Sub DrawMe()
    Console.Writeline("Square.DrawMe")
  End Sub

End Class
```

Here we have two classes, a base class, and a derived class with an overriding method that does a link demand for all permissions. That means that the Shape.DrawMe() method cannot possibly be called by partially trusted code, right? Wrong.

> **Remember: a link demand is done when the caller is jitted, not when the caller executes.**

All the hostile untrusted caller has to do is something like this:

```
' ExploitBadLinkDemand.vb

Module Exploit

  Public Sub Main()
    Dim MySquare As Shape
    MySquare = New Square()
    MySquare.DrawMe()
  End Sub

End Module
```

When the JIT compiler runs it sees a call to DrawMe() on an object of type Shape. That method has no link demand, so no link demand is performed. The fact that later, when the code actually runs it will be an instance of Square is irrelevant to the jitter. This code calls the Square version of DrawMe() but never does the link demand.

> **If you put a link demand on an overriding method in the derived class then you also have to put it on the overridden base class method.**

Worst Practice: Inconsistent Link Demands on Interfaces

Be careful as well for the analogous flaw involving interfaces. Interfaces are types. If your class implements an interface and one of the implemented methods has a link demand but the interface does not then all the attacker has to do is call via the interface. Similarly, if the interface declares the method as taking a link demand then every implementation of that method should have the same link demand:

```
Imports System.Security
Imports System.Security.Permissions

Public Interface IPayment
  <PermissionSetAttribute(SecurityAction.LinkDemand,_
  Name:="FullTrust")> _
  Sub PayBill()
End Interface

Public Class Creditor
Implements IPayment

' Whoops, forgot the link demand
  Public Sub PayBill() _
  Implements IPayment.PayBill
    ' ...
  End Sub
End Class
```

The caller of this public class gets a link demand if the call goes via the interface but no link demand if the call is made directly on the class.

> **When interfaces are involved, it is almost never correct to use a link demand. If you must then every implementation of the interface must explicitly make the right link demands.**

Worst Practice: Inconsistent Class and Method Link Demands

We've seen this before, but it bears repeating. If you put a link demand attribute on both a class and a method of that class, only the demand on the method is checked:

```
<SecurityPermissionAttribute(SecurityAction.LinkDemand, _
Unrestricted:=True)> _
Public Class Alpha
```

```
        <EnvironmentPermissionAttribute(SecurityAction.LinkDemand, _
        Unrestricted:=True)> _
        Public Sub Bravo()  ' This _only_ checks for environment permission.
        End Sub
End Class
```

> **Declarative security attributes on methods replace declarative security attributes on classes. They do not combine.**

Actually, the above guideline is not quite accurate. If, for instance, you have a regular demand attribute on a class and a link demand attribute on a method then the method will do both a link demand and a run-time demand. However, given they are easily confused you should not mix class attributes and method attributes. If you find yourself in this situation just put the explicit attributes on each method.

Worst Practice: Structure Constructors

There is one more link demand "gotcha" – consider this structure definition:

```
' Somewhere in Assembly Alpha.DLL:
<SecurityPermissionAttribute(SecurityAction.LinkDemand, _
Unrestricted:=True)> _
Public Structure Sierra
    Public Tango As Integer
End Structure
```

Now consider the call site – does this do a link demand?

```
' Somewhere in Assembly Bravo.DLL:
MySierra = New Sierra
MySierra.Tango = 0
```

Yes, it does – how about this?

```
' Somewhere else in Assembly Bravo:
MySierra = New Sierra
```

These two pieces of code do exactly the same thing: create a structure with a value initialized to zero. However, the latter does not make a link demand! If Sierra were a class then a constructor method (marked with the appropriate link demand) would be automatically generated, but structures do not get an automatically generated constructor! (Instead, the runtime just automatically initializes each element to a sensible default without calling a constructor method.) This could potentially be a security risk if you need to restrict the creation of the structure.

> **If you must make a link demand when a structure is created then you must explicitly define the constructor.**

How to Implement Insecure Exception Handling Code

Implementing the code that handles error conditions is one of those things many programmers leave until the end of the development cycle. The same goes for testing. By the end of any development cycle both testers and developers are usually rushed and willing to blow off flaws caused by incorrect exception handling. Exceptions are by definition unexpected, so it might seem a waste to spend a lot of effort ensuring that the program works correctly even in rare error conditions.

Obviously, that attitude contributes to the development of brittle programs that behave unpredictably and unhelpfully when exceptional cases happen. Fortunately, VB.NET gives you tools such as structured exception handling (the `Try...Catch...Finally` statement) to make exception handling code easier to write. Even with structured exception handling, however, it is still quite easy to introduce security vulnerabilities through poor implementation of exception handling code.

Furthermore, bad exception handling gives you more problems than security vulnerabilities. Users expect and deserve programs, which gracefully and robustly handle all conditions, even exceptional ones. Take the time to ensure that your programs work well and work securely even when exceptions crop up.

Worst Practice: Leaking Privileged Information

One of the major design problems encountered when creating good exception handling is deciding how much information to include in the exception. On the one hand, you want enough information so that a benign caller is able to inform the user that some error has occurred and give them enough information (if appropriate) so they can diagnose and fix the problem. On the other hand, your caller may be hostile and use that information as part of an attack.

A great way to ensure that your programs are vulnerable to this kind of attack is to check for code security last. Suppose, for example, that your fully-trusted component needs to call into unmanaged code to do some operation on a caller-supplied file name. (Normally you would use one of the file stream classes to do file operations, but suppose for the sake of the example that you need to call some specific unmanaged API not represented in the .NET Framework.)

You probably want to throw an exception if the file does not exist, if the path is to a directory rather than a file, or if the caller does not have the right to read the file. As we will see, that is the right list in the wrong order!

Here's an extremely bad way to do it. The code below superficially looks correct, but in fact has a number of flaws in its exception handling that could be exploited.

What we're going to do here is call into an unmanaged Win32 API (FindFirstFile). First, we need to define the structure that we pass to the unmanaged API:

```
' BadFile.vb

Imports System
Imports System.Runtime.InteropServices
Imports System.Security.Permissions

<StructLayout(LayoutKind.Sequential, CharSet := CharSet.Auto), _
SerializableAttribute()> _
Public Class FindData
    Public FileAttributes      As Integer
    Public CreationTimeLow     As Integer
    Public CreationTimeHigh    As Integer
    Public LastAccessTimeLow   As Integer
    Public LastAccessTimeHigh  As Integer
    Public LastWriteTimeLow    As Integer
    Public LastWriteTimeHigh   As Integer
    Public FileSizeHigh        As Integer
    Public FileSizeLow         As Integer
    Public Reserved0           As Integer
    Public Reserved1           As Integer
<MarshalAs(UnmanagedType.ByValTStr, SizeConst := 260)> _
    Public FileName As String
<MarshalAs(UnmanagedType.ByValTStr, SizeConst := 14)> _
    Public AlternateFileName As String
End Class
```

Next, we shall define what unmanaged methods we are going to call:

```
Public Class FileExample

    <DllImport("kernel32.dll", CharSet := CharSet.Auto, _
    SetLastError := True)> _
    Private Shared Function FindFirstFile(pFileName As String, _
    <[In](), Out()> pFindFileData As FindData) As IntPtr
    End Function

    <DllImport("kernel32.dll")> _
    Private Shared Function FindClose(Handle As IntPtr) As Boolean
    End Function

    Public Shared Sub SomeFileOperation(FileName As String)
```

Now we shall actually use the unmanaged APIs that we have named above. First, we check to see if the file exists. Normally you would use the `System.IO.File.Exists()` method but suppose for the sake of argument that you later needed to do something special with the handle that could only be done through unmanaged code.

Since the caller might not have the right to call unmanaged code we shall assert the right to do so, and later demand the right to access the file system.

```
Dim UMCPerm As New SecurityPermission( _
    SecurityPermissionFlag.UnmanagedCode)

UMCPerm.Assert()
```

We shall be using some of these "magic numbers" defined by the Win32 APIs so we'll give them friendlier names to make the meaning more clear:

```
Dim Handle As IntPtr
Dim Data As New FindData
Dim Win32Error As Integer
Dim InvalidHandle As New IntPtr(-1)
Const FileNotFound As Integer = 2
Const PathNotFound As Integer = 3
Const FileAttributeDirectory As Integer = 16

Handle = FindFirstFile(FileName, Data)
```

Now we have some code that handles the error cases and throws appropriate exceptions.

```
If IntPtr.op_Equality(Handle, InvalidHandle) Then
   Win32Error = Marshal.GetLastWin32Error()
   If Win32Error = FileNotFound Then
     Throw New Exception("File " & FileName & " not found")
   ElseIf Win32Error = PathNotFound Then
     Throw New Exception("Path " & FileName & " not found")
   Else
     Throw New Exception("File " & FileName & " caused error " _
        & Win32Error)
   End If
End If

If CType(Data.FileAttributes, Boolean) And _
   CType(FileAttributeDirectory, Boolean) Then
   Throw New Exception("Path " & FileName & " is a directory")
End If

FindClose(Handle)
```

Now we know we have a good file, so make sure that the caller has permission to read it.

```
    Dim FilePerm As New FileIOPermission( _
      FileIOPermissionAccess.Read, FileName)
    FilePerm.Demand()
    ' Now do something
```

Then the code would continue to do whatever it needed to do using the file system.

```
    End Sub
  End Class
```

Does the code above look pretty reasonable? This implementation has a long list of problems. It has both correctness problems and security problems. Since we're talking about exception handling, let's look at those vulnerabilities first.

Problem 1: Path Discovery

This is the most serious problem in this code, and is a direct result of putting the security check after the checks for file validity.

Suppose this fully trusted component is called by a caller from the Internet zone, Internet programs are not allowed to determine what applications you have installed on your machine. First, that is none of their business, and second, they might be looking for applications that have known security vulnerabilities in order to mount an attack later.

Suppose you distribute the code above as part of a library of useful functions. An attacker could obtain your binary code and start looking for vulnerabilities. They could then write an assembly that exploited those vulnerabilities, put it up on a web site (disguised, perhaps, as a game or other harmless application) and hope people download it. Even if your users have good security policies that grant only a small set of permissions to code from the Internet, the attacker does not need many permissions at all to use the flawed fully trusted code above against the users.

An attacker could write code like this that runs just fine from the Internet zone:

```
' BadFileExploit1.vb

Module Exploit
  Sub Main()
    ' I wonder if Office is installed on the C drive?
    Try
      FileExample.SomeFileOperation( _
        "C:\Program Files\Microsoft Office")
    Catch E As System.Exception
      If E.Message.endswith("is a directory") Then
        System.Console.Writeline("Office is installed on C:\")
      Else
        System.Console.Writeline("no, Office is not installed on C:\")
      End If
```

```
    ' [Omitted] continue to analyze the user's file system
    ' [Omitted] report findings back to the attacker's web site.
      End Try
    End Sub
  End Module
```

Vulnerabilities like this that leak private information about the layout of a user's disk are called **path discovery vulnerabilities**. Given enough time, hostile code can enumerate your entire directory structure through a combination of clever guessing and brute force. This may not sound particularly hazardous, but it is. Even if the attacker can only read the file and directory names (but not the actual file contents) there is a lot of interesting information stored in those names.

For example, all the users on a particular machine have their own documents and settings directory named the same as the user's name. If your machine has a path discovery vulnerability then attackers can determine the names of everyone who uses your machine. That's a big help if the attacker later wants to try to guess passwords.

If the code did the security check first, then all the attacker could determine was that their code did not have access to the file system, not the organization of that file system.

This flaw is not limited to scenarios that involve calling unmanaged code. It is certainly possible to write fully managed programs that leak information out of exceptions.

> **Perform security checks as early as possible. Unauthorized callers should get no information other than the fact that they are not authorized.**

For another information leaking attack, see the *Fail to Demand on Cached Data* section below.

Problem 2: Denial of Service

Another problem with the exception handling in the code above is that the call to FindClose() is after an exception. If the exception is thrown then the handle will leak.

This is particularly bad if this code is running on a server and the client has some way of forcing the code to throw an exception by passing in bogus data. An attacker could keep on calling this method with a directory name until every handle in the kernel is allocated, using up all the server's memory. Eventually the machine will become unusable.

You should close the handle immediately or even better; use a Finally block to ensure the handle is cleaned up.

Note also that the code does not check to see if `FindClose()` failed. Secure code aggressively looks for errors and handles them appropriately. Even if the right thing to do is to ignore the failure, that fact should be explicit in the code so that future maintainers understand the intended semantics.

Problem 3: The Assert Lives On

There are also some security problems with this code that are not related to the exception handling. For instance, the assert for unmanaged code permission is not reverted when the method is done calling unmanaged code. This means that if this method later calls into some other method that demands the right to call unmanaged code, the stack walk will terminate without checking the caller of `SomeFileOperation()`. If the assert is intended to allow only one call into unmanaged code then that is all it should allow.

Problem 4: Unintended Side Effects

Whenever you call into unmanaged code, it is extremely important to understand all possible behaviors of that code. For example, the call to `FindFirstFile()` can produce a dialog box if it is passed a path to a floppy drive with no disk in it. For example, suppose an attacker writes an assembly that does this and puts it on the Internet:

```
' BadFileExploit4.vb

Module Exploit
    Sub Main()
        ' I feel like being irritating!
        Dim I As Integer
        For I = 1 To 1000000
            Try
                FileExample.SomeFileOperation("A:\Foo\Bar")
            Catch E As System.Exception
            End Try
        Next
    End Sub
End Module
```

That "feature" is almost certainly not what the author of this code intended. It is a security issue because the caller may not have the right to produce user interface elements, but the call happens before security is checked.

Fortunately, this is an extremely weak "attack", more of an irritation than anything else. Still, if a user sets policy stating that no user interface elements shall be produced then there ought to be no way for untrusted code to produce user interface elements.

Fortunately, services such as the web server restrict creation of user interface elements using the underlying Windows security system, so there is no way for a hostile client to cause a server running the vulnerable code to pop up message boxes on the server console.

146

Problem 5: Fit and Finish

The FindData class is public. Why? As we mentioned above, if there is no good reason to make a class public then make it private. Similarly, the FileExample class is not sealed. Is there some reason why another assembly should be able to subclass this class? If not, make sure that it cannot be subclassed.

Worst Practice: Fail to a Non-Secure Mode

This particular kind of flaw is fortunately becoming less common thanks to structured exception handling. However, it still crops up occasionally, particularly when calling unmanaged code.

Suppose we have a method CheckPassword() that returns a descriptive error code rather than throwing an exception. Here's an example that demonstrates the "fail to a non-secure mode" pattern:

```
ErrorCode = CheckPassword(UserName, Password)
If ErrorCode = ErrorBadNameOrPassword Then
   Throw New Exception("Bad name or password")
End If
' User is authenticated, now do appropriate custom role-based security
```

Do you see what the problem is here? Suppose CheckPassword() returns ErrorOutOfMemory, or ErrorTooManyUsers, or ErrorNetworkUnavailable, or some other error.

All the attacker has to do to fool your authenticator into authenticating them is do something to make CheckPassword() fail without returning ErrorBadNameOrPassword. Perhaps the attacker will launch a DoS attack to eat up all the memory or network bandwidth before calling your code. This code is far more secure:

```
ErrorCode = CheckPassword(UserName, Password)
If ErrorCode <> Success Then
   Throw New Exception("Password check failed with error " & ErrorCode)
End If
' User is authenticated, now do appropriate custom role-based security
```

This flawed design is much less likely if CheckPassword() throws an exception rather than returning an error code. This is because of one of the major advantages of exceptions over error codes. That is:

> **If an error code is not explicitly checked then the error is ignored. If an exception is not explicitly handled then it propagates up the stack until a handler is found (or the program terminates as there are no handlers).**

Exceptions *insist* upon being handled and therefore discourage sloppy programming that ignores errors.

> **Use structured exception handling wherever possible. If you must check error return codes then always check for success, not for specific failure.**

Note also that returning the same error message for both a bad user name and a bad password prevents attackers from discovering which user names are valid. You might also consider not returning the error number but rather just reporting that an unspecified error occurred, particularly if some error codes could allow an untrusted caller to deduce any sensitive information.

Use good judgment to find the balance between producing error messages that inform benign users how to solve their problems and ones that will inform attackers how to mount better attacks. The last thing you want to do is produce an error message such as:

```
Security exception: GetDirectoryName: You are not authorized to
read the name of directory "C:\Indigo"
```

Canonicalization Issues

A large number of common exception-handling flaws that involving failure to a non-secure mode, are **canonicalization flaws**. A canonicalization flaw is a vulnerability introduced because you incorrectly assume that data you have been given is always in some standard form. Let's look at some examples of code that fails to a non-secure mode because of canonicalization flaws:

User Names

Suppose you want to check a username to see if it is has the form ROMEO\username so that you can disallow members of the Romeo team from accessing some feature:

```
Public Sub CheckUserName(Username as String)
   If UCase(Left(Username, 5)) = "ROMEO" Then
      Throw New Exception("The Romeo team does not have access")
   End If
End Sub
```

First, this is automatically suspicious code because you should probably be using security objects such as principals and identities to implement role-based security. However, even leaving that aside this code is simply broken in that it does not keep anyone on the Romeo team out and it might stop authorized people from getting in.

The code assumes that a valid user name is always of the form domain\username but in Windows 2000 and later, username@domain.company.com is a legal username as well. Though this code would block romeo\bob correctly, it would block romeo_smith@sierra.somebigcompany.com incorrectly, and would incorrectly let bob@romeo.somebigcompany.com through.

Essentially the code is flawed because it makes an unchecked assumption about the format of a string. Secure code would verify that the string is in the correct format first; we shall discuss techniques for doing this below.

Finally, even without the canonicalization flaw the code is insecure because it fails to an insecure mode. Any time a new untrusted domain is set up this code must be changed. It is far safer to have a list of domains you allow in than a list of domains you keep out.

File Names

A similar mistake is easy to make with file names and paths. Suppose you want to ensure that a particular application only reads and writes files in a particular application-specific directory. The obvious thing to do is to check the directory string. Directory strings are case insensitive, so we'll convert it to upper case and compare it to a static string.

That seems reasonable. What is wrong with this file path code?

```
' Make sure that the user only reads from our directory.
Public Sub DoFileThing(FilePath As String)
   If UCase(Left(FilePath, 9)) <> "C:\MYAPP\" Then
      Throw New System.Exception("Illegal path.")
   End If
End Sub
```

Again, first this is wrong because you should be using the isolated storage classes to keep application-specific files somewhere safe. That is what isolated storage is for.

Leaving that aside, this code is also completely broken because it allows paths such as C:\MYAPP\..\OTHERAPP\BLAH.TXT through.

There are many similar mistakes you can make with files. From the operating system's perspective, "LONGFILENAME.TXT", "LONGFI~1.TXT", "LONGFILENAME.TXT$DATA" and "LONGFI~1.TXT." are all the same filename. Windows recognizes short file names and file names with periods on the end as legal aliases for the full file name. In fact, there are other legal aliases for this file name not listed here. If your code says that one of those is an invalid file name then it must also reject all the non-canonical forms.

> You must never make a denial decision based on the name
> of a file or a path. Specifically, never use Deny on a
> FileIOPermission object naming a specific file or path. The
> .NET Framework is not immune to these
> canonicalization issues.

URLs

Not to labor the point, there are many canonicalization issues involving URLs as well.
For example, all these URLs are essentially synonyms for each other:

```
http://www.microsoft.com/
http://www.microsoft.com./
http://207.46.197.102/
http://207.46.197.102:80/
http://%57%57%57%2E%4D%49%43%52%4F%53%4F%46%54%2E%43%4F%4D/
http://www.wrox.com@www.microsoft.com/
```

These are only a small fraction of the URLs that ultimately resolve to the same address.

That last one can lead to some particularly unpleasant canonicalization errors. A
relatively little-known feature of URLs is that a user name (and password) may be
specified before the address. If the site does not support user logins then the user
name will simply be ignored, but it certainly does look like an URL for an entirely
different site to the uninitiated. For example, you could introduce a canonicalization
flaw like this:

```
' Make sure that the caller only posts to our web site.
Public Sub PostResultsToWeb(Url As String)
    If UCase(Left(Url, 21)) <> "HTTP://WWW.MYSITE.COM" Then
        Throw New System.Exception("Bad Url")
    End If
End Sub
```

All a hostile caller must do is pass in the string
"http://www.mysite.com@www.evilsite.com/" to get past this check.

Canonicalizing Correctly

> If you possibly can, simply do not ever make a security
> decision based on the name of something – the odds are
> very good that it will be exploitable in some way. Many
> things that can be named can be named in multiple ways.

This principle generalizes to more than just names: any time you are parsing information out of a string it is a good idea to first check to see that the string is in fact in the form you expected. If it deviates even slightly from your allowed format, then fail to a secure mode and deny access. This means that you will sometimes have false negatives; perhaps legal file names in an unusual format will be rejected unnecessarily. That is unfortunate, but it is better to force your users to use a canonical form as a workaround then to allow attackers to circumvent your security.

Some good tools for checking to see if data is in a canonical form are the regular expression classes in the .NET Framework. Regular expressions allow you compactly and efficiently describe patterns and check strings to see if they match the patterns. A full exploration of regular expressions is beyond the scope of this book, but here is a brief example to give you an idea.

A regular expression is a description of a string pattern written in a quite dense, hard-to-read format. Here we shall give a regular expression for "good user name", where a good user name is something like "YANKEE123\Bob". We'll specify it quite precisely:

```
' regularexpresion.vb

Imports System
Imports System.Text.RegularExpressions

Module RegexExample

  Private Function GoodUserName(User As String) As Boolean
    GoodUserName = Regex.IsMatch(User, "(^\w{1,32})\\(\w{1,32}$)")
  End Function
```

The shared `IsMatch()` method of the `Regex` class takes two strings, one input string and one regular expression string. The meaning of expressions in our regular string is given below:

^	Beginning of string
\w	Any word character, that is a through z, A through Z, 0 through 9 or _
{1,32}	Between 1 and 32 characters of the pattern to the left
\\	Backslash
$	End of string

This pattern matches a string in the form "DOMAIN\USERNAME" where domain and username must be 1 to 32 letters, numbers or underscores.

Now that we have the pattern, we can simply see if the user string matches it. If not, then we can reject it out of hand. If it does match then we know that we can parse out the user name and domain name with some confidence that we shall not introduce a canonicalization flaw.

```
Sub Main()
  Console.Writeline("YANKEE123\Bob: " & _
                   GoodUserName("YANKEE123\Bob"))
  Console.Writeline("YANKEE123@Bob: " & _
                   GoodUserName("YANKEE123@Bob"))
End Sub

End Module
```

If you run the program above, you should see the following results:

```
YANKEE123\Bob: True
YANKEE123@Bob: False
```

We will use regular expressions further when we discuss server-side validation below.

For much more information on the correct use of regular expressions, see the *Visual Basic .NET Text Manipulation Handbook* (Wrox Press, ISBN: 1-86100-730-2).

Worst Practice: Change State without Handling Exceptions

Computer programs are ultimately "state machines". Programs take in information from users, represent that information by changing the values of bits of memory, and then manipulate that state information. You can introduce several vulnerabilities by failing to correctly handle exceptions during critical state-altering operations. Let's look at some examples:

Worst Practice: Make your State Inconsistent

One of the simplest ways to cause problems through poor exception handling is to do things in the wrong order. Suppose you have some sort of simple client-server architecture (not necessarily over the Internet; client-server architectures are a common design pattern for many applications). You might have a priority queue used by the server to keep track of pending jobs for clients:

```
Public Sub CreateNewRequest()
  QueuedRequests = QueuedRequests + 1
  If QueuedRequests >= 100 Then
    Throw New Exception("Sorry, the server is too busy, " _
                    & "try again later")
  End If
  ' Now create objects to represent the request,
  RequestInfo = New RequestInfo()
  ' Put the object in a queue, etc...
End Sub
```

Well, what if the code was called by an untrusted caller? What if the caller could force New RequestInfo() to throw an out-of-memory exception, which the untrusted caller then caught?

The untrusted caller might attempt to eat up lots of memory temporarily, call your method one hundred times, and release the memory. Suddenly the service throws nothing but "server too busy" errors even if there is nothing in the queue!

This sort of pattern applies far more generally than just to client-server applications. The essential problem here is that there is a way to make the state of the program (the request count member variable) inconsistent with reality (the actual number of pending requests.) Any time it is possible for an untrusted caller to force you into an inconsistent state is a potentially serious flaw.

Worst Practice: Use Bad Defaults

Another potential vulnerability caused by forgetting about exceptions is to have bad default behavior. For example, suppose you are adding a new customer to your customer database and want to generate a new random password that expires immediately for that customer:

```
NewCustomer = CustomerDatabase.AddNewCustomer(Name)
NewCustomer.PasswordExpires = Now()
NewCustomer.Password = GenerateRandomPassword()
```

Here's a good question: what is the password before the random password is set? Suppose it is a blank string by default. What happens if the call to Now() throws an out-of-memory exception? (Now() allocates a DateTime structure internally and therefore can throw an exception). If you said "there is now a user in the database with a good user name and a blank password", you win.

Is there a realistic attack here? That is hard to say. An attacker would have to make your program run out of memory at *exactly* the right time, between two statements. On a client machine, that would not be particularly difficult but it could be quite hard to do so if your code is running on a remote server.

However, the question of whether the attack is realistic is not particularly relevant. If there is any doubt as to whether a section of code is secure, then take steps to secure it.

> **Always remember that attackers have plenty of time on their hands. If there is only a one-in-a-million chance that a particular piece of code will fail then the attacker just needs to launch a million automated attacks.**

There are many ways to improve this design and mitigate the vulnerability. For instance, the customer database object could run a stored procedure that automatically generates a random password or the customer object could have a property Activated that is only set to True when the object is completely initialized.

The vulnerable code above may also be exploitable through a multi-threading attack, see the section *Threading Issues* later in the chapter for details.

Vulnerabilities Involving Exception Filters

The exception filter attack is a general attack, which can be used to take advantage of either of the two vulnerabilities discussed above. However, it is a particularly dangerous attack when you are using role-based security and impersonation.

Consider this scenario: You provide a fully-trusted library of useful objects to your customers. One of the methods in the library calls some unmanaged code that requires full administrator rights.

In accordance with the Principle of Least Privilege, you want to gracefully handle the case where the current user is an administrator who is not currently logged in to an administrator account. You do not want to make the user have to save their work, log out, log back in as administrator, call your library method again, log back out and log back in as a normal user.

Your code therefore prompts the user for the admin password, which you then use to create an authenticated WindowsIdentity object. (In Chapter 3 we discussed how to create a new WindowsIdentity object given a username, domain, and password.) The code then impersonates the administrator, does whatever it needs to do as administrator, and reverts to the regular user:

```
Public Class BadExample

Public Shared Sub DoTheThing()
    Dim NewIdentity As WindowsIdentity
    Dim NewContext As WindowsImpersonationContext
    Dim UserName As String, Domain As String, Password As String
    Dim WP As WindowsPrincipal = Thread.CurrentPrincipal

    ' Check to see if we are already running as admin.
    If NOT WP.IsInRole(WindowsBuiltInRole.Administrator) Then

        ' [ommitted], Obtain the username, domain and password
```

As there is not a direct way to create a new authenticated user we'll use the GetWindowsIdentity() method that we created in Chapter 3, in the section *Impersonation with WindowsIdentity Objects*.

```
        NewIdentity = GetWindowsIdentity(UserName, Domain, Password)

        NewContext = NewIdentity.Impersonate()
        ' This thread now behaves as though it was started by the
        ' authenticated user identified by NewIdentity
    End If

    DoTheAdminThing()
    ' (Calls unmanaged code that requires admin rights)
```

```
    NewContext.Undo()

    ' Now the thread reverts to the identity of its creator
  End Sub
  Private Shared Sub DoTheAdminThing()
    ' ...
  End Sub
End Class
```

Does this "code" look correct? Based on the previous discussion in this section you should immediately notice that if `DoTheAdminThing()` throws an exception then the thread impersonation is never revoked. If the untrusted caller catches the exception then the untrusted caller will be running in the impersonated context of the administrator!

The interaction between the .NET security system and the underlying Windows security system is a little unusual in this situation. Essentially, what the managed code above has done is tell the underlying Windows security system "this program is now being run by an administrator".

Fortunately, the code above has not told the .NET security system anything; no grant sets have changed and the managed principal object associated with the current thread has not changed. All the managed security restrictions continue to be in effect.

However, that is no reason for complacency. Remember that good code has multiple redundant systems to ensure security. The code above can accidentally cede administrative rights to untrustworthy code, which is unlikely to be a good thing.

Furthermore, this is just one example of a general flaw pattern: code that temporarily changes some global state information (such as the current impersonation information) and fails to revert the change because of an exception. If the exception is caught by an untrusted caller, the caller can then take advantage of the unintentionally exposed change.

How can we mitigate this vulnerability?

Finally does not Help

The obvious mitigation strategy for this vulnerability is to use a `Finally` block. A `Finally` block guarantees that whatever is inside it will actually run even if there is an exception. Unfortunately, this is not sufficient:

```
    NewContext = NewIdentity.Impersonate()
    Try
      DoTheAdminThing()
    Finally
      NewContext.Undo()
    End Try
```

Suppose an exception is thrown in `DoTheAdminThing()`. What happens? First the .NET Runtime searches up the managed call stack for a `Catch` block. Suppose it finds one. It executes the code in the `Finally` block and then immediately branches to the `Catch` block.

Unfortunately, there is a problem:

> **A `Finally` block only guarantees that certain code will run. A `Finally` block does *not* guarantee that no code will run *between* the point of the exception and the contents of the `Finally` block.**

VB.NET even provides a convenient syntax to run code between the point of the error and the `Finally` block: the exception filter. Suppose the hostile, partially trusted caller has called your method like this:

```
' Hostile code:
Public Sub CallTheObject()
  Try
    BadExample.DoTheThing()
  Catch Ex As System.Exception When ExploitFlaw()
    DoSomethingElse() ' This code runs after the Finally in DoTheThing
  End Try
End Sub

Public Function ExploitFlaw() As Boolean
  ' This code now runs before the Finally in DoTheThing
  DoSomethingEvil()
  ExploitFlaw = True
End Function
```

Let's trace through what happens.

❑   First, the hostile `CallTheObject()` calls the trusted `DoTheThing()` method.

❑   `DoTheThing()` impersonates the administrator and calls `DoTheAdminThing()`.

❑   `DoTheAdminThing()` throws an exception, possibly because the untrusted code has previously eaten up lots of memory or otherwise caused error conditions to become more likely.

❑   The .NET Runtime finds the `Catch` block in `CallTheObject()` and runs `ExploitFlaw()` to see if this block can handle the exception.

❑   `DoEvil()` calls `DoSomethingEvil()`. Note that at this point the operating system still thinks that the current user is an administrator. Something the attacker will definitely try to exploit.

- ❑ DoSomethingEvil() finishes its attempt at an exploit and returns.

- ❑ ExploitFlaw() returns True. The .NET Runtime stops its search for exception handlers.

- ❑ The .NET Runtime runs the code in the Finally block of DoTheThing(). The admin impersonation is reverted.

- ❑ The .NET Runtime runs DoSomethingElse() in the Catch block of DoTheThing().

Again, remember that this pattern applies not just to impersonation, but to any situation where trusted code temporarily changes global state in a manner that can be exploited by untrusted callers.

If Finally does not solve the problem, what does?

Catch It Yourself

Unfortunately, the only thing you can really do in this situation is to have both a Catch block and a Finally block. The code is somewhat repetitious, but secure:

```
Dim Reverted As Boolean
Reverted = False
NewContext = NewIdentity.Impersonate()
Try
   DoTheAdminThing()
Catch Ex As Exception
   NewContext.Undo()
   Reverted = True
   Throw Ex
Finally
   If Not Reverted Then
     NewContext.Undo()
   End If
End Try
```

This ensures that the reversion to self happens before code up the call stack gets to run, that it runs exactly once, and that the exception still gets passed up to the caller.

The coding pattern above is only necessary when you are changing global state in such a manner that untrusted code absolutely must not run until the change is completed.

One More Note about Impersonation

While we are on the subject of impersonation, you might have noticed that we are always talking about code temporarily impersonating administrators or other privileged users. It might occur to you that we could do things the other way around, always run as administrator but impersonate some low privilege account such as Guest except when absolutely necessary.

There is a good reason why that technique is not used: it doesn't work! Though impersonating a given user is a privileged operation, reverting the thread to the original security token can be done by anyone. If you have an administrator impersonating a normal user then untrusted code can revert the thread back to the more privileged state.

What about Imperative Security and Exception Filters?

Is this a security hole?

```
FileIOPermission.Assert() ' This could be any permission
Try
   DoSomething()
Finally
   CodeAccessPermission.RevertAssert() ' Revert all previous asserts
End Try
```

If DoSomething() throws an exception then an untrusted exception filter could run before the RevertAssert(). Won't that essentially give the asserted permission to the untrusted filter code?

Fortunately, no. Suppose the hostile, less-trusted exception filter calls trusted code that demands the permission asserted before the exception. If the hostile assembly was not granted the privilege then the stack walk would terminate unsuccessfully before it reached the assert.

If you're thinking deviously though, you'll note that there is a variation on this idea with a potential luring attack. Suppose now that the untrusted code calls trusted code that has an exception filter that does some dangerous thing. (This is extremely unlikely; trustworthy code does not normally attempt to, say, delete files from its exception filters. However, for the sake of argument, suppose it did.)

The attacker now reasons, "Suppose I can cause an exception to happen after a privilege is asserted. The exception filter will then run and the assert will ensure that my grant set is never checked."

Figure 1

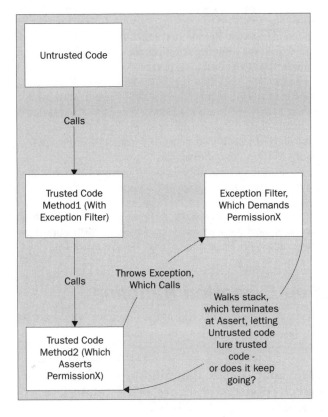

In Figure 1 it now it looks like the demand for PermissionX will succeed even though Trusted Code Method1's caller is untrusted. Fortunately, the .NET security system takes this into account:

> **If there is an assert on the stack when an exception filter is called then the assert is suppressed while the exception filter runs.**

A Deny or PermitOnly will remain on the stack in this scenario, so if Trusted Code Method2 denies a permission then any exception filter that makes a demand will not succeed.

> **You do not have to worry about hostile exception filters taking advantage of your imperative security.**

Worst Practice: Fail to Audit Security Exceptions

Security auditing is the practice of creating information to track attackers' attempts to violate your security. The first step in tracking down any attacker has to be discovering that the attacker is attacking you! Remember, most attacks do not succeed the first time. The attacker will probably make many attempts that are easily defended against by your security system before they find a vulnerability.

A discussion of specific auditing technologies would take us rather far a field. IIS and SQL Server have their own configurable auditing mechanisms and the Windows NT, Windows 2000, and Windows XP operating systems have the ability to automatically audit any ACL-controlled object. If you need to do some custom auditing not covered by one of these systems then you can use the `System.Diagnostics.EventLog` class in the .NET Framework to create security-auditing entries (or any other kinds of auditing you need to perform; not all logs are security-related).

Note that the right to write to the event log requires high trust; if untrusted code could create fake audit entries then it could really confuse administrators! You will probably need to demand `EventLogPermission` to write to the event log.

Summing up Exception Handling

There are many ways to write bad exception handling; it is very easy to do. The key takeaway here is simply this:

> **"Error-case" code is code that might run and therefore must be as correct, robust, and secure as the "main-line" code in your programs.**

Think about the state of your program and ensure that it is always secure, even on those irksome exceptional cases. Attackers love to force error conditions because they know that they often force execution of poorly tested code that reveals juicy secrets useful for mounting more attacks.

How to Reveal Secrets

A secret is anything that you do not want less-trusted code to know about. We have already seen that it is possible to leak secrets such as the state of the user's hard disk to untrusted code through poor exception handling. In this section, we'll cover some more discovery flaws as well as some of the perils of encryption. We will finish up with a discussion of some general information-stealing attacks that the .NET security system cannot defend against on it own.

Worst Practice: Fail to Demand on Cached Data

A common technique for improving performance is to cache data, particularly data that is expensive to generate and frequently requested. That way the first fetch is expensive but every fetch after it is fast. However, you must ensure that if the initial fetch demands some permission that every subsequent fetch demands it as well! For example, what is wrong with this program fragment?

```
Public Shared Function GetFileInformation(FileName As String) _
As MyFileInformation()
  Dim MFI As MyFileInformation()
  If Not MyCache.Contains(FileName) Then
    MFI = ReallyGetFileInformation(FileName)
    MyCache.Add(FileName, MFI)
    Dim Perm As New FileIOPermission( _
      FileIOPermissionAccess.PathDiscovery, FileName)
    Perm.Demand()
    GetFileInformation = MFI
  Else
    GetFileInformation = MyCache.Lookup(FileName)
  End If
End Function
```

Suppose that the caller lacks the right to discover paths. Here's our first potential flaw: that `ReallyGetFileInformation()` might not demand the `PathDiscovery` permission. In that case, the first call to `GetFileInformation()` will fail but the cache will be populated. When the caller calls a second time, it succeeds without doing a demand.

With that in mind you add a demand to `ReallyGetFileInformation()` and/or move the demand to before the call:

```
Public Shared Function GetFileInformation(FileName As String) _
As MyFileInformation()
  Dim MFI As MyFileInformation()
  If Not MyCache.Contains(FileName) Then
    Dim Perm As New FileIOPermission( _
      FileIOPermissionAccess.PathDiscovery, FileName)
    Perm.Demand()
    MFI = ReallyGetFileInformation(FileName)
    MyCache.Add(FileName, MFI)
    GetFileInformation = MFI
  Else
    GetFileInformation = MyCache.Lookup(FileName)
  End If
End Function
```

Now here's our second flaw: suppose trusted code populates the cache by calling `GetFileInformation()` first. Once the cache is populated by trusted code then any untrusted code can just grab information right out of the cache.

161

There is no way around it: this method has to make the demand every single time it is called.

```
Public Shared Function GetFileInformation(FileName As String) _
As MyFileInformation()
  Dim MFI As MyFileInformation()
  Dim Perm As New FileIOPermission( _
    FileIOPermissionAccess.PathDiscovery, FileName)
  Perm.Demand()
  If Not MyCache.Contains(FileName) Then
    MFI = ReallyGetFileInformation(FileName)
    MyCache.Add(FileName, MFI)
    GetFileInformation = MFI
  Else
    GetFileInformation = MyCache.Lookup(FileName)
  End If
End Function
```

Lest you think this is just a hypothetical example, code functionally equivalent to the first example above was found in the .NET Framework source code during a security code review. (Fortunately, it was found and fixed long before the code shipped to customers!) The actual flaw was considerably harder to see because the flawed method was quite long and complex.

> **This flaw pattern applies to any cached secret normally protected by a demand. Paths, file contents, environment variables, registry key names and contents, user names, and so on are all privileged information that you must handle carefully once your trusted code obtains them.**

Worst Practice: Write your own Encryption

> **Don't ever even consider writing your own encryption.**

That is the best advice we can possibly give you on the subject of writing your own encryption code to try to keep something a secret. Feel free to repair your own car, replace your own plumbing, and refinish your own furniture, but leave encryption implementation to professionals.

If your encryption algorithm is your own invention then odds are good that there are subtle weaknesses that a cryptanalyst could break. Even if you do manage to come up with a good cipher there are many more complex issues that must be correctly handled by a cryptographic system, such as revocation of compromised keys and so on. Furthermore, actually implementing the algorithm correctly and securely is extremely difficult. Most exploits of cryptographic software result from flaws in implementation rather than weaknesses in the cryptographic algorithms.

Worst Practice: Use XOR "Encryption"

For some reason this particular encoding algorithm is very popular among build-it-yourself encryption aficionados – perhaps because the same algorithm can be used to encrypt and decrypt.

Here we take a plaintext string and a key string. We XOR every character in the plaintext with the corresponding character in the key (starting over at the beginning of the key if the key is shorter than the message). The result is the ciphertext, which looks like unreadable garbage.

```
' Xor.vb

Imports System
Imports Microsoft.VisualBasic

Module XOREncoding

  Public Function XOrEncrypt(PlainText As String, Key As String) _
    As String
    Dim CurPlain As Integer, CurKey As Integer
    Dim PlainChar As Integer, KeyChar As Integer, CipherChar _
      As Integer
    Dim CipherText As String
    CipherText = ""

    For CurPlain = 1 To Len(PlainText)
      CurKey = 1 + (CurPlain Mod Len(Key))
      PlainChar = ASCW(Mid(PlainText, CurPlain, 1))
      KeyChar = ASCW(Mid(Key, CurKey, 1))
      CipherChar = PlainChar XOr KeyChar
      CipherText = CipherText & ChrW(CipherChar)
    Next
      XOrEncrypt = CipherText
  End Function
```

> **This is just about the worst "encryption" algorithm ever. Do not use it.**

```
Public Sub Main()

  Dim EncodedText AS String
  Dim DecodedText As String
  Dim Plaintext AS String
  Dim Key As String

  Plaintext = "I Want to keep this secret"
  Key = "Secret"
```

```
        EncodedText = XOrEncrypt(PlainText, Key )
        DecodedText = XOrEncrypt(EncodedText, Key)

        Console.WriteLine("The plain string  = " & PlainText)
        Console.WriteLine("The encoded string = " & EncodedText)
        Console.WriteLine("The decoded string = " & decodedText)

    End Sub

End Module
```

If we just run it you should see:

```
The plain string =   I Want to keep this secret
The encoded string = ,C%♦→'E↕↔E▼6 ‖R◀⌐:─C☺ ↕! ↕
The decoded string = I Want to keep this secret
```

The encoded string might look secure, but there are many, many weaknesses in this cipher. Just a few are: if the key length is less than the message length then it is susceptible to frequency analysis. (If the key length is longer than the message then you have the problem of communicating a long secret key; if you can communicate the key securely then use the same communication technique for the message!) If any part of the message is guessable then the key can be partially determined, which then allows the attacker to decrypt more and more of the message and recover more and more of the key.

Do not attempt to reinvent the wheel! Which is more likely? That you can come up with a secure implementation of a novel, unbreakable encryption technique, or that the thousands of cryptography experts who have analyzed existing "off the shelf" algorithms looking for flaws have all missed a serious flaw? Off-the-shelf cryptography packages are extremely robust when used correctly.

Spend the time you would have spent coming up with a clever algorithm reading up on the System.Security.Cryptography namespace. It contains classes to help you implement secure communication over insecure networks, digital signing, and secure encryption and decryption of files. Cryptography experts implemented these classes.

Worst Practice: Try to Keep Secrets from the User

There is an obvious temptation to try to keep secrets (proprietary algorithms, server passwords, and so on) from users. Unfortunately, it is generally impossible to keep software-based secrets from the user account, which is running your code, or from the machine administrator. They own the machine and can analyze every byte of code running on it to their hearts content until they know all your secrets. It is possible (if difficult and expensive) to design hardware that keeps secrets from its users, but this book is about software.

For example, suppose your program is a client-server application and you want to ensure that only your client speaks to your server. As we will see, this is practically impossible. Some common ways that people attempt to do the impossible follow:

Worst Practice: Embed Secret Strings

The simplest way to keep a secret is to make it a constant local string inside an inaccessible private method, right?

```
' MyObject.vb

Class MyObject

  Private Sub ConnectToServer()
    Const SecretPassword AS String = "drowssaPterceSyM"
    OpenConnection(SecretPassword)
  End Sub

  Private Sub OpenConnection(Password AS String)
    ' ...
  End Sub

End Class
```

Wrong, this is the easiest kind of "secret" for any user to find out. It is quite easy to write a program that scans an executable looking for things that look like constant strings. In fact, here's a little trick that uses the ILDASM utility (which ships with the .NET SDK) to find every constant string loaded onto the stack in a program:

```
> ildasm MyObject.DLL /text | findstr ldstr

IL_0000: ldstr        "drowssaPterceSyM"
```

> **Assume that your users know about all the constant strings in your program.**

The findstr command-line utility can be found in the System32 directory of your Windows installation, if that command is not in your path.

A Brief Note about Spelling Backwards

It is almost embarrassing to have to say so, but here goes:

> **Spelling your secret strings backwards does *not* magically prevent anyone from finding them. Many people can read English even if it is written backwards.**

Many people can also decipher Pig Latin; so don't try that one either.

It would be nice to be able to say that actual professional engineers would never resort to cheap tricks like embedding "secret" keys containing backwards, English strings, in products shipped to millions of users. Unfortunately, it happens all too often. Microsoft had a major public relations nightmare in the early part of 2000 when someone discovered that an algorithm in FrontPage Server Extensions had this constant string embedded in it:

```
"!seineew era sreenigne epacsteN"
```

Though there was not actually a serious security flaw associated with this secret string, having even the appearance of a possible security flaw caused by an easily compromised secret is bad enough for your public relations.

If you want more information on this particular issue just do a search for "weenies" at http://www.ntbugtraq.com.

Worst Practice: Construct or Encrypt Secret Strings

You can certainly make your strings harder to find but it doesn't help much though. For example, what if we just stored a bunch of numbers rather than a string? We could then reconstitute the string when we need it:

```
Dim SecretPassword As String
Dim CurChar AS Integer
Dim PasswordData As Integer() = {65, 32, 83, 69, 67, 82, 69, 84}
For CurChar = 0 To UBound(PasswordData)
   SecretPassword = SecretPassword & ChrW(PasswordData(CurChar))
Next
   OpenConnection(SecretPassword)
```

You can scatter the bits that make up the string all over your code and just put them back together again before you call into the server. Unfortunately, the user can still determine what the string is very easily, even without analyzing your algorithm. The user can simply run a debugger and step through your code, watching the string-reconstitution algorithm doing its work.

No system that requires the plain text to be in memory on the machine can prevent the user from determining the contents of that memory. After all, your program acts on behalf of the user, so the capabilities of your program are a subset of the capabilities of the user. Since your program knows its own secrets, so can the user running the program.

A secret shared is a secret no longer. If you do not want your client users to know your secrets, then keep your secrets on the server. Of course, if you sell the server software then your server-hosting customers will know your secrets, but hopefully you can trust the people hosting your servers. If you cannot trust even them then you are going to have to keep your secrets on your own servers. More generally:

> **Suppose you are designing a client-server application and you do not own every single client and server machine involved. You cannot predicate the security of the server on a guarantee that the client is benign.**

Attackers *will* write hostile clients. We will cover some of the ways that hostile clients attack servers below.

You Can't Keep your Algorithms Secret Either

Client-server issues aside, what about algorithms? Can those be kept secret?

Again, no; not if you ship the code to customers. Anyone can use ILDASM and a debugger to learn everything there is to know about your algorithms. You will have to rely on non-technical mechanisms such as patents, copyrights, trade secrets, and other legal defenses to prevent unauthorized people from stealing your intellectual property if you ship code implementing your algorithms it to customers.

Some third parties are making "obfuscators" available that claim to take IL and transform it into equivalent IL that works the same as the input program but which cannot be understood by mere mortals. As a security-conscious developer, you should take these claims with a rather large grain of salt.

It is easy to write an obfuscator that merely changes the names of internal methods around so that debuggers will see names like `"AA()"` instead of `"RebalanceBinaryTree()"`, but that is quite weak obfuscation. More sophisticated obfuscators actually reorganize the flow of algorithms to make them harder to debug. However, two risks immediately spring to mind: first, how do you know that the obfuscated program actually is equivalent? It would be rather irksome if a bug in the obfuscator introduced a serious flaw in the obfuscated assembly. Second, if someone can write a "de-optimizer" that blows your carefully crafted algorithms apart into incomprehensible spaghetti code, then someone can also write a "re-optimizer" that puts it back together again.

It is far better simply not to rely on the impossible task of keeping a secret from the user; assume that your algorithms are known and code them accordingly. An algorithm only has to be figured out *once*. After it is posted on the Internet by the first person to figure it out, all the obfuscation in the world will not help.

A Brief Note about Source Code

Given that your algorithms and their secrets are public knowledge, you may as well act as though your source code is available to the public. Third parties have already written IL decompilers that transform IL back into source code. The only useful information in your source code that is not represented in the generated executable, is the comments and local variable names.

Source code ends up in the hands of outsiders in many ways. In this more security-conscious era, an increasing number of customers are demanding to do independent reviews of source code. Source code can be subpoenaed if you are sued. In addition, of course, source code can fall into the hands of attackers if they successfully attack your server.

> **Your application's security cannot rely on secrecy of the source code.**

Decompilers do not reveal comments, but the other channels for leaking source code to the public mentioned above do. Given that your source code may fall into the hands of attackers, be careful about what information your comments reveal. Most comments in code are harmless and fulfill their purpose of making the code easier to understand. However, comments such as the following reveal tasty sensitive information to attackers:

```
' Function QueryLightbulbWindow
' Written by Stephanie King, April 2002
' If you have questions about this code you can reach me at
' 425 555-1212 x1234
' st_king@bitbucketsoftware.com
' or drop by my office at the Seattle branch office
'
' This code is to work around the security flaw described
' by bug #60298 in the BITBUCKET_BUGS database.
'
' Note that this code is not threadsafe but a race condition
' is very unlikely.
```

Any attacker who reads that now knows that there is a security flaw somewhere that has something to do with this code, and that there may be an exploitable race condition. If they want more information, they could pose as a colleague from another office and pump the author directly over the telephone.

We will further discuss the perils of storing secrets in source code below, when we discuss server-side security.

Security through Obscurity

Security professionals might call all of the above worst practices examples of "attempting security through obscurity". Security through obscurity **alone** is very weak security indeed. Ideally, you want a good mix of real security **and** obscurity.

By way of analogy, keeping your gold bars in a secure vault is a good idea. Keeping your gold bars a secure vault the location of which is only known to a small number of people is even better. Keeping your gold bars in a cardboard box the location of which is only known to a few people and hoping no bad people find out is a very bad idea.

> **Make sure that your code is sufficiently robust that even if all the source code was available to attackers, they could not find easily exploitable weaknesses.**

How to Write Insecure Server-Side Code

More and more code these days is being written using a client-server architecture where the Internet is used as the connecting layer. This new world introduces new challenges when writing secure code. In this section, we will consider ASP.NET as our primary example of a server platform. However, most of these common vulnerabilities apply to any system that serves up information over the Internet.

On the one hand, there are considerable security advantages to running code on the server over running code on the client. Consider IIS for instance. Code on the server by default runs in a thread with either a security token for an account with few rights (if you are using anonymous access) or with a validated user's rights. That makes it easy to keep to the principle of least privilege.

In addition, it is much easier to keep secrets from the client. (Though any successful attacker who compromises server security once will immediately download all the files they possibly can. As we mentioned above, do not rely on keeping any of your source code secret.) In addition, you are much less likely to have your code called by untrusted code on the server; most server applications use trusted components from end to end. Server administrators can carefully restrict what software is installed and ensure that only trustworthy applications are on their servers.

On the other hand, servers are targets that can be attacked from anywhere in the world with little chance of tracking down attackers. If a server is compromised then it is likely that the exploit will steal or damage valuable information on the server. DoS attacks are also much more dangerous on a server machine than on a client machine; if a client is denied service then you can just reboot the machine, if you have to. If the server is attacked then hundreds or thousands of users may be unable to get their work done.

When thinking specifically about server code we need to consider two main types of vulnerabilities. First, we will briefly discuss some ways of mitigating DoS attacks. We will then go into a more in-depth look at vulnerabilities caused by inadequate vetting of client-supplied data.

Don't forget that almost all of the other possible vulnerabilities discussed in this chapter apply to server code as well.

169

Denial of Service Attacks

Mitigating DoS attacks on a server is extremely difficult. Generally, however, the techniques for mitigating DoS attacks can be summed up as follows:

> **First, if you are going to fail then fail as early as possible. Second, design your system to have good worst-case performance.**

Fail Early

This is always good advice – how many times have you been half an hour into installing some software only to get a "disk full" error message? This is intensely frustrating – good installers check early to see that there is enough space, that the user is an administrator who holds a valid license key, and so on. If failure is inevitable then it is far better to fail immediately rather than waste the user's time.

The same goes for denial-of-service attacks. The attacker does not particularly care what the results of their request are. They do not care if they get a "permission denied" error. What they care about is that their attack is eating up your server's processor and memory in order to keep them from other people.

Aggressively verify all input from the client and if any of it is malformed just produce an error page. (As we discussed above, be careful to not give away too much information in this error page! We will cover a specific server vulnerability involving error pages below.) Do not do anything expensive, such as opening database connections, running queries, or doing anything else that consumes lots of memory, disk space, CPU, or kernel objects until you absolutely have to.

Consider the Worst Case

Consider also the cost of a given request when deciding whether to honor that request. For example, if one of your algorithms involves parsing a user-supplied string what happens if the user supplies a million-character string? Does your parsing algorithm bog down, eating up all the CPU trying to parse all the data?

If so, then there are things you can do to mitigate the potential DoS vulnerability. The easiest thing to do is to simply check the strings passed in and if any are too long, return an error. If there are legitimate cases where large or hard-to-analyze data must be accepted, then consider tuning your algorithms to have good worst-case performance. Many algorithms trade bad performance on atypical data for excellent performance on typical data – the QuickSort algorithm, for instance. It may be better to use algorithms that have reasonably good performance in every case. MergeSort, for example, tends to be slower (on average) than QuickSort, but performs equally well for every possible input.

The only way to determine what your code performance is under DoS attack conditions is to simulate some attacks. When you do performance testing make sure that you include cases where large numbers of simulated clients all pass bogus data at the same time, request non-existing resources, and so on. See what happens to the response time and throughput for the non-hostile clients. Tools like Microsoft's Web Application Stress Tool (http://webtool.rte.microsoft.com) can help with this process.

There are even better reasons for aggressively vetting client data, which we will explore in the next section.

Worst Practice: Trust the Client

In most legal systems, innocence is assumed until guilt is proven. Fortunately, there is no good reason to apply the same standard to client-server interactions.

> **Servers must treat every bit that comes from the client as potentially hostile until proven otherwise; failure to do this can introduce a number of serious vulnerabilities.**

We have already seen in this chapter that there is essentially no effective way to determine that data sent from a client to your server is really coming from the client that you wrote. Any sufficiently clever attacker could take your client apart, figure out how it works and build their own client. The malicious client could send malformed data, and if your server is not robust in the face of hostile data then you have a serious problem.

Let's look at a couple particularly egregious cases where trusting the client leads to serious vulnerabilities: the SQL Injection and Cross Site Scripting vulnerabilities.

The SQL Injection Vulnerability

Here is a very typical server-side program. It takes a parameter passed in the client's request, builds a SQL query based on the parameter and then displays the results of the query back to the client.

Do you see anything wrong with this code fragment from a security perspective?

```
<%@page language="VB" %>
<script runat="server">

Private Function DoDatabaseThing()
    Dim myConnection As SqlConnection
    Dim myCommand As SqlCommand
    Dim myReader As SqlDataReader
    Dim myQuery As String
    Dim ProductType As String
```

```
' Obtain the product type from the client request.
ProductType = Request.Params("producttype")

' Build the query.
Query = "SELECT Name, Cost FROM Products WHERE ProductType = "
Query = Query & "'" & ProductType & "'"

' Execute the query.
myCommand = New SqlClient.SqlCommand()
myConnection = New SqlClient.SqlConnection(GetConnectionString())
myCommand.Connection = myConnection
myCommand.CommandText = Query
myConnection.Open()
myReader = myCommand.ExecuteReader()
' Display the results . . .
```

The flaw is this: the code implicitly trusts that the client has actually put "Skis" or "Televisions" or some such thing into the request object, so that Query must contain something like:

```
SELECT Name, Cost FROM Products WHERE ProductType = 'Televisions'
```

Perhaps your site's web page can only pass good strings, but an untrustworthy client can pass any string it chooses. Suppose a hostile client passes in this as the product type string:

```
"Televisions' UPDATE Products SET Price = '99.99'
WHERE Model = 'SONY KV-32FS13' --"
```

That would then produce the query string

```
SELECT Name, Cost FROM Products
  WHERE ProductType = 'Televisions'
UPDATE Products SET Price='99.99'
  WHERE Model = 'SONY KV-32FS13' --'
```

This is a legal query string, which not only fetches the requested data but also discounts a nice 32-inch flat screen television by 80%. That is probably not something you want your clients to be able to do!

> **Once you allow untrustworthy, unchecked user data to mix freely with your SQL queries you have essentially given access to your database to any client who wants it.**

Worst Practice: Telling the Client what went Wrong

We have already discussed leaking information in exceptions, but it bears repeating. Suppose you have the vulnerability described above. It is bad enough to have a vulnerability; do not make it easily discoverable! That is, do not do something like this:

```
Try
    ' [ ... database code ... ]
Catch E As Exception
    ' Something went wrong! Give debug info.
    Response.Write("Error processing query " & Query)
    Throw E
End Try
```

First off, this makes it very easy for attackers to determine that you have a SQL injection vulnerability; the attacker can just send any random malformed data and get enough information to determine how your query string is laid out. Once they know that it is quite easy to start injecting SQL that reveals the entire structure of the database table by table.

Second, as we will see below, the code above also contains a cross-site scripting vulnerability.

Third, in the vast majority of cases your users do not need to know exactly what went wrong. Error messages should ideally be "actionable". If there is no way that a client can diagnose and fix the problem, then do not give them a whole lot of stack traces and other technical information. Just give them a simple "something went wrong" page.

Best Practice: Vet the Data, then use Parameterized Queries

The safest approach is, as you know by now, is to have multiply nested defenses. First, do a fast, easy check to see that the data is at least reasonable. That will probably eliminate any injection attack right there, but "probably" is not very strong. Second, use a parameterized stored procedure rather than a query string. That is, let the stored procedure manipulate the client-supplied parameter string itself rather than building a custom query every time. Finally, if there is an error do not echo the user-supplied data back to the client:

```
Private Function DoDatabaseThing()
    Dim myConnection As SqlConnection
    Dim myCommand As SqlCommand
    Dim myReader As SqlDataReader
```

First, we'll vet the client-supplied string before doing any expensive database calls. If the string is malformed we are probably dealing with a hostile client, so bail out as soon as possible:

```
Dim ProductParam As SqlParameter
Dim ProductRegEx As Regex = New Regex("^[a-zA-Z ]{1,30}$")
' A valid product type has only letters and spaces and is between
' one and thirty characters long.
Dim ProductType As String
ProductType = Request.Params("producttype")

If Not ProductRegEx.IsMatch(ProductType) Then
  Throw New Exception("Bad input")
End If
```

Note that we do not echo back the supplied string. We shall see why that is important in the next section on Cross Site Scripting. Next, we simply pass the client string to a stored procedure:

```
myConnection = New SqlConnection(GetConnectionString())
myCommand = New SqlCommand("CostByType", myConnection)
myCommand.CommandType = CommandType.StoredProcedure
ProductParam = New SqlParameter("@ProductType", _
                               SqlDbType.NVarChar, 30)
ProductParam.Value = ProductType
myCommand.Parameters.Add(ProductParam)
myConnection.Open()
myReader = myCommand.ExecuteReader()
' ...
```

You can then add a stored procedure to your database to do the query for you. For example, a SQL server stored procedure might look something like:

```
CREATE PROCEDURE CostByType
(
  @ProductType nvarchar(50)
)
AS
  SELECT Name, Cost FROM Products WHERE @ProductType = ProductType
GO
```

This actually compiles up into a method that takes a string as an argument rather than substituting the parameter as text Even if somehow an "UPDATE" query gets past the server checks there is no way this stored procedure can actually do an update query.

> **Consider using stored procedures. Stored procedures enhance performance because the query can be parsed and optimized ahead of time. They are secure because the arguments are true arguments, not elements of the query language.**

Worst Practice: Run as Database Administrator

The code samples above call out to a helper function to build the database connection string. What is wrong with this helper function implementation?

```
Private Function GetConnectionString() As String
  GetConnectionString = "server=localhost;" & _
                        "uid=sa; & _
                        "pwd=;" & _
                        "database=MyOnlineStore"
End Function
```

Just about everything is wrong with it! Almost every line of this short method is indicative of some violation of our model of multiple nested defenses.

❑ The web server and the database server are running on the same machine. Often this is unavoidable; multiple machines are expensive after all. However, this means that if an attacker ever compromises the web server then they get to mess with your database server "for free" and vice versa. If you keep your data on a different machine then you reduce the risk of having your data stolen or modified if the web server has some vulnerability. (There are also potential performance advantages to having separate data and web servers.)

❑ The user ID is the SQL database administrator account, violating the principle "always run with the least possible privilege". If the attacker manages to pull off a SQL injection attack, it will be done with the full rights of the database administrator. If you use a more restricted user account then you can limit the successful attacker to only reading and writing a subset of your data.

❑ The administrator password is blank! We do not need to labor the point here; this is obviously a terrible practice.

❑ Suppose an attacker does not manage to compromise the server entirely but does manage to see your source code somehow. (Perhaps an unrelated vulnerability has allowed the attacker to download the source of the ASP.NET page rather than running it). Even if you fixed the previous three problems, an attacker who can see this source code now knows the SQL server machine name, your database name, and the name and password of a user authorized to read the database. That is information of considerable interest and value to an attacker!

The whole point of our strategy of multiple nested defenses is that if you accidentally introduce an exploitable vulnerability somewhere you can at least limit the severity of the exploit. To mitigate the risk of both SQL injection attacks and information leakage if your source code is stolen the .NET Framework provides a convenient application configuration storage object to parse configuration information out of XML files. For example, you could store the connection string in a configuration file and read it like this:

175

```
Private Function GetConnectionString() As String
  GetConnectionString = _
  System.Configuration.ConfigurationSettings.AppSettings( _
                                        "DBReadConnection")
End Function
```

You can then store the connection string in your web.config file. (Note that the machine, user ID and password are much improved as well.)

```
<?xml version="1.0" encoding="utf-8" ?>
<configuration>
  <appSettings>
    <add key="DBReadConnection"
         value="server=sqlbox1;uid=dbreader;pwd=N1t$4a@2C2;
             database= MyOnlineStore"/>
  </appSettings>
  ...
```

It would not hurt to put an appropriate Access Control List (ACL) on that file while you are at it.

The connection string could also be stored in an ACL'd registry key. Regardless of where you put the information, the point is that you should make attackers surmount one hurdle after another if they want to attack your servers successfully. Do not allow small vulnerabilities (such as a source code leak) to be easily turned into large ones (such as giving away the database administrator's password).

The Cross Site Scripting (CSS) Vulnerability

The CSS vulnerability is a little trickier conceptually than the SQL injection vulnerability, but CSS attacks have gained considerable prominence recently. Unlike the SQL injection attack, the CSS attack does not go after the server itself. Rather, the target is a client of the server. The vulnerability allows the attacker to make the server attack another client for them.

There are three players in a CSS scenario, the "Evil Attacker", the "Nice Trustworthy Site" (a server), and the "Unwitting Victim" (a client). The Evil Attacker would like to run some malicious script code on the Unwitting Victim's machine and starts looking for ways to do so.

Let's suppose that the cookies for www.NiceTrustworthyGuys.com have valuable information in them such as passwords, credit card numbers, or authentication data. It does not matter for the sake of this discussion what the data is exactly, just that the Unwitting Victim would like it to remain a secret. The Evil Attacker would like to read these cookies and steal this information.

176

Evil Makes Attempt Number One

The Attacker might put some evil script code on their web site, http://www.IAmSoEvil.com/, that attempts to read the cookies for the trustworthy site. They could then send spam to the Unwitting Victim enticing the Victim to click a link and visit the evil site. If the Victim has a modern HTML-aware e-mail client, the Evil Attacker could just send out mail containing something like:

```
<html><a href="http://www.IAmSoEvil.com">
Click here for [something enticing: stock tips, free beer giveaways,
whatever.]
</a></html>
```

However, even if the Victim falls for it and clicks the link, this attack is unlikely to be effective; odds are very good that the Victim will use the browser security system to sandbox the script. Any attempt to read cookie files for other web sites will be foiled thereby. By default, most browsers do not allow web pages to read cookies from other sites.

Evil Makes Attempt Number Two

The Evil Attacker then gets a bright idea: can they trick the Unwitting Victim into *believing that the evil code comes from the trusted site?* The Evil Attacker could, say, intercept information coming over the Internet and replace it with different information. This might be technically difficult, but both software and hardware exists that can "sniff" the packets sent between a client and a server over the Internet. With a little cleverness, the Evil Attacker could intercept the packets, destroy them, and replace them with packets containing hostile script. The Attacker could thereby spoof the Unwitting Victim's browser into believing that it was talking to www.NiceTrustworthyGuys.com when really it was getting its information directly from the Evil Attacker.

Unfortunately, for the Evil Attacker, this attack is simply not practicable if www.NiceTrustworthyGuys.com uses a secure, encrypted HTTPS connection. Even if it does not, setting up a packet sniffer and intercepting packets is not easy. The Evil Attacker would rather not have to work that hard!

Evil Makes Attempt Number Three

Here's an easier idea though: can the Evil Attacker actually *make* www.NiceTrustworthyGuys.com serve up an evil script? Yes! They can if the authors of the Nice Trustworthy Site left a CSS vulnerability in their server side code.

Suppose, for example, that the Nice Trustworthy Site had a page with a method something like this:

```
Private Sub SayHello()
  Response.Write = "<html>"
  Response.Write = "Hello, " & Request.Params("username") & "!"
  Response.Write = "</html>"
End Sub
```

This page takes a string from the client and sends it right back to the client. This might look harmless, but the Evil Attacker's job just got a whole lot easier, as we shall see.

Of course, in order to take advantage of this vulnerability, the Evil Attacker has to know that the vulnerability is there. Unfortunately, these sorts of vulnerabilities can be easy to find even if the Evil Attacker does not have the source code to the server pages. All the Evil Attacker needs to do is write a hostile client that sends garbage strings to every page on the web site and then see if there is a page that echoes that garbage right back. It would not be particularly hard to write a program that automatically does so to every page on a web site.

How the Evil Attacker finds out about this vulnerability is not particularly important though. How does the exploit actually work?

The Nice Guy's web page echoes back anything you throw at it. All the Evil Attacker needs to do to make the Nice Guy's server serve up their evil code is to convince the Unwitting Victim to send the evil code to the server in the first place. How are they going to do that?

That is the easy part. The Evil Attacker just modifies their spam mail a little:

```
<html><a href=
"https://www.NiceTrustworthyGuys.com?username=Bob[..evilscript..]">
Click here for [something enticing: stock tips, free beer giveaways,
whatever.]
</a></html>
```

Now what happens when the Unwitting Victim clicks on the link? The victim browses to www.NiceTrustworthyGuys.com over a secure connection, which then serves up:

```
<html>
Hello, Bob <script>[ evil script here ]</script>!
</html>
```

The Damage Done

The evil script can now read the contents of the trusted site's cookies and post them to www.IAmSoEvil.com, thereby stealing the valuable data stored therein. That's not all. It can also insert scripts that track your behavior on the trusted web site. It can post any information you post to the trusted web site to the evil web site as well. The attacker's ability to track your usage of the trusted site is limited only by their cleverness. Note also that this vulnerability is not mitigated by encrypting the HTTP traffic.

Essentially the client's browser has every reason to believe that the hostile script was *intentionally* served up by the trusted web site, so the script can do anything that the trusted site can do. For instance, if the user's policy allows the trusted site to create .NET objects then it can do so. That would be subject to the security zone restrictions on the trusted site, but if the trusted site is in the user's Local Intranet zone then that is considerably more damage than if it were restricted to the Internet zone.

Mitigating a CSS Vulnerability

As we have seen, secure HTTPS connections do not mitigate the vulnerability. The Unwitting Victim cannot mitigate their vulnerability through firewall hardware or software either; both the initial request to the trusted server and the posting of stolen data to the evil server originate from inside the Victim's firewall. The only thing the Victim can really do is decide to never click on any web link that comes from an untrustworthy source, which is an unrealistic, unworkable solution. There is nothing that the Unwitting Victim can do about this problem because the vulnerability is on the trusted server.

This means that you as a developer of trusted server-side code have a considerable responsibility. Unfortunately, CSS vulnerabilities are seldom as easy to spot as the one above. ASP.NET makes it very easy to combine untrustworthy client-supplied data with the trustworthy data served up by the site. Even worse, the nature of the attack is that a single flawed page on a trusted domain is enough to enable the exploit.

Mitigating the CSS vulnerability on the server requires a two-pronged approach:

> **Vet and/or filter the data on the way in. Vet and/or encode the data on the way out.**

In theory, either of these prongs would be sufficient to solve the problem, but our multiple defenses model calls for as many redundant defenses as possible. If a maintenance programmer adds some new code and accidentally forgets to filter some input then the mistake will likely be caught on the way out.

Filtering

As we suggested with the SQL injection vulnerability, it is a good idea to aggressively validate your user-supplied data. For instance, if a field can only contain numbers, letters, and spaces, then say so:

```
Dim UserRegEx As Regex = New Regex("^[a-zA-Z0-9 ]*$")
' Zero or more letters, numbers or spaces.
Dim UserString As String = Request.Params("whatever")
If Not UserRegEx.IsMatch(UserString) Then
    ' If we get here then the
    ' client might be either buggy or hostile.
    Throw New Exception("Bad input")
End If
```

In some circumstances, a non-hostile user will accidentally give you a bad string. For instance, you might be writing a web-based message board, which by its very nature echoes user-supplied strings to other users. Users will probably type in messages with punctuation and so on. In such a situation, it might be a better user experience to just filter the potentially bad characters out of the string:

179

```
Dim UserRegEx As Regex = New Regex("[^a-zA-Z0-9 \.\?\!\,]")
' Match everything but letter, number, space, punctuation
Dim UserString As String = Request.Params("whatever")
UserString = UserRegex.Replace(UserString, "")
```

Which technique you use depends on your application. Consider the user scenarios carefully when deciding what kinds of input are valid and how to treat invalid data.

If you want to filter on only the minimal set of characters with meaning in HTML you can filter out only these:

```
Dim HTMLRegEx As Regex = New Regex("[\<\>\'\"\(\)\%\&\;\+]")
' Matches any of < > ' " ( ) & ; +
UserString = HTMLRegex.Replace(UserString, "")
```

However, that would violate our guideline of always checking for valid data rather than attempting to enumerate all invalid data. Furthermore, there may be legitimate users who need to pass these characters in to your server code.

Encoding

In the interests of multiple lines of defense, it is a reasonably good idea to also check the data before it goes back out to the user, and occasionally you really do need to allow *any* user data in, do some transformation on it and spit it back out. In that case, you cannot filter the data on the way in and must encode it on the way out. For example, you might have a web-based forum discussing programming languages. Obviously, it is necessary for users in such a forum to be able to use characters such as angle brackets and parentheses!

Fortunately, the ASP.NET object model provides you with a method that does this:

```
Dim UserString As String = Request.Params("whatever")
' ... vet or filter as necessary ...
' ... transform as necessary ...
' Now safely encode it:
UserString = Server.HtmlEncode(UserString)
Response.Write(UserString)
```

The HtmlEncode() method takes a string and replaces the HTML-sensitive characters with their HTML entity representations. The browser will then interpret these as text, not as markup. For example, this string containing a script markup tags:

```
<script>alert("you are toast!");</script>
```

becomes this string containing no markup:

```
&lt;script&gt;alert(&quot;you are toast!&quot;);&lt;/script&gt;
```

which is then rendered by the client as looking like the original string rather than being interpreted as code.

Other Issues

Some worst practices don't fit well into any of the broad categories above but that is not to say that these are less dangerous or less important vulnerabilities!

In this section, we will look at some bad coding practices, which may introduce security problems involving multi-threading, caching user data to disk, delegates, and Reflection.

Threading Issues

In the section on writing bad exception handling above, we gave this example:

```
NewCustomer = CustomerDatabase.AddNewCustomer(Name)
NewCustomer.PasswordExpires = Now()
NewCustomer.Password = GenerateRandomPassword()
```

Recall that this is vulnerable code because if Now() throws an exception it leaves a customer in the database with a blank password. There may be another way to exploit this code; it is not threadsafe.

A Brief Refresher on Threading

Modern multi-threaded operating systems give the illusion that many more processes are running "at the same time" than there are physical processors in the machine. Essentially, they do this by rapidly switching between applications. Each thread of each application gets its own brief time slice to do some processing. When the time slice is up the state of the CPU is stored away in memory and the context of the next thread is loaded in. The only situation in which the machine is actually running two different programs at exactly the same time is when you have a multi-processor machine.

All the threads in a process share the same memory and machine code, but the point at which they are executing in that code is usually not the same. Occasionally, either by chance or by design two threads will be executing in the same code one after the other. These sorts of situations lend themselves to race conditions: conditions where the exact timing of CPU context switches makes a real difference in the data manipulated by the thread.

The canonical example of a race condition looks something like this:

```
Public Class Rocket
    Private GlobalCount As Integer

    Sub CountDown()
        GlobalCount = GlobalCount - 1
        If GlobalCount = 0 Then BlastOff()
    End Sub
```

```
Public Sub BlastOff()
' ...
End Sub
End Class
```

Let's say that GlobalCount currently equals two. Suppose two threads, Alpha and Bravo are running and the operating system switches back and forth between them like this:

```
Alpha:   GlobalCount = GlobalCount - 1     ' GlobalCount = 1
Bravo:   GlobalCount = GlobalCount - 1     ' GlobalCount = 0
Bravo:   If GlobalCount = 0 Then BlastOff()  ' BlastOff!
Alpha:   If GlobalCount = 0 Then BlastOff()  ' BlastOff again! Oops.
```

It gets even more awful when you start to break the statements down into their component parts; after all, there is no magic rule that forces the processor to execute entire statements before switching threads. If we break down this statement:

```
GlobalCount = GlobalCount - 1
```

down into the actual "atomic" (that is, the smallest non-interruptible) operations it looks something like this:

```
Put Value From GlobalCount Into Temporary Storage
Decrement Temporary Storage
Store value in Temporary Storage into GlobalCount
```

Suppose then the order of operations goes something like this, starting with GlobalCount set to 2:

```
Alpha:   GlobalCount --> Alpha's Temporary storage     (GlobalCount = 2)
Bravo:   GlobalCount --> Bravo's Temporary storage     (GlobalCount = 2)
Bravo:   Decrement Bravo's Temporary storage           (GlobalCount = 2)
Bravo:   GlobalCount <-- Bravo's Temporary Storage     (GlobalCount = 1)
Bravo:   If GlobalCount = 0 Then BlastOff()            (No blastoff)
Alpha:   Decrement Alpha's Temporary storage           (GlobalCount = 1)
Alpha:   GlobalCount <-- Alpha's Temporary Storage     (GlobalCount = 1)
Alpha:   If GlobalCount = 0 Then BlastOff()            (No blastoff)
```

In this case, effectively one of the calls has been lost. Though there have been two calls the count has only been decremented once. Situations like this where bizarre outcomes result from specific code running at specific times on different threads are examples of race conditions.

So Where is the Vulnerability?

There are two possible vulnerabilities involving non-threadsafe objects. The first is, essentially, what we have already seen; if untrusted code ever manages to be running on two different threads then both threads may call your more-trusted code in a tight loop on each thread. The attacker hopes to cause a race condition that leads to some exploitable logic error in your program. In the example above the attacker might have a good reason to want BlastOff() to happen twice (or never). One can imagine situations in which financial transactions happening twice (or never) might be desirable to an attacker.

This vulnerability can be mitigated by making the code threadsafe: putting appropriate locks in place so that only one thread can read or write a global object at one time.

The second vulnerability is similar to the first except that it depends on a race condition between two different pieces of code. An attacker could construct a method specifically designed to introduce an exploitable race condition in non-threadsafe code.

For example, consider once more our example of some benign, trusted code adding a new customer to a database: Perhaps this is some code in a highly trusted customizable database application.

```
' Your code on thread Alpha
NewCustomer = CustomerDatabase.AddNewCustomer(Name)
NewCustomer.PasswordExpires = Now()
NewCustomer.Password = GenerateRandomPassword()
```

An attacker writes up a hostile customization for your database application and tricks a user into downloading it. Even if the user does not fully trust the hostile customization, it can still do harm to the user by exploiting the threading flaw. Suppose the customization is running on a different thread, Bravo: The hostile customization first determines the user's name – possibly through some other exploit – and then attempts to take advantage of the threading flaw by constantly trying to cause race conditions:

```
' Attacker's code on thread Bravo
Dim KeepGoing As Boolean
Do
   KeepGoing = False
   ' [ omitted: Figure out current Name through some exploit]
   Try
     Customer = CustomerDatabase.Logon(Name, "")
     Customer.CreditLimit = "$10000000"
     Customer.Password = "GOTCHA"
   Catch
      KeepGoing = True
   End Try
   If Not KeepGoing Then Exit Loop
Loop
```

The attacker is hoping that eventually just by chance the order of thread execution goes

```
Alpha: NewCustomer = CustomerDatabase.AddNewCustomer(Name)
Alpha: NewCustomer.PasswordExpires = Now()
Bravo: Customer = CustomerDatabase.Logon(Name, "")
Bravo: Customer.CreditLimit = "$10000000"
Alpha: NewCustomer.Password = GenerateRandomPassword()
Bravo: Customer.Password = "GOTCHA"
```

If this unlikely sequence ever happens then the hostile customization can send back to the attacker the name of a customer with a known password and a high credit limit.

What is the Risk?

Race condition exploits are by their nature difficult to pull off, but attackers have time on their side. If a race condition can only possibly occur if two threads are running particular code then the attacker will ensure that one thread is always running their code. If the race condition is a one-in-a-million chance then the attacker only has to run the exploit a million times (on average) to make it work. With desktop machines that run over a billion operations per second, a million failed attacks is not as many as you might think.

This is another good reason to implement effective auditing. If you find out you're being attacked after "only" a few thousand failed logon attempts then you can begin to search for ways to discourage the attack.

What Should I Do?

Also, think also about the risks associated with other code running between your statements (the same as you would for the exception filter exploit). If there is a potential vulnerability there, then consider tightening up the order in which things happen so that the default is always secure.

If you have code that if called on the wrong thread could leak sensitive information to untrusted callers or otherwise cause harm then there are two possibilities for mitigating the vulnerability. The first is to carefully design and implement the object so that it can be safely called on multiple threads. If, on the other hand, you have no supported scenario in which the code ought to be called on multiple threads then you can write code to prevent the object from being called on multiple threads by attackers.

Consider our "blastoff" example above, where the attacker runs the same code on two different threads in order to exploit a race condition. One way to mitigate this problem is to make the code threadsafe by using a `Mutex` (short for "mutually exclusive") object. A `Mutex` is essentially a gatekeeper that only lets one thread into the code at a time. Once a thread is in the code, the `Mutex` puts any other thread that tries to get in to sleep until the current occupant leaves.

```
Public Sub CountDown()
  GlobalMutex.WaitOne()
  Try
```

```
      GlobalCount = GlobalCount - 1
      If GlobalCount = 0 Then BlastOff()
    Finally
      GlobalMutex.ReleaseMutex()
    End Try
  End Sub
```

Now it is impossible for thread Bravo to decrement the counter in the middle of Alpha's decrement. Only one thread can be between the calls to `WaitOne()` and `ReleaseMutex()`.

Notice that we must guarantee that the mutex is released! If we neglected to put that exception handling code in and the call to `BlastOff()` throws an exception then the mutex would never be released. Any other thread that attempted to access this method would halt, waiting for the mutex to be released, and therefore halt forever. (That itself could be an exploitable vulnerability.)

Fortunately, there is a more elegant solution to this problem. A nice feature in VB.NET is the `SyncLock` statement, which essentially allows you to use any object as a mutex:

```
  Public Sub CountDown()
    SyncLock Me
      GlobalCount = GlobalCount - 1
      If GlobalCount = 0 Then BlastOff()
    End SyncLock
  End Sub
```

Any object can be used in a `SyncLock`. In this case, the `Me` object itself is a convenient object to use. This code will ensure that the `CountDown()` methods of two different `Rocket` objects can be running at the same time on different threads, but any one object's method can only be running in one thread at a time.

Whether you use mutexes or sync locks, to do it right you must ensure that every read or write to the protected data is protected. Writing proper threadsafe code can be difficult. A proper discussion of good multithreaded design is beyond the scope of this text. See the *Visual Basic .NET Threading Handbook* (Wrox Press, ISBN 1-86100-713-2) for more information on this complex topic.

If on the other hand you have no need for the object to ever be called on multiple threads then simply do not allow the object to be called on multiple threads. This is yet another example of a more general principle we have come across several times so far in this book:

> **Defensively detect attempts at misusing your code. Throw an exception as soon as you detect some suspicious behavior.**

In this particular case, the suspicious behavior is "calling a method on an unexpected thread". If that is the suspicious, unsupported behavior, then simply check for that behavior and abort if you find it. This is essentially the same design pattern as taking possibly hostile data and verifying that it is in canonical form:

```
Public Class Rocket
   Private GlobalCount As Integer
   Private Dim InitialThread As Thread
   ' . . .
   Public Sub New()
     InitialThread = Thread.CurrentThread()
     GlobalCount = 10
   End Sub

   Public Sub CountDown()
     CheckThread()
     GlobalCount = GlobalCount - 1
     If GlobalCount = 0 Then BlastOff()
   End Sub

   Private Sub CheckThread()
     If Thread.CurrentThread() <> InitialThread Then
       Throw New Exception("Method called on incorrect thread.")
     End If
   End Sub

   Private Sub BlastOff()
     ' ...
   End Sub

End Class
```

A quick check to make sure you are still on the same thread is much easier than actually making the object multi-threaded.

The added bonus of such a check is that you not only mitigate a possible vulnerability, but you also prevent bugs caused by benign callers calling your object on the wrong thread. Note also that the error message returned is descriptive enough to enable a benign caller to troubleshoot the problem but does not give a hostile caller any more information than they already have. The hostile caller knows that the object is being called on the wrong thread because they did it deliberately.

Finally, note that neither technique will work in this case:

```
NewCustomer = CustomerDatabase.AddNewCustomer(Name)
NewCustomer.PasswordExpires = Now()
NewCustomer.Password = GenerateRandomPassword()
```

Here, the vulnerability is not caused by two instances of trusted code running on different threads, but rather has trusted code running on one thread and hostile code running on another thread. Adding any kind of threading checks to the trusted code will not help. The only way to mitigate this vulnerability is to make the code inherently more secure; for instance, by having a more sensible default value for the password.

How to Write Bad Serialization Code

Serialization is the process of translating the state of objects into a format amenable to storage and/or transmission. It's called serialization because the state of a set of objects must be converted from its "live" representation stored all over your memory to a series of consecutive bytes. The opposite process, taking the bytes of the stream and reconstituting the state of the objects is called **deserialization**.

Serialization is used for transmitting the state of an object over some kind of barrier. For example, if you have a child AppDomain that produces an uncaught exception then the exception object can be serialized and moved across the AppDomain boundary into the parent domain. Serialization is also used to "freeze dry" the state of an application, save it to some storage system (such as a disk or database) and "reconstitute" it later.

A Brief Refresher on Serialization

In .NET an object is serializable if it implements the `ISerializable` interface and is marked with the `Serializable` attribute. A serializable object writes information into a table of named information fields called a `SerializationInfo`. An object called a formatter determines the actual bytes of the serialized state. The deserializer reads the data back out of the `SerializationInfo`. A deserializer is usually implemented as a constructor of an object.

Here's an example of how an object serializes its state to an information structure: We have a class that represents a car with three properties. We wish to be able to write instances of this object out to disk and read them back in again later.

We start with the class definition and some public properties:

```
' Car.vb

Imports System
Imports System.Runtime.Serialization

' Note: This code may have a security flaw because it does not
' check to ensure that the caller has serialization permissions.
<Serializable()> _
Public Class Car
Implements ISerializable
    Public Make As String
    Public Model As String
    Public MSRP As Decimal
```

The class has one "regular" constructor that initializes it exactly as you might expect:

```
' Regular constructor
Public Sub New(NewMake As String, NewModel As String, NewMSRP _
```

```
                          As Decimal)
        Make = NewMake
        Model = NewModel
        MSRP = NewMSRP
    End Sub
```

The "freeze drying" method takes an object that can store name-value pairs:

```
    'Serializer
    Public Sub GetObjectData(Info As SerializationInfo, _
                            Context As StreamingContext) _
        Implements ISerializable.GetObjectData
        Info.AddValue("Make", Make)
        Info.AddValue("Model", Model)
        Info.AddValue("MSRP", MSRP)
    End Sub
```

Finally, the "reconstituter" is a special constructor that takes the information back out of the storage object and rebuilds the object:

```
    ' Deserializer
    Public Sub New(Info As SerializationInfo, Context As _
                StreamingContext)
        ' The info object can return any type, so we have to do a type
        ' cast to avoid a compiler error
        Make = CType(Info.GetValue("Make", GetType(String)), String)
        Model = CType(Info.GetValue("Model", GetType(String)), String)
        MSRP = CType(Info.GetValue("MSRP", GetType(Decimal)), Decimal)
    End Sub
End Class
```

The user of the object can then decide how it is to be serialized. For instance, it might be serialized into a compact binary format and saved to disk:

```
' SerializeCar.vb

Imports System.IO
Imports System.Runtime.Serialization.Formatters.Binary

Module SerializeCar

    Public Sub Main()

        Dim MyCar AS Car
        Dim MyStream As Stream
        Dim MyFormatter As New BinaryFormatter()

        MyCar = New Car("Ford", "Explorer", 30000)
        Mystream = File.Open("MyFile", FileMode.Create)
        MyFormatter.Serialize(MyStream, MyCar)
```

```
        MyStream.Close()

    End Sub

End Module
```

The call to `MyFormatter.Serialize()` creates a `SerializationInfo` object. As `Car` implements the `ISerializable` interface the `BinaryFormatter` knows that it pass the `SerializationInfo` to `MyCar.GetObjectData()`. That does its work, storing the object into the `SerializationInfo`. The formatter then extracts the stored information from the `SerializationInfo` and stores it in `MyStream` using a compact binary format. The stored object could then be e-mailed to someone else and reconstituted on their machine, as long as the same class definition and formatter were used.

To deserialize the opposite process occurs. Here the formatter reads the bytes out of the stream and reconstructs the `SerializationInfo`. It then passes the `SerializationInfo` to the appropriate `Car` constructor and the object is reconstituted.

```
MyStream = File.Open("MyFile", FileMode.Open)
MyFormatter = New BinaryFormatter()
MyCar = CType(MyFormatter.Deserialize(MyStream), Car)
MyStream.Close()
```

Worst Practice: Write to Predictable Locations

No matter whether you use the convenient built-in serialization objects or develop your own, you will probably end up putting the serialized state on disk at some point. Where you put it is important. There are several potential vulnerabilities to watch out for any time you write to the disk. Firstly:

> **You must not allow untrusted code to decide where a file goes.**

Paths and file names should not be derived from data supplied by untrusted code (or by untrusted clients, if you are implementing server-side code) unless that data has been thoroughly vetted. We shall see why not below. The second is:

> **You should also avoid writing out data supplied by untrustworthy sources.**

The reasoning behind these seemingly unnecessary restrictions becomes clearer if you think like an attacker. Attackers want (maybe more than anything else) to get executable files on to your machine, whether those files are .NET assemblies, native code assemblies, or scripts. Getting the exploit code onto the target machine is the obvious first step required to execute it.

The next problem the attacker has is making the exploit code run once it is on your machine. There are several ways to do this. For example, the exploit code could be written into `c:\windows\notepad.exe` or some other commonly used program, overwriting the existing benign program with a hostile one. The next time the target user edits a text file the exploit runs with full trust. Another way to make hostile code run with full rights is to store it in the startup folder, so that when the machine reboots the code runs automatically.

If the exploit code is in the form of a .NET assembly and it is stored in the right directory, the attacker could put a helper object on a web page and wait for vulnerable people to download and run the helper object. When the helper object runs it is in the Internet zone (although by default the internet zone does not contain any permissions may people will change this as they will want to run code from the Internet), but it can load the fully trusted (because it is on the local machine) exploit code, if it is stored in the right location.

An example of this class of vulnerabilities shipped with Internet Explorer many years ago. An object that could store state on disk was accidentally marked as "safe for scripting" so that it could be used by web page scripts. The object allowed the untrusted caller to supply both the path and some of the information persisted out. Some of the security vulnerabilities this caused were:

❏ Any web page could launch a DoS attack against a client machine by simply filling up the client's disk with thousands and thousands of files.

❏ Any web page could discover paths on a client machine by attempting to write files to guessed paths and checking for failure.

❏ Worst of all, any web page could write a file called `hack.hta` into the startup folder of a client. An HTA file is an "HTML Application", essentially an application written in HTML and script. Since HTAs are not downloaded from the Internet but rather act like local executables they do not run with the usual Internet Explorer security restrictions. Furthermore, when IE loads an HTA it ignores all the random junk in the file that it does not understand; it just extracts the scripts and markup it needs to run.

The practical upshot was that an attacker could use this control to write executable code to any client's hard disk, which would then execute using the full rights of that client the next time the machine was rebooted. Remember, fully trusted hostile programs can do anything you can do. They can post all your files to some usenet group, change your password, anything.

Saving State Safely

If you are saving code on behalf of a user then it is probably best to simply create a file dialog and let the user decide where the file should go. Users are bad at making security decisions but they can be presumed to be smart enough to not save documents into the global assembly cache directories or to overwrite executable files!

If you are saving state for your application then the best thing to do is to use the `IsolatedStorage` classes to manage your application state for you. This is a good idea for three reasons:

First, the isolated storage directories use carefully constructed paths that are hard for untrusted code to find. Determining where a given isolated storage is on disk should require `PathDiscovery` permissions at the very least.

Second, the right to use isolated storage is granted by the `IsolatedStoragePermission`, not the `FileIOPermission` object. Good security policies can safely grant `IsolatedStoragePermission` to less-trustworthy code but `FileIOPermission` must only be granted to fully trusted code. If your assembly never needs to access the file system, and is not granted permission to access the file system, then the odds are very good that no file-system-attacking vulnerability will be found in your code by attackers!

Third, the local Intranet code group is granted the right to unlimited isolated storage but not granted full file system access. If you ever want your program to be run from a network share, you should plan to require only the rights granted to the local Intranet code group.

Worst Practice: Allow Untrusted Code to Serialize Sensitive State

In our `Car` example above, there were no private data members, and none of the data was particularly security-sensitive. However, you might have a serializable object with private fields such as:

```
<Serializable()> _
Public Class Person
Implements ISerializable

    ' ...
    Private SocialSecurityNumber As String
    Private BankAccountNumber As String
    Private MothersMaidenName As String
    ' ...

End Class
```

Now, as we discussed above in the section on failing to keep secrets, there is no way to hide this information from the user or even from any fully-trusted code. However, this information should be hidden from untrusted code that may have obtained a reference to a `Person` object.

If that untrusted code can create a `BinaryFormatter` object and an in-memory stream then the untrusted code can simply serialize the object into its stream. The binary format of that stream is not at all difficult to reverse engineer. In short:

> **Serialization makes every serialized field of an object readable by the caller.**

You should protect your security-sensitive objects from being serialized by untrustworthy callers by adding a declarative demand to your `GetObjectData()` method:

```
<SecurityPermission(SecurityAction.Demand, SerializationFormatter _
                    := True)> _
  Public Sub GetObjectData(Info As SerializationInfo, _
                           Context As StreamingContext) _
   Implements ISerializable.GetObjectData
```

The `SerializationFormatter` demand ensures that everyone on the call stack has the right to inspect the serialized format of your object. Like the other permissions, that allow code to override visibility rules, this permission is usually only granted to fully trusted code.

Worst Practice: Allow Untrusted Code to Deserialize Sensitive State

The same warning goes when going the other way. The untrusted code can create a binary stream, which contains data that looks like the serialized state of your object. If the untrusted code is allowed to deserialize an object that contains sensitive data then the untrusted code may cause the reconstituted object to have a bad internal state.

You should therefore protect the deserializing constructor of security-sensitive objects with the same demand for `SerializationFormatter` rights.

A Brief Note about the Default Serializer

Serialization code is a good example of the sort of boring-to-write "boilerplate" code that ends up with bugs because you added a new field and forgot to add the serialization code. To make the common case easier, the .NET Runtime provides a default serializer and deserializer to any class that is marked with the `SerializableAttribute` but does not implement the `ISerializable` interface.

This default serializer will serialize every member of the class (no matter what its visibility is) recursively serializing any member objects. If for any reason you do not want a field serialized by the default serializer then be sure to mark it with the `NonSerialized` attribute:

```
<Serializable()> _
Public Class DefaultSerializer

   <NonSerialized()> Private Temporary As String
   Private Important As String

   '...

End Class
```

Err On the Side of Caution

If you are not sure whether a given serializable object contains "sensitive" data then err on the side of caution – put demands on the serialize/deserialize methods. In fact, even if the object does not contain "sensitive" data you should consider whether an untrusted object would ever really need to serialize the object. If the answer is "no", then make the demand.

> **Avoid "repurposing" attacks; if there is no partial trust scenario then disallow partially trusted callers.**

How to Write Bad Event Handlers and other Delegates

So far we have not talked at all about event-driven programming, a style of programming commonly used by Visual Basic programmers. Event handlers in VB.NET are actually a special case of a more general concept, the **delegate**. We shall first quickly define what exactly a delegate is and then discuss some of the security problems associated with delegates.

A Brief Refresher on Delegates

Delegates are a new concept to Visual Basic; they are analogous to function pointers in C/C++ or function objects in JScript. A delegate is an object that represents a call to a method; this is useful where the exact method to be called is not known at compile time. The delegate type of the delegate object constrains the sorts of methods (the number and types of arguments and so on) that may be represented by that object. You can the bind the delegate to a particular method at run time based on what ever conditions you want.

Behind the scenes Visual Basic's event handling code always worked using delegate-like objects, but this implementation detail was not exposed to VB developers. VB.NET's event handling mechanism works the same way, but more of the infrastructure is now visible – if you want it to be. Events in VB.NET still work the same way they used to with similar syntax, but direct manipulation of the underlying delegates is now possible as well.

Behind the scenes event binding works something like this:

When you declare an event handler for a particular event on a particular event source object VB.NET actually creates a delegate to your event handler. It passes that delegate object to the event source object. The event source object maintains a list of event sink delegates. (The "sources and sinks" terminology comes from engineering jargon; a source is some device that produces something, a sink consumes something.) When the event source raises an event, behind the scenes it simply invokes everything on its list of delegates one at a time and thereby executes all the event handlers.

For example, consider the declaration of a standard button-click event handler in a managed form. The button is declared as a known event source (by the `WithEvents` keyword) and the handler is declared as an event sink (with the `Handles` keyword). The constructor simply initializes the object and VB.NET takes it from there to actually do the hookup:

```
Public Class Form1
    Inherits System.Windows.Forms.Form

    Friend WithEvents Button1 As System.Windows.Forms.Button

    Private Sub Button1_Click(ByVal sender As System.Object, _
    ByVal e As System.EventArgs) Handles Button1.Click
        ' ...
    End Sub

    Public Sub New()
        ' ...
        Me.Button1 = New System.Windows.Forms.Button()
        ' ...
    End Sub

End Class
```

To make explicit what is actually happening here, this code is exactly equivalent:

```
Public Class Form1
    Inherits System.Windows.Forms.Form

    Friend Button1 As System.Windows.Forms.Button ' No WithEvents

    Private Sub MyHandler(ByVal sender As System.Object, _
    ByVal e As System.EventArgs) ' no Handles clause
        ' ...
    End Sub
    Public Sub New()
        ' ...
        Me.Button1 = New System.Windows.Forms.Button()
        AddHandler Button1.Click, New EventHandler(AddressOf MyHandler)
        ' ...
    End Sub
End Class
```

Now the delegate creation and binding is more explicit. The `EventHandler` constructor produces an `EventHandler` delegate that represents the `MyHandler()` subroutine. (VB.NET requires the `AddressOf` operator to make it explicit that the `MyHandler()` method is being bound, and it is not an expression in itself).

Delegates are powerful and useful programming tool. They can be used in any situation where some code must call some arbitrary, externally determined method when some condition is met; events are just one example of such a situation.

Security Issues with Delegates

Delegates, though powerful and useful, should be used carefully to avoid introducing vulnerabilities. The essential problem is that a delegate is a little package of functionality just waiting to run. Suppose you are writing an event source, some code that raises an event. Your code is handed delegate objects representing the subroutines to automatically call when the event is raised. You have no idea what those methods do or where they came from. All you know is that someone wants you to call the method when you raise an event.

Calling Delegates

Normally one constructs methods not knowing who is going to call them. The hard part about writing secure code, as we have seen so far, is ensuring that methods are robust in the face of hostile, unknown, untrustworthy callers. At least you have some idea what methods *your* function implementation calls; with delegates, you do not know what the delegate is going to do when you invoke it.

It is somewhat analogous to the problems of taking data from untrusted clients in server-side code, as we discussed above; invoking delegates given to you by untrusted code is essentially taking candy from strangers. The danger comes in part from this important fact:

> **The delegate object (an event handler, for example) may represent a method from a highly trusted assembly. The delegate's invoker (an event source, for example) may also be from a highly trusted assembly. However, the code that called AddHandler may be from some less trusted, possibly hostile assembly.**

Let's think about an example not involving event handling for a change. Suppose you have a method that takes a delegate so that it can call an arbitrary function when some condition is met. For example, you might write a method that takes a string and a delegate and calls the delegate back for each place where the string matches a pattern read from a configuration file.

Here is an implementation that has some serious security holes. First, we declare the type of the delegate and the method that takes the delegate:

```vb
' delegate.vb

Imports Microsoft.VisualBasic
Imports System.Security.Permissions

Public Class DelegateExample

  Private Const PatternFile As String = "C:\Patterns.Txt"
```

```
Public Delegate Sub MatchCallback(Source As String, _
                                  Index As Integer)

Private Shared Function FetchPatternFromFile(ByVal PatternFile _
                                        As String) As String
    ' we'll just provide a very simple implementation
    Dim MyStream As StreamReader = File.OpenText(PatternFile)
    FetchPatternFromFile = MyStream.ReadLine()
    MyStream.Close()
End Function

Public Shared Sub Match(Source As String, MCB As MatchCallback)
    Dim Pattern As String
    Dim Index As Integer
```

Now suppose we need to assert a permission for some reason. Perhaps the default pattern is stored in a configuration file. Since it is safe to read the file we can assert the right to read the file system:

```
Dim FilePerm As New FileIOPermission(PermissionState.Unrestricted)
FilePerm.Assert()
Pattern = FetchPatternFromFile(PatternFile)
```

Now we can continue with the actual work of the method: searching the string and calling the caller back on every match.

```
    Index = 1
    Do
        Index = InStr(Index, Source, Pattern)
        If Index = 0 Then Exit Sub
        MCB(Source, Index)
        Index = Index + Len(Pattern)
    Loop
    End Sub
End Class
```

A benign caller might call this method like this:

```
Public Module MainMod

    Public Sub OnMatch(Source As String, Index As Integer)
        System.Console.WriteLine(Index)
    End Sub

    Public Sub Main()
        ' Suppose the pattern is "abc".
        DelegateExample.Match("abc    abc abcabc", _
        New DelegateExample.MatchCallback(AddressOf OnMatch))
        ' This will then write out 1/7/11/14.
    End Sub

End Module
```

The vulnerability arises in the following manner. Suppose somewhere on the user's machine there is a fully trusted assembly – perhaps also written by you, or perhaps not – that requires permission to access the file system and takes a string and an index. As a (somewhat contrived) example, suppose the user has installed a fully trusted assembly with this method:

```
Public Shared Sub UpdateStockList(Company As String, _
   Rating As Integer)
   ' [ omitted ] open configuration file for stock tracking
   ' application, write company name and rating into file.
   ' This demands FileIOPermission of course.
End Sub
```

An untrusted hostile assembly downloaded from the Internet could not successfully call UpdateStockList() directly because the demand would fail. However, the untrusted hostile assembly could trick your flawed string-searching program into asserting the privilege:

```
DelegateExample.Match("abcCorporation", _
   New DelegateExample.MatchCallback( _
   AddressOf StockUtilities.UpdateStockList))
```

This then writes out "abcCorporation" as being a number one rated stock pick in the configuration file for a completely different program.

The example is somewhat contrived, but you take the point I'm sure: DelegateExample is badly flawed in several ways. First, it asserts far more rights than it actually uses. It ought to assert the least privilege required:

```
Dim FilePerm As New FileIOPermission( _
   FileIOPermissionAccess.Read, PatternFile)
```

Second, it does not revert the assert before calling the delegate. Remember, an assert says "I know that there is no luring attack; please temporarily suspend full stack walks for this permission." If you call an arbitrary delegate then how do you know that there is no luring attack? You do not.

Essentially any code with this design pattern is potentially vulnerable:

Figure 2

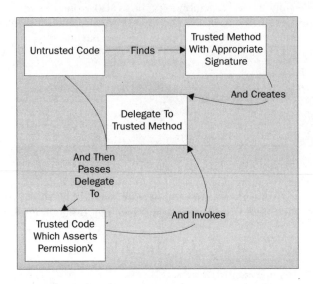

When the delegate is invoked, it will call a fully trusted method.

> **Do not assert rights before calling delegates. If the delegate is sufficiently trusted it can assert its own rights if it needs to.**

Producing Delegates

The converse of the case above also indicates a potential vulnerability. The untrustworthy code was able to do its dirty work because some other trustworthy code left a dangerous public method lying around just waiting to be snapped up and used as a delegate. In the case above, the trustworthy code is not responsible for its misuse of course; the problem lies with the poorly implemented delegate caller.

However, writing public, dangerous methods is a particularly poor programming practice when you implement methods intended to be used by delegates such as event handlers. In many cases, it is not necessary for the event source to be badly written. If the benign event source and the benign-but-dangerous event sink, are both fully trusted then an untrusted caller can lure the source into calling the handler. At this point if the event fires and the handler demands a permission the stack walk may have only fully trusted code on it.

Let's look at this a little closer. Suppose that your fully trusted customizable program exposes a couple of public event sources:

```
Public Class Form1
  Inherits System.Windows.Forms.Form
  Public ButtonDeleteFile As System.Windows.Forms.Button
  Public ButtonCreateFile As System.Windows.Forms.Button
  ' Note: No WithEvents, Public instead of Friend
  ' ...
```

Furthermore, suppose that it exposes its handlers publicly as well:

```
Public Sub DeleteButtonHandler(ByVal sender As System.Object, _
ByVal e As System.EventArgs)
  ' [ omitted: delete a file ]
End Sub

Public Sub CreateButtonHandler(ByVal sender As System.Object, _
ByVal e As System.EventArgs)
  ' [ omitted: create a file ]
End Sub
```

The constructor for the form then hooks up the events:

```
Public Sub New()
  ' ...
  Me.ButtonDeleteFile = New System.Windows.Forms.Button()
  Me.ButtonCreateFile = New System.Windows.Forms.Button()
  AddHandler Me.ButtonDeleteFile.Click, _
  New EventHandler(AddressOf Me.DeleteButtonHandler)
  AddHandler Me.ButtonCreateFile.Click, _
  New EventHandler(AddressOf Me.CreateButtonHandler)
  ' ...
```

So far, all is well. Suppose, however, this is a customizable application and you carefully set the evidence and the policy to ensure that the customization is granted only a small permission set.

The code above is still highly vulnerable because hooking up public event sources to public event handlers requires no particular permissions. If at any time this forms-based application passes a reference to the form to any hostile customization code there is nothing stopping the hostile code from doing something like:

```
AddHandler TheForm.ButtonCreateFile.Click, _
New EventHandler(AddressOf TheForm.DeleteButtonHandler)
```

Suppose the hostile code does that and returns. Ten minutes later, the user clicks the "create file" button and a file is created *and then deleted*. All of the stack walks succeed because the untrusted code is long gone; it is no longer on the stack. When the event handler runs every frame on the stack is fully trusted.

Any time you make the event sources and handlers available to untrusted code you are essentially handing over control of your event-based programming model. This is particularly dangerous when the untrusted code can manipulate what various user interface elements do.

Figure 3

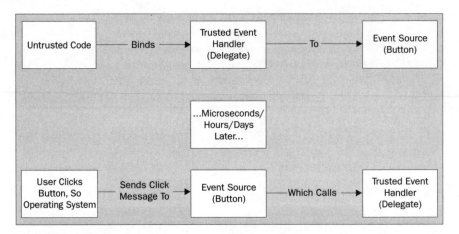

> **Be extremely careful when mixing public event handlers and untrusted code. The best thing to do is to restrict the visibility of the event sources and handlers.**

Using Reflection Safely

The purpose of the Reflection layer is to discover information about objects. Typically this is used so that callers may call methods without having to know exactly what the method looks like at compile time. Essentially Reflection is a smart proxy layer that makes calls on the caller's behalf.

That is fundamentally a dangerous thing to do; the luring attack is all about getting some highly trusted assembly to make a dangerous call on behalf of untrusted code. The Framework code that implements Reflection is always fully trusted. Keep this in mind when designing your own code, particularly if it can be called by untrusted code and it uses Reflection.

We have already covered how link demands work with Reflection in Chapter 3. From a security perspective there is one more important rule about Reflection that we have not yet covered, namely:

Do not Proxy Reflection

We know that the key thing about link demands is that they put the onus for avoiding luring attacks onto their callers. There are a few methods in the .NET Framework that might not actually make a link demand but have behavior reminiscent of a link demand in this regard. Consider the in-memory version of `Assembly.Load()`, for example. This method has the signature.

```
Overloads Public Shared Function Load( ByVal rawAssembly() As Byte ) _
   As Assembly
```

If for some reason you have an assembly in memory instead of on disk, you may still load it. You might wonder: if the assembly is not on disk then how does the policy engine determine what evidence to use? It can determine the hash but not the zone or path.

In this case the policy engine gives the same evidence to the created assembly as the assembly that called the `Load()` method. If you call this method from a fully trusted assembly then the loaded assembly will also be fully trusted!

The behavior is somewhat like a link demand in the sense that only the immediate caller's evidence is considered, much as a link demand only checks the immediate caller's grant set.

Recall that if you call a method with a link demand via Reflection, the Reflection layer converts the link demand into a regular stack-walking demand, ensuring that hostile callers cannot get around the link demand by using the fully trusted Reflection layer as an intermediary. You therefore might expect that if you call the in-memory version of `Assembly.Load()` via Reflection the policy engine skips the Reflection layer when attempting to determine what evidence to associate with the newly loaded assembly.

You would be correct. However, this implies two very important things. First, for this specific case: you must never call `Assembly.Load()` with a byte stream provided to you by an untrusted source unless you use the overloaded version that takes an explicit `Evidence` object. If your more-trusted code for some bizarre reason takes a byte stream from an untrusted source and loads it then the untrusted source may provide you with the bytes of a hostile assembly that would then obtain your permissions.

It is rather unlikely that you would actually write that specific code, however. There is a second, more general rule that we can derive from this example:

> **You must never write a proxy for the Reflection layer. That is, you must not write highly trusted code that takes in arbitrary `MethodInfo` objects and arbitrary arguments from untrusted sources then blindly invokes the methods.**

An untrusted caller could give you a `MethodInfo` object for `Assembly.Load()` or some other security-sensitive method and pass in any arguments it wanted. If your Reflection proxy calls any method that has behavior, based only on the immediate caller rather than the full call stack then essentially you are allowing less trusted code to use your evidence.

This is not to say, "Never use Reflection." Reflection is very useful, but can only be used securely when you know where the invoked objects came from! If you want to use Reflection then ensure that trustworthy code is the only source of the invoked `MethodInfo` objects, either by writing the code yourself or using a Demand to ensure that your callers are highly trusted.

Summary

We have just seen an awful lot of awful code in this chapter. The scary thing is that though some of the code is clearly contrived, all of these flaws can easily creep into real-world code. Real-world code tends to be longer and more complex than short samples, which makes the vulnerabilities much less obvious.

We can sum up the litany of specific common problems listed above into just three principal mistakes. Any one of these mistakes can lead you to write insecure code that makes your users vulnerable to attackers:

- ❏ First mistake: **try to do the impossible**. For example, try to keep secrets by implementing your own encryption or try to hide implementation details from your users.

- ❏ Second mistake: **write sloppy code**. For example, make everything public, write bad error handling code, or write inconsistent link demands.

❑   Third mistake: **trust everyone**. For example, assume that data from untrusted sources is well-formed and not hostile.

In the next chapter, we will look at some best practices. We will look both at specific ways to write good code and general techniques for managing the whole development cycle. We will finish Chapter 6 with a checklist summarizing the things you should be thinking about when attempting to write solid, secure code.

VB.NET

Code Security

Handbook

6

How to Make Code Secure

In the previous chapter, we examined a considerable number of mistakes that even seasoned developers make all the time. In this chapter, rather than looking at worst practices for writing insecure code we shall look at some of the best practices for writing secure code. We will finish off the chapter with an extensive checklist summarizing what to look out for when writing or reviewing code.

Secure Code is Solid Code

If you build your bank on sand rather than bedrock then you automatically make the task of securing the vault much harder. Worse, if the infrastructure of the building cannot support the weight of the vault then you have a considerable re-engineering problem on your hands.

The same is true of coding projects; it is much harder to make an application secure if it is poorly written in the first place. Let's think about some of the characteristics of well-engineered code but look at them from a security perspective. Well-engineered code is **correct**, **testable**, **performant**, and **maintainable**.

Correctness

Firstly, insecure code is often just a special case of **incorrect** code; which does not actually implement the semantics intended by the developer. Alternatively, the code may work as intended but have a fundamentally insecure design.

Robustness is one important aspect of correctness, and is particularly important with regard to security. The robustness of a piece of code is a measure of its ability to withstand unusual situations. Does the program perform well in low memory conditions or does it fail to an insecure mode? Does it detect invalid input and reject it immediately, or will it cheerfully attempt to schedule a package delivery in the year 1902 and automatically give a price reduction for a late package?

> **Do not cut corners; attackers look for the "corner cases" that might be handled incorrectly in the hopes that some of those flaws might lead to exploitable vulnerabilities. Every possible code path must be secure.**

Fixing It

Fixing any coding mistake is expensive. Furthermore, it is well understood that the later a flaw is found, the more expensive it is to fix. Fixing a major mistake the day after you introduce it might inconvenience your testers. It is not a particularly good idea to inconvenience your testers, but compare that to inconveniencing customers! Fixing a major mistake the day after it ships to customers can be immensely expensive and have a cost not only measured in monetary terms but in reputation as well.

Bug Triage

To help manage this process developers and software project managers normally prioritize mistakes – deciding which to fix and which to live with. This process is often called "bug triage", an analogy to the practice of classifying battlefield casualties by the severity of the injury. Triagers usually give the highest priority to those coding mistakes that cause unwanted behavior during the normal operation of the product by normal users. If the flaw causes the program to terminate abnormally or behave badly when a user does something only slightly out-of-the-ordinary, then it should probably be fixed straight away. If on the other hand the flaw can only be exposed by an extremely unlikely series of user actions, then it might be documented in a "readme" file and the fix postponed until the next service release.

From the "usability" perspective, this seems like it is clearly the right thing to do. Why waste a whole lot of expensive developer and tester time fixing a bug that no user will ever run into because it is only exposed by some obscure sequence of events no normal user would ever perform?

This entirely understandable attitude misses a key point though. Yes, a software flaw that causes a user to lose data because you forgot to handle an exception somewhere in main-line code is bad. However, even an obscure software flaw that allows a wily attacker to steal or modify that user's data is potentially worse.

> **It is often the obscure flaws (which no normal user will ever encounter) that lead to vulnerabilities. The first question you should ask when triaging a bug is "can attackers exploit this flaw to hurt the user?"**

If you have identified a flaw that you believe may introduce a security vulnerability there are a few questions you should ask to try to determine just how bad the vulnerability is. Here are a few examples of the sorts of things to think about when triaging security issues:

First, think about how bad it is for your customers/users:

❑　How severe is the vulnerability? Can the attacker gain complete control of the machine, just discover paths, or could they mount a denial of service attack?

❑　How many customers could be affected by this attack? All of them, only customers who have configured your product in a certain way, or even none?

❑　Is there anything your customers can do to mitigate the risk themselves? Will rebooting the machine eliminate the denial of service? Is there some configuration of the software that will prevent the attack without crippling the application entirely?

Then think about how much work the attacker has to do:

❑　Just how hard would it be to exploit the vulnerability? Does exploiting the vulnerability require the resources of the National Security Agency, a typical university network, or a single attacker working from a home machine? Could one knowledgeable attacker write a recipe for the attack that could be posted to a newsgroup and then followed by a thousand unskilled "script kiddies"?

❑　Does the attack work every time, or will the attacker likely fail a million times before succeeding? Exploits that depend on race conditions, out-of-memory conditions, and so on are unlikely to be easily pulled off the first time, but may happen eventually if the attacker is persistent. Will your auditing catch the million unsuccessful attacks?

All security flaws are serious but some are more serious than others. A security flaw that only affects a few users and requires enormous resources to exploit is one thing; a gaping hole that allows any teenager with too much time on their hands to gain full trust on ten thousand machines is another.

There is no magic formula to determine whether a given security flaw meets the bar for fixing in the next version, issuing a "hot fix", or recalling your product. All you can do is analyze the problem carefully, think about the customer impact, and decide accordingly. Consider the full cost of fixing the flaw (developer time, testing time, support calls, bad publicity) against the cost of not fixing the flaw and having a well-publicized attack against your customers or systems as a result.

Telling Users

Suppose you discover a serious security vulnerability in one of your shipped applications. Perhaps you discover it in-house, or perhaps some clever "white-hat hackers" have discovered the vulnerability and sent the details to you rather than taking advantage of it themselves. Either way, what do you tell your customers between discovering the problem and issuing a fix?

Obviously a trustworthy company admits its mistakes, takes responsibility for those mistakes and exercises due diligence in fixing them. That is not at issue. The more interesting question is whether you tell users they are at risk before you release a patch. On the one hand, you want your customers to be aware that there is a potential problem so that they can attempt to protect themselves until there is a patch available. On the other hand, doing so is effectively broadcasting your vulnerabilities to attackers who then have a window of opportunity to take advantage of it.

A complete discussion of all the issues involved in what has come to be known as the "responsible disclosure" debate is beyond the scope of this book. For a good overview of the issues associated with responsible disclosure, see http://www.ietf.org/internet-drafts/draft-christey-wysopal-vuln-disclosure-00.txt.

Manage the Risk by Planning for Mistakes

Possibly the most important thing to take away from this discussion of correctness is this:

> **Plan for security vulnerabilities in your product the same way you would plan for a physical disaster like a fire or flood. Do everything you can to ensure that it will not happen and have a clear, well-thought-out disaster plan just in case it does.**

Testability

Writing software that cannot be tested effectively is a recipe for disaster. If you cannot easily test your programs then you have no data upon which to make a judgment of how correct or secure your product is! However, testing software for security is somewhat different from normal software testing.

As we discussed above in the section on triaging bugs, most testers concentrate on three things.

- ❏ First, they ensure that the "mainline" scenarios work extremely well so that users do not run into flaws during the normal operation of the product.

❑ Second, they check "corner cases", those possible-but-rare cases that may have been overlooked by the developers. Does the family-tree database recognize that there was no February 29 in 1900? Does it handle the case where there are two brothers both named George?

❑ Third, they may attempt to "stress" the software by throwing garbage input or massive input at it and ensuring that it produces sensible error messages.

Mainline testing is focused on ensuring that the application does what the user wants when used normally. It is focused as much on verifying usability as finding bugs. Security testing is much more like the second and third tasks; it is often focused on ensuring that the application fails gracefully when badly misused.

The best part about security testing is that it gives the testers a chance to get away from the occasionally tedious work of verifying that the code works in mainline scenarios and really exercise their devious minds. In order for them to be able to do so effectively, however, testers need as much knowledge of potential vulnerabilities as the developers who are trying to avoid them. Make sure that testers as well as developers understand how the .NET Framework security system works so that they can test effectively. They should also know about common techniques used by attackers.

Things to Look for When Testing Security

As we have already said, many security vulnerabilities are just new occurrences of common themes. Here are some things to take in to consideration when testing software:

❑ Try running the software in a restricted security environment: run the code from the Internet to restrict its code-based permissions or the Guest account to reduce its role-based permissions. Does it succeed? If it fails, does it fail early and give sensible error messages? Do those error messages give away any sensitive information?

❑ Do not forget about stress testing, particularly for server applications. Identify every possible avenue for hostile data to get into an application and see what happens when bad data is passed. Does the application detect it and abort, or does something bad happen?

❑ Bad data can be too long, too short, random, inconsistent, and so on. Inconsistent data is particularly interesting. If a public method expects, say, an object representing a family tree what happens if you pass in a tree with cycles in it? (That is a tree where two people are both listed as each other's mother, for example.) Does the machine go into an infinite loop? That might introduce a DoS attack if the code was running on a server. Attackers will pass in illogical, unrealistic data in the hopes that something fails in a vulnerable manner.

❑ The previous example generalizes somewhat: look for combinations of code that may individually be perfectly safe but which might introduce vulnerabilities when used together.

❑ Bad data can also be actively hostile data, particularly on servers. If you suspect that you might have a cross-site-scripting flaw, or a SQL injection flaw, then write a custom client that can post any data to your server. Try posting chunks of HTML containing script, SQL expressions and so on for every possible input field.

❑ Go back through your bug database and review old bugs, particularly those that were not fixed and were postponed to be fixed in later service releases. (If you don't have a bug database, there is no time like the present to start one.) Those old bugs may give you ideas for possible security flaws, or may in fact be security flaws.

❑ Stress the code by testing it under unusual conditions: run it on machines with heavy CPU load, run your tests on multiple threads in the same process and see what breaks, eats up all the memory or disk space on a machine, and what fails.

❑ Look for ways to force your code to eat up memory or disk space itself. If untrustworthy callers can force the code to consume resources then your code may be vulnerable to a DoS attack.

One thing to not look for when testing software for security is this:

Do not waste time coming up with luring attacks that would require a fully-trusted hostile caller or a hostile caller with administrative privileges to successfully lure your code into doing something harmful. If a hostile program becomes fully trusted or gains administrator rights then the hostile program need not lure your code into doing something harmful; it can just do it itself.

Server Performance

Far too often developers get the attitude that performance and security are at odds. They are not. The old adage is true: you can make it go as fast as you want if you just stop worrying about correctness. Raw performance as measured by benchmarks is only one aspect of server performance, and a highly artificial one at that. A server that serves up hundreds of hacker-defaced pages per second cannot really be considered to be performing well!

Furthermore, the same principles that keep servers secure, such as careful vetting of client-supplied data, also enhance server performance. Checking user data that is valid does consumes machine cycles, it's true, but those cycles are preventing DoS attacks from chewing up even more cycles and cross-site scripting attacks from stealing your users' data. Those checks are a necessary investment in security.

Security and performance are connected in many ways. For example, a key performance metric for server software is performance under stress conditions (such as thousands of simultaneous requests under low memory conditions). Remember that attackers bent on causing DoS attacks often attempt to artificially stress the server. Recall also our discussion in Chapter 5 on exception handling; attackers will stress the server in the hopes of exposing exploitable vulnerabilities in poorly tested exception-handling code. If you know that your code runs in a performant, robust manner, even when under stress conditions then it is less likely that such an attack on the server will succeed.

Again, a full discussion of writing performant code is well beyond the scope of this book. However, if you know only one thing about performance tuning applications (whether on the client or the server), know this:

> **The only way to achieve high performance is to set specific performance goals and make careful measurements to see if you have reached those goals.**

Performance and Security

When writing performant code it is a good idea to keep a few orders of magnitude in mind:

❑ A machine cycle on a modern machine takes a few **nanoseconds** (or less).

❑ Typical disk operations such as opening a file take a few **milliseconds**. Refreshing a monitor screen takes around twenty milliseconds.

❑ Typical string operations such as concatenation take a few **microseconds**.

❑ Typical Internet operations such as fetching a web page can take a few **seconds**.

You can expect that a successful Demand on a permission object will take in the order of a few microseconds. (The performance of unsuccessful Demands is not particularly interesting; an unsuccessful Demand is often followed by returning an error and refusing to do any more work!) A successful Demand is one that walked the entire call stack until it either found the top or found a suitable Assert. Successful Demands that must traverse large call stacks with many assemblies will obviously be more expensive than ones with short call stacks in few assemblies.

The point is this: on a client machine you can probably get away with thousands of Demands before you slow your program down so much that it causes a noticeable change to the user. After all, it takes around twenty thousand microseconds to redraw the screen and, obviously, users cannot perceive any change that takes less than that amount of time. If you want to write high performance code then concentrate on eliminating expensive things, such as disk or network access, first.

The situation is slightly different on servers; after all, the difference between a page that takes 10,000 microseconds to render and one that takes 12,000 microseconds is the difference between 100 pages served per second and 80 pages served per second. Heavily loaded servers are more sensitive to small increases in the average CPU time spent per page. However, the general rule of thumb is just as true on servers: eliminate the slowest thing first. Well-written security code is unlikely to be the slowest thing.

If, however, you are doing some highly performance-sensitive operation in a tight loop millions of times a second and must make a Demand in there, and the Demand is the most expensive thing then you might have a problem. In this sort of situation, there really is a tradeoff between performance and security. If you find yourself in this situation, consider doing things such as:

❑   Look for places where your code makes a Demand and then calls code that makes the same Demand.

For example, perhaps you have a method that you know will need File IO permission so you demand it up front. This is in keeping with good design practices anyway, always clearly documenting your security requirements and checking for permissions sooner rather than later. However doing two Demands is redundant and expensive. You might want to carefully review the code and eliminate the outer Demand.

An even better idea is to keep the outer Demand, Assert the relevant permission and then do the tight loop. The Demand will be less expensive because the Assert will terminate the stack walk early but there will be no change in the overall security.

❑   If justified, replace the innermost Demand with a LinkDemand. LinkDemands have no per-call cost because the demand is only done once when the caller is JIT compiled. However, this decreases your security by imposing the burden of preventing luring attacks upon your caller.

❑   As a last resort, if the performance problem is the result of repeated demands for the right to call unmanaged code there is a special attribute used to eliminate this problem. You can use the SuppressUnmanagedCodeSecurity attribute on a method to turn off all checks for the right to call unmanaged code during the execution of the method. Using this attribute automatically adds a link demand for the right to call unmanaged code to the method.

> **Get your security story right first and then see if it is fast enough. Do not change security code for performance reasons unless you have a clear, measurable benefit and the change has been carefully thought through.**

Maintainability

There is a good chance that your code is likely to be around for a long time in one form or another. You will have to fix mistakes, write new versions of old software, and borrow code from past projects to use in new projects, and so on. Clearly, if you cannot understand the code then you cannot fix mistakes without risking worse ones; effectively you cannot correctly extend or repurpose the code. If you design the code to be clear and maintainable in the first place, it is far more likely to turn out that way.

This is particularly true when it comes to the security semantics of your code. If ever there was a proper place to write incredibly clear, straightforward code, your security code is it. Remember that your code may be maintained by people who do not understand the semantics of the security system or the VB.NET language as well as the authors.

Does this contradict our earlier advice regarding source code? Recall that we recommended you not to reveal excessive details that attackers could use against you should they obtain your source code. More generally, we also recommended that anything that slows attackers down is a good thing. Does it then follow that your source code should be deliberately hard to read?

Of course not; do not make it hard for attackers to find flaws by making the code hard to understand. Make it hard for attackers to find flaws by ensuring that you have very few flaws! Make sure that it is easy for you to find and fix flaws by making the code clear, maintainable, robust, and modular. Further, make sure that both source code and supplemental documentation (such as your bug database) is kept both secure and up-to-date.

Good Assemblies

The first thing that the .NET security system sees when it loads your code is the **assembly manifest**. The manifest lists **attributes** such as the name and version of the assembly. It also lists the **security requirements** for the assembly to work correctly, such as "this assembly must always be granted the right to call unmanaged code". The manifest also lists the **dependencies**: the list of other assemblies that must be present on the machine in order for it to work correctly.

> You can view the manifest of any assembly with the ILDASM utility.

In this section, we will discuss one of the most important attributes of any assembly: its strong name. We will also discuss other informational assembly attributes and have a quick refresher on using security attributes on assemblies to document security requirements.

Strong Names

Suppose you write a library of useful classes in VB.NET and want to distribute them to customers. You call it `FooCorp.Gadgets.dll` and sell it over the Internet. Everything goes well until some attacker takes your DLL, modifies it slightly to do something harmful, and starts distributing it. When your customers go to load `FooCorp.Gadgets.DLL` they expect that they are getting the same DLL that you produced, but of course anyone can name any DLL anything they want. An attacker might be distributing a hostile DLL with the same name.

Strong names solve this problem. Unlike a regular name, which is merely a string, a strong name consists of four parts: a **regular name**, a **version number,** a **culture identifier**, and a **digital signature**.

The strong name system allows your customers to load your class library based on its strong name, not its file name. The version number allows your customers to load a specific version of an assembly, and to know that two assemblies with the same file name and same signature but different version numbers were in fact produced by the same publisher.

Note that a strong name may also include an optional "culture" parameter. You may have distributed several different assemblies localized for different regions. If you do not have localized assemblies or do not care which one you get, then just set the culture parameter to "neutral" and the loader will ignore it.

For example, the strong name of the DLL mentioned above might be

```
"FooCorp.Gadgets,Version=1.0.0.0,Culture=neutral,PublicKeyToken=5c8e8f
345ff71bd6"
```

As we shall see, the security system compares information in the strong name against information derived from the actual bytes of the assembly. If an attacker managed to get a bogus `FooCorp.Gadgets.dll` on a user's machine this strong name would not load it. Users should be encouraged to use strong names whenever possible for exactly this reason; they will always know what they are getting.

> **Note that a strong name is not the same thing as an Authenticode publisher signature. We will cover the difference in detail below.**

All you really need to understand about strong names is that when you load an assembly by its strong name you are guaranteed that you are loading an untampered assembly written by a particular publisher. However, a somewhat deeper understanding of the public key cryptography used to make strong names strong is a good thing to have.

Public Key Cryptography in a Nutshell

Public key cryptosystems provide a system whereby any binary information (such as an assembly or an e-mail or even just a number) can be encrypted using a pair of keys called the public and private keys. If the file is encrypted with one key it can only be decrypted with the other.

Recall from our discussion of evidence in Chapter 2 that every assembly has a unique number associated with it called the hash. If a publisher includes with the assembly the hash encrypted with the publisher's private key then you can decrypt the hash with the public key. If the hash of the assembly and the decrypted hash match then you know that the publisher vouches for that assembly; only someone who knows the private key could have produced a hash decryptable by the public key, and only the publisher knows the private key.

That is a rather brief explanation. If you want to know how this works in more detail, see Appendix A, which explains how public key cryptography is used to ensure that code actually came from a trusted source.

How to Sign an Assembly with a Strong Name

The .NET Framework SDK ships with a useful utility called SN.EXE that performs most of the tasks associated with strong-naming an assembly. To strong-name assemblies the tasks you need to perform are as follows:

❑ Designate a **signing authority**, that is, some highly trusted and security-conscious person in your organization who can ensure the secrecy of the private key.

❑ Create a **key pair** (that is, a public key and a corresponding private key). Extract the public key from the key pair.

❑ Developers doing day-to-day work on the assembly should **delay-sign** it with the public key. Delay signing is the process by which space is reserved in the assembly for the strong name signature so that the signing authority can later emit the signature into the file.

❑ Once you are ready to ship, the signing authority **signs** the assembly with the private key.

The Signing Authority Must Keep Your Private Keys Private

> **It is vitally important that your strong name private key never fall into the hands of a hostile person.**

Suppose you have just shipped version 1.0 of FooCorp.Gadgets.DLL with a strong name.

```
"FooCorp.Gadgets,Version=1.0.0.0,Culture=neutral,PublicKeyToken=5c8e8f
345ff71bd6"
```

Suppose further that some disaster strikes; an attacker makes off with your private key. What is the worst that can happen?

For instance, can the attacker then create a hostile DLL with exactly the same strong name as your just-shipped DLL? If that were the case then the attacker could create a hostile DLL with the same strong name and distribute it, hoping that users who load the DLL based on the strong name will in fact load the hostile DLL, which would then be a highly trusted hostile DLL.

Fortunately, that is not the case. If the private key is revealed then an attacker *cannot* create a hostile DLL with exactly the same strong name.

Why not? Recall that a strong name consists of a regular name, a culture, a version, and a digital signature. If the attacker changes even a single bit of your assembly then the digital signature produced with your stolen private key will be different and therefore the strong name will be different. Any customers who have bound against your strong named assembly will continue to load your version, not the attacker's version.

The attacker could create a hostile version 1.0 of the DLL and attempt to convince people that this strong name referred to a valid DLL produced by you, but the attacker actually has a much more clever option available: produce a hostile version 1.1.

Though an attacker with your private key cannot produce a hostile DLL with exactly the same strong name, your versioning story is now completely shot. The attacker can create a hostile version 1.1 of `FooCorp.Gadgets.DLL` and create a strong name using your private key. If the attacker convinces a customer that his version is in fact a newer, more feature-rich version of your code then the customer cannot detect the attack by comparing the public key in version 1.0 to the one in version 1.1. They could be the same public key and both signatures could be valid but only one actually came from you.

The best way to keep a secret is to share it with as few people as possible. Designate a small number of highly trusted people in your organization as signing authorities and make sure that they are the only people who have access to the machines containing the private key files. Ideally, the private key files should be kept on removable media and stored in a physically safe location until needed. This will prevent accidents; the last thing you want is for every developer in your company to have a copy of the private key and then have a laptop stolen.

Creating a Key Pair

When you need a key pair for your organization, have the signing authority run the strong name utility to create a key pair file and a public key file:

```
> sn.exe -k private.snk
```

```
Microsoft (R) .NET Framework Strong Name Utility  Version 1.0.3705.0
Copyright (C) Microsoft Corporation 1998-2001. All rights reserved.

Key pair written to private.snk
```

> **sn.exe -p private.snk public.snk**

```
Microsoft (R) .NET Framework Strong Name Utility  Version 1.0.3705.0
Copyright (C) Microsoft Corporation 1998-2001. All rights reserved.

Public key written to public.snk
```

This will create two files. The private.snk file contains the public and private keys; the public.snk file contains only the public key. Do whatever is necessary to secure the private.snk file; put it on a floppy in a locked room, put it in a safety deposit box, or use some other physical security to keep it safe. The public.snk file is public. You can e-mail it to all your developers, publish it on the Internet; whatever you want.

Delay Sign the Assembly

The day-to-day work on the assembly may now be done by developers who do not have access to the private key. You should add the public key file to your source code management system and add the following two attributes to your source code:

```
<Assembly: System.Reflection.AssemblyKeyFileAttribute("public.snk")>
<Assembly: System.Reflection.AssemblyDelaySignAttribute(true)>
```

The first attribute embeds the public key into the assembly. This provides the public key portion of the digital signature but not the signed hash. By embedding the public key into the assembly your developers and testers can write other assemblies that reference the assembly under development by its strong name. See below for the details on how to reference an assembly by its strong name.

How can that be, if the signed hash is missing? For that matter, how can the assembly run at all, if the .NET Runtime will immediately detect that it has an invalid strong name? For testing purposes, you can temporarily override the strong name validation checking on a specific assembly based on its file name. This allows you to test scenarios that require the file to be strong named without actually having to get the signing authority to get the private key floppy disk (or whatever) out of the safe.

> **sn.exe -Vr FooCorp.Gadgets.DLL**

The Vr argument simply tells the compiler that eventually the signed hash will be embedded in the assembly so that the compiler can reserve a block of empty space in the assembly.

Really Sign the Assembly

Finally, when you have completed development and are ready to ship the assembly to customers you can send the delay-signed assembly to the signing authority. The signing authority has access to the file containing both the private and public keys:

```
> sn.exe -R FooCorp.Gadgets.DLL private.snk
```

Once the real version is available, it would probably be a good idea to have all the developers and testers turn verification back on:

```
> sn exe -Vu FooCorp.Gadgets.DLL
```

Consuming Strong Named Assemblies at Compile Time

When you are compiling an assembly that has compile-time references to other assemblies, the compiler will generate the appropriate strong-name references in the manifest for you. For example, suppose we compiled up this executable:

```
' snexample.vb

<Assembly: System.Reflection.AssemblyKeyFile("public.snk")>
<Assembly: System.Reflection.AssemblyDelaySign(true)>
<Assembly: System.Reflection.AssemblyVersion("1.0.0.0")>
Public Class SNExample
   ' ...
End Class
```

```
> vbc /t:library /debug snexample.vb
```

If some other assembly "test" references that DLL then the strong name information is automatically included. We can view the manifest with the ILDASM utility:

```
> vbc /debug /r:snexample.dll test.vb
> ildasm test.exe
```

This shows that the manifest contains three strong name bindings. This assembly will attempt to load strong-named versions of the mscorlib, Microsoft.VisualBasic, and snexample assemblies.

```
.assembly extern mscorlib
{
  .publickeytoken = (B7 7A 5C 56 19 34 E0 89 )
  .ver 1:0:3300:0
}
.assembly extern Microsoft.VisualBasic
{
  .publickeytoken = (B0 3F 5F 7F 11 D5 0A 3A )
  .ver 7:0:3300:0
}
.assembly extern snexample
{
  .publickeytoken = (5B 7D 7F 91 8F F7 7B D5 )
  .ver 1:0:0:0
}
```

The manifest contains all the information necessary to resolve the strong name of an assembly: the assembly name, the public key token, the optional culture information token, and the version number. When the strong named assembly is loaded then the .NET Runtime will ensure that the public key token, version number, culture information, and name match and that the public key can be used to successfully decrypt the hash.

> **Note that a strong named assembly may only reference other strong named assemblies! The whole point of the strong name system is to ensure that only a specific, well defined set of assemblies are loaded by an application.**

You might have noticed that the manifest refers to a public key token, not a public key. A public key is often a rather unwieldy string of over a hundred bytes. A public key token is essentially a more manageable eight-byte hash of the public key. Again, the hash algorithm is designed so that for all practical purposes there will never be two public keys that have the same token.

You can view the actual public key and public key token of a strong-named assembly with the SN utility:

```
> sn.exe -Tp snexample.dll
```

```
Public key is
00240000048000009400000006020000002400005253413100040000010001000b30
b57f6b6aab45d9f75b759caea9bd621fea827ae53321cc8f6d9c56318019cea565c
f9bb65502c8744b89e38aa9062193744890a8a2b062f68661862af490f281528b8a
97b5eb4c22adf2e3f115a9740a14fd697cb1f50cb7d85c32c7ea3831ec7e3ca5e65
fa23253afbc4d55c49c9f761bd1488b465d8

Public key token is 5b7d7f918ff77bd5
```

Consuming Strong Named Assemblies at Run Time

There are scenarios where you might have to bind to a strong-named assembly at run time using reflection methods such as `Assembly.Load()`. Applications such as ASP.NET may also allow administrators to configure which strong named assemblies are used by specifying strong names in configuration files. In both cases, there is a simple string format to specify a strong name:

```
"snExample,Version=1.0.0.0,Culture=neutral,PublicKeyToken=5b7d7f918ff7
7bd5"
```

`Assembly.Load()` and other methods that take assembly names, will accept strings in this format. Again, this string has all the information necessary for the loader to find right assembly. The loader will verify authenticity and integrity by ensuring that the encrypted hash in the assembly can be decoded with the public key.

Authenticode and Strong Names

It is important to understand that Authenticode and strong names are distinct, complementary technologies.

> **Strong naming is all about naming assemblies in such a way that users can have confidence that they really are loading the assembly they want to load. Authenticode is all about establishing trust relationships between users and code publishers.**

Fundamentally, the purpose of the strong name system is to provide a secure, unique name for every assembly. However the strong name mechanism is also used to establish trust; for example, if you look at your default security policy you will see that two subgroups of the "My Computer" zone grant full trust to any assembly that contains a Microsoft or ECMA strong name. Strong names are both a binding mechanism and evidence that a particular entity produced an assembly.

This idea of granting trust based on cryptographically strong evidence such as strong names is a good idea, but perhaps you can see how this could get unwieldy. What if there are a hundred or a thousand software publishers that you would like to trust? What happens when new publishers are created as new companies are formed? If strong names are the only mechanism for determining trust relationships with publishers then life quickly becomes a maintenance nightmare for the security administrator.

Maintenance nightmares are very bad for security. Remember that users will choose expediency over security; they will attempt to work around the security system if they cannot run the software they need to run.

The Authenticode digital signature system is intended to help solve this maintenance problem by putting the burden of determining identities and trustworthiness onto third parties.

License and Registration Please

A strong name is like the Vehicle Identification Number found in various places around a car. Like the strong name system, the VIN system is designed to uniquely identify a car. It may tell you who made the car but it certainly tells you very little about whether the manufacturer was trustworthy.

An Authenticode **certificate** is by way of analogy essentially a driver's license. A driver's license not only uniquely identifies an individual but more importantly, *it provides evidence of the ability to perform a task*. A driver's license says, "The Department of Motor Vehicles vouches for the fact that the person identified by this card has demonstrated the ability to drive".

Most society's systems of credentials allow us to let credentialing organizations to do the due diligence required to weed out the qualified from the unqualified. If you are looking to hire a driver, you do not have to do all the work of testing for competence yourself: just check the candidates' licenses and automatically reject anyone not trusted by the DMV. You might reject some people who can drive safely but that is a price you are probably willing to pay! Of course, if you do not trust the DMV to do an adequate job of vetting drivers then you are stuck with the task of either finding some other credentialing organization or doing it yourself.

Furthermore, a driver's license is not a guarantee that an individual is a 100% safe driver, only that they have passed some minimum criteria. The DMV reserves the right to revoke their certification should the driver prove to be a poor driver.

How Authenticode Works

The Authenticode system is quite similar, though it is about vouching for the right to run code on your machine, not to drive a car.

The Authenticode system works like this: First, a software publisher obtains a certificate from a **certifying authority** (CA). The CA's job is to verify that the publisher named on the certificate is in fact a real entity (whether an individual developer or an entire company). Furthermore, the CA vouches for the **trustworthiness** of the publisher. The CA vouches for trustworthiness by promising to revoke the certificate if the publisher is ever found to be distributing hostile code. (The details of how the information about revoked certificates flows around the Internet are somewhat complex; we will not discuss the technical details of certificate revocation here.)

The publisher's certificate is simply an electronic document. It uses the same digital signature technology used by the strong name system to ensure that certificates cannot be counterfeited. The CA digitally signs the publisher's certificate with its private key so that users can use the public key to verify that the publisher's certificate did in fact come from the named CA.

The publisher's certificate contains the public key corresponding to the publisher's private key. When the publisher signs an assembly the Authenticode system takes a hash of the assembly, encrypts it with the private key, and embeds the certificate and encrypted hash into the assembly.

This is quite similar to the way that the strong naming utility produces a strong name; both the strong name system and the Authenticode system guarantee that an assembly has not been tampered with by embedding into the assembly information including an encrypted hash of the assembly. Remember though that they do this for different purposes: the strong name is intended as a mechanism to ensure that only the assemblies desired by the user are loaded, whereas the Authenticode signature is intended to establish a trust relationship with the publisher via a trusted third-party certifying authority.

This publisher signature can now be used as evidence to establish trust. For example, suppose my administrator has configured my machine policy to say "Any code written by an entity trusted by Verisign is trusted by me." Now it is no longer that administrator's job to keep track of every new software publisher in the world and whether they are trustworthy or not. It is Verisign's job to keep track of which certificates were used to sign malicious code so that they can be revoked.

> **This is actually a somewhat simplified scenario. The Authenticode system allows "trust chains" of considerable length. For instance, there might be a chain where a developer is trusted by an "intermediate" CA (such as a publisher) who is in turn is trusted by a "root" CA.**

When the end user attempts to load an assembly the policy system searches the assembly for an Authenticode signature, since the loader is looking for evidence and an Authenticode signature is evidence. It verifies that the signature is in fact valid, that is that the public key provided by the certificate can be used to decode the encrypted assembly hash. It verifies that the publisher's certificate was properly signed with a CA's private key by decrypting it with the CA's public key. If this all checks out then the evidence is valid and may be used by the policy system. It checks policy to see what rights the machine policy grants to code vouched for by that CA.

This is extremely similar to the process by which strong names are used as evidence: if the encrypted hash in the assembly can be correctly decrypted with the public key corresponding to a trusted publisher then the policy engine has evidence that the assembly was produced by a trusted publisher. The differences are that first, the Authenticode information does not uniquely identify the assembly; it identifies a publisher, and second that the Authenticode information establishes a trust relationship via a third party whereas a strong name does not.

> **You can see what specific publishers and CA's you trust by running the `certmgr.exe` utility. You might be surprised to find out exactly whom you trust to make trust decisions on your behalf. The operating system ships with many default CA's in the list of trusted roots.**

Every step in the verification process is important: think about the analogy to checking a bus driver's license.

❑ First, you have to verify that the picture (the hash) on the license matches the person (the assembly). If it does not match then it does not matter what the license says!

- Assuming it does match, then you need to check to see that the license issuer vouches for the ability of the bearer to drive large vehicles rather than, say, being a fishing license. (The CA must have issued a "code signing" certificate, not some other sort of certificate.)

- Finally, you must determine what authority issued the license. A valid bus driver's license issued by "Big Bob's Bargain Basement Print Shop" might not carry any weight. (You must declare that the CA is allowed to make trust decisions on your behalf.)

Signing an Assembly with an Authenticode Certificate

If you would like to sign an assembly with an Authenticode certificate then the first step is to obtain a certificate from the appropriate certifying authority. Consider who is going to be running your code and whether they will trust that authority. For example, if you are writing code to be run internally in your own company then you might consider setting up a certificate server of your own internally to sign internal-only applications. If you want, the assembly to be trusted by the public then consider using one of the commercial certifying authorities such as Verisign.

The CA will issue a "signing" certificate that contains a key pair. When the code is actually signed, only the public key is embedded in the code. The private key never leaves the original certificate.

> **Again, treat the private-key-containing version of the certificate extremely carefully. Anyone who possesses the private key can produce software that looks exactly as if you wrote it.**

Actually, signing the finished assembly with the Authenticode certificate is quite straightforward; just run the `signcode.exe` utility and it will start up a wizard that goes through all the necessary steps with you.

One very important thing to remember when signing a strong-named assembly with an Authenticode signature is this:

> **Always apply the Authenticode signature after the assembly is fully strong named (that is, has the strong name signed hash.) If you delay-sign an assembly to reserve space for the strong name, then apply the Authenticode signature and then put the strong name in the Authenticode security system will detect that someone has "tampered" with the bits of the assembly. The Authenticode signature needs to be applied last to be valid.**

You can then verify that any assembly is signed with a trusted Authenticode certificate by running the chktrust.exe utility. If the assembly is not signed, signed, but tampered with, or contains an untrusted certificate in the certificate chain then it will produce a dialog box explaining the problem.

Assembly Security Attributes

One last thing to look at before we leave assembly-level security behind is to quickly recap the assembly attributes discussed in Chapters 2 and 3.

There are three main purposes of the assembly security attributes:

❑　To ensure that developers have thought about luring attacks before they ship their code

❑　To clearly document the security requirements of an assembly

❑　To prevent luring attacks by running with least privilege

The first purpose is accomplished by the AllowPartiallyTrustedCallersAttribute. All strong named assemblies that lack this attribute will do a link demand for full trust when called. Do not put this attribute on any assembly if you have not performed a thorough security review looking for luring attacks. The combination of this attribute and your strong name is essentially a statement that you have diligently looked for security vulnerabilities before shipping the code. Furthermore, if none of your user scenarios involves your code being called by partially trusted code, then do not allow partially trusted callers.

The second purpose is accomplished by the RequestMinimum and RequestOptional assembly attributes. If your program will always require certain permissions then use RequestMinimum to clearly document this requirement. Documenting your requirements makes the trust level required by your code clear both to your customers and to future maintainers of the code base.

It also allows users with restrictive security policies to deny access early. If you know ahead of time that your code will need to be fully trusted in all scenarios then do not waste user's time by failing after the program has already been running for a while.

If there are permissions that your code might demand but which are not strictly necessary then use RequestOptional to document this fact. For example, your program might demand the right to print a document if the user chooses a menu item, this feature is nice to have but in many cases the applications core functionality would be unaffected if it is not available. By documenting your optional requests, you give information to administrators about what sort of demands your program is expected to make. They can use this information to decide whether to restrict access to those permissions or not.

The third purpose is accomplished by the `RequestRefuse` attribute. If your program will never require certain permissions then you can ensure they are never granted. In particular, if there are no scenarios in which your code should be used to call code that requires powerful permissions (such as the right to call unmanaged code or set policy) then consider ensuring that they are never granted. After all, luring attacks are all about untrusted, less privileged code convincing more privileged code to do work for it; if your trusted code is not actually more privileged then the luring attack will fail.

> **Remember that attackers look for ways to repurpose highly trusted code; a security vulnerability in a fully trusted program that keeps track of your muffin recipe database could compromise your entire machine. Ensure that your assemblies run with the least privilege required. That can greatly limit the scope of a potential exploit.**

Summing Up Assembly Security

Though that was a lot of material, it reduces to one simple fact:

> **Secure assemblies clearly and strongly identify where they came from and what they do.**

All of the foregoing material is merely the implementation of this general principle.

- ❑ **Strong names** use public key cryptography to uniquely identify an assembly so that its users know that they are getting what they expect: a specific, assembly that has not been tampered with.

- ❑ **Authenticode** signatures provide evidence that the assembly was authored by a trustworthy entity vouched for by a third party.

- ❑ The **security attributes** clearly define what level of trust is required and what permissions will never be used.

Write Securable Code

There are many tradeoffs in software design. It is hard to make code both feature-rich and small, for example. There are many such tradeoffs: on time versus bug free, easy to learn versus powerful, and secure versus usable. The entire point of a security system, after all, is to prevent undesirable work from being done by restricting who can do the work.

Fortunately, it is only hard to overcome these tradeoffs, not impossible. It is possible to write code that is feature-rich and tight, on time and (mostly!) bug free, easy to learn and powerful, and both secure and usable. All it takes to do any of these things is careful design, attention to detail, and lots of work.

One of the keys to writing code that is both useful and secure is to allow administrators to customize the security settings. In most cases, you will not have much to do here: the policy system is designed to allow administrators to customize security settings. If administrators want to allow your software to have some level of trust then they can use the existing policy mechanisms to do so. Using assembly attributes to indicate exactly what permissions your software requires in order to run; will make the administrators' jobs easier.

If your software supports advanced security features, such as auditing, then make the software configurable so that administrators can turn the feature on or off. Features that increase the security of the software should generally be turned on by default, even at the cost of usability or performance. If the software is highly configurable then administrators can always turn off the unneeded features. Administrators should not have to learn how to turn features on in the event of an attack.

> **Security is often the antithesis of productivity. Software should be as secure as possible without seriously compromising functionality by default. Let the administrators consciously choose to lower their security if they need to in order to unlock more features.**

A good example is Internet Explorer. IE ships with somewhat risky features required for rendering common pages turned on, such as the ability for web pages to contain scripts.

Conversely, if your code provides risky, optional non-security features that are not used by 80% of your users then consider turning the feature soff by default or not installing them by default. Administrators can choose to install and enable the features if they want to.

For example, in the early days of Internet Information Server (IIS) the web server was installed and enabled by default with certain versions of Windows. This meant that millions of machines were running web servers whether they were intended to be web servers or not. Though that was very convenient for the relatively small percentage of users who wanted to run a web server, it was also an attractive target for attackers.

Attackers like "software monocultures" because they know that if they can find vulnerabilities on one machine they can probably exploit them on many machines. When these attackers found exploitable vulnerabilities in IIS, they could then write hostile code that would successfully exploit all of those millions of machines.

IIS is turned off by default when you install Windows XP and Windows .NET Server. If you need a web server, it is easy enough to turn it on. If you do not want to be running a web server then it will not be on, which means that you are likely to be immune to any attack against the server.

> **If most users do not use a potentially risky feature then disable it by default.**

If possible, ensure that security administration features are sufficiently discoverable that the administrators do not have to read your documentation to secure the installation. Remember, attackers are more likely to read and understand your manuals than overworked network administrators.

Finally, note that throughout this section we have been referring to administrators making security decisions via policy and other configuration options. Try never to leave a security decision up to a regular user at run time.

Experience has shown that users make terrible security decisions. They choose the expedient option rather than the safe option. They do not understand the security model. They do not read the text on the dialog boxes! Usability tests show that many users just click on the leftmost button on any dialog without actually reading the text because usually that does what they want.

Users typically do not understand the risks associated with or the consequences of their decisions, they do not have enough information to make good decisions, and they do not know how to get that information. The accountants, fire fighters, or medical students who use your software are experts on accounting, fighting fires, or setting broken legs, not security. Let their (hopefully) security-savvy administrators make these decisions.

If you absolutely must ask a user to make a security decision – for instance, if they are home computer users with no administration bureaucracy – then there are some good guidelines for how to talk to users about security on the MSDN web site. See http://msdn.microsoft.com/library/en-us/dnsecure/html/securityerrormessages.asp.

The Big Checklist

This is a long list but by no means a complete one. Here we are going to concisely summarize most of the material we have covered so far.

❑ **Write Solid Object-Oriented Code**

- Write straightforward, maintainable code with easily understood and well-documented security semantics.

- Lock down your code: make classes final and methods nonoverridable if possible.

- If a class must be overridable then consider using inheritance demands to restrict who can extend a base class.

- Try to keep as many fields as possible `Private` or `Friend`. Untrusted code can read and modify `Public` fields and possibly `Protected` fields if the class is overridable.

- Use property accessor methods to make read-only (or write-only) fields if appropriate. Property accessor methods can also restrict access to fields containing sensitive information by demanding permissions on attempts to get or set the value.

- The same goes for classes, interfaces, and enumerations. Clearly mark them as `Friend` and only mark ones that need to be as `Public`.

- Spell out the attributes rather than depending on defaults; this makes the code more easily understood.

- `Friend Overridable` methods are overridable by classes in other (potentially hostile) assemblies. (The hostile assembly would have to be written in another language; there is no way to override a `Friend` method from another VB.NET assembly.)

❏ **Use Policy**

- Never ask a user to make a trust decision. The purpose of the policy system is to allow users and their administrators to make consistent security decisions based on evidence. When asked to make security decisions at run time users usually make the most expedient decision; not the safest one.

  If you absolutely, positively have to ask a user to make some decision about their own security, then design the user interface elements extremely carefully. See http://msdn.microsoft.com/library/en-us/dnsecure/html/securityerrormessages.asp for some good advice.

❏ **Turn Security on by Default**

- If your code supports optional security features such as auditing then turn them on by default. Your customer's administrators can always turn them off if they choose to. Administrators should not have to turn security features on in the event of a disaster.

- Do not require that administrators or users read long and complex documentation in order to secure your software.

- Conversely, if your code supports risky optional non-security features that are not used by 80% of your users then consider turning the features off by default. Let administrators turn the features on if they need to.

❏ **Write Good Assemblies**

- Use `RequestMinimum` to clearly document your must-have grant set.

- Use `RequestRefuse` to run with least privilege.

- Use `RequestOptional` to clearly document permissions you might demand but can do without.

- Strong-name your assemblies.

- Only give a strong-named assembly the "allow partially trusted callers" attribute if (a) you have performed a thorough security review and believe there are no "luring attack" vulnerabilities, and (b) you support scenarios where partially trusted code can call your code.

❏ **Use Declarative Attributes on Classes and Methods**

- Use declarative attributes to clearly document the security requirements of your classes and methods.

- Ensure that you have not mixed class attributes and method attributes incorrectly. Remember that a method attribute replaces any attribute with the same action on its class, rather than combining with it. It is probably wise to not mix class attributes and method attributes at all.

❏ **Use Assert, Deny, PermitOnly, and Demand Correctly**

- If you need to `Demand` a permission, doing it earlier is usually better.

- Use `Demand` to help prevent "repurposing" of your code. For example, if you write a method that is intended to always be called by a fully trusted caller, demand full trust.

- Remember to `Demand` every time sensitive cached data is accessed, not just the first time.

- If you do not need an imperative `Assert` to be active for the rest of the method then use `RevertAssert` to cancel it when you no longer need it.

- Do not use `Deny` to prevent access to specific files or registry keys. These kinds of denials are susceptible to canonicalization errors.

- Remember that `PermitOnly` and `Deny` are overridable by `Assert`. Code that is granted a permission and the right to assert permissions can always obtain that permission.

❏ **Use Link Demands Carefully, if at All**

- Consider the options very carefully when writing link demand attributes. A link demand puts the burden of preventing luring attacks upon the caller.

- Remember that link demands on a method happen only once per caller. Furthermore, they happen when the callers are jitted, not when the protected methods are called.

- Remember that a link demand does not do a stack walk; it only checks the assembly calling the protected method.

- Ensure that every way to call a link-demand-protected method is identically protected; interfaces, subclasses, and superclasses with inconsistent attributes may cause vulnerabilities.

- Structures do not necessarily have a constructor method. Do not assume that a link demand on a structure definition will prevent the structure from being created by an untrusted caller.

❑ **Audit Security Failures**

- Auditing is particularly important when writing server-side code. If your customers have no way to tell that your code is being probed or attacked by an attacker then they are unlikely to detect the problem before the attack succeeds. Without audit trails, it is difficult to track an attacker down. Worst of all, you might never even know that you had been successfully attacked.

- Auditing security failures is also very helpful when testing the security of your code.

- Remember that writing to the security log is a highly privileged operation. Effectively your code must be fully trusted and may need to Assert the right to write to the log.

❑ **Do Not Keep Secrets**

- Be very careful when caching sensitive data. For instance, data obtained from a method that did a demand should ensure that it demands a similar permission when handing out the data to other code.

- Ensure that the security of your software does not rely on keeping secrets from hostile users. Hostile users can discover all your secrets. There is no way to keep, say, a password in your executable code that cannot be discovered by a clever user. In addition, fully trusted code has all the capabilities of the aforementioned clever user. However, if you have hostile, fully trusted, code running then you have bigger problems than losing your secrets!

- Ensure that the security of your code does not rely on keeping your source code a secret. Source code can be revealed to third parties in many ways, such as outright theft, reverse engineering, litigation, or licensing.

- In particular, assume that even your server-side code will be compromised. Keep secret information such as database passwords in configuration files, registry keys or other stores. That way an attacker who gets your source code cannot immediately learn the secret.

- Use encryption extremely carefully; encryption is not a panacea. Even good encryption technologies do little good if they are used incorrectly.

- Never attempt to implement your own encryption algorithms.

- If you need to generate truly random, unpredictable data then use a cryptographic-strength random number generator. The standard "random number" generator produces easily guessed sequences. Easily guessed secrets do not stay secret for long.

❏ **Err On the Side of Caution**

- Ensure that error messages are informative enough to diagnose the problem but do not reveal sensitive information that an attacker could use. Remember that most regular users are not technically savvy, but many attackers are.

- Design your error code paths as carefully as your normal code paths.

- Remember that (possibly hostile) exception filters can run any time an exception is thrown, and almost any line of code can throw an exception under some circumstance. This is particularly important to consider when performing operations that alter sensitive global state, such as when impersonating other users.

- Fail to a secure mode.

- Use structured exception handling rather than passing back error codes. It is easy to forget to check an error code and thereby fail to an insecure mode.

- Use sensible, secure defaults when creating and initializing new objects. Do not allow an unexpected exception to leave your data inconsistent or insecure.

- Avoid canonicalization errors. User names, file paths, URLs, e-mail addresses, and other common string-based data formats may be more complex than you think. Avoid making decisions based on the name of something. If you must do so then only accept data in a canonical form; use regular expressions or other tools to ensure that the data is in an acceptable form.

- Always check to see that data is valid, rather than invalid. You can always add a valid case you missed later; it is hard to know that you have caught all the invalid cases.

- Do not echo caller-supplied data back in an exception, particularly in client-server scenarios; this could create a cross-site scripting vulnerability in the code that displays the exception to the user.

❏ **Call Unmanaged Code with Extreme Caution**

- If you assert the right to call unmanaged code you should ensure that you make a demand appropriate for the unmanaged API you are about to call.

- Make sure you understand all possible behaviors of the unmanaged API. Many Win32 APIs have many parameters and can do several tasks. In particular, some Win32 APIs produce user interface elements such as message boxes when they fail, which you might not want.

- Avoid repurposing attacks by carefully validating parameters. In particular, remember that hostile code can pass integers outside the range of an enumerated type.

- Never allow untrusted code to obtain information about kernel handles, pointers, or other details of the unmanaged code world.

- Be careful with scarce unmanaged resources. A memory or handle leak is never a good thing. Attackers might attempt to force the leak as part of a DoS attack.

❏ **Vet Untrusted Data with Extreme Prejudice**

- Your server code should not trust anything that comes from the client. The client could be a custom-built hostile client designed to compromise your server.

- Your server code should never echo client-supplied data back to any client without checking it for safety or encoding it (or better, both).

- Always vet client-supplied data to build SQL queries or connection strings. Consider using stored procedures instead.

- Check all client-supplied data; make sure that numbers are in sensible ranges, strings are sensible lengths, and so on.

- Fail early. The less processor time and memory you consume before denying a hostile request, the harder it is to create a successful DoS attack.

- Consider the worst possible performance of your algorithms. Choose algorithms based on both their worst-case performance and typical-case performance. Attackers may try to force the worst case to produce DoS conditions.

❏ **Restrict Serialization to Privileged Code**

- Demand the permission to serialize data in your serialization code, even if the information being serialized is not sensitive. There should be an extremely good reason **not** to demand the right to serialize data.

- If a class's normal constructor demands a permission then the serialization constructor should probably demand the same permission.

❏ **Be Careful with the File System**

- Never allow untrusted code to determine the location and contents of a file. The untrusted code could be attempting to create a hostile program in the My Computer zone, or it could be attempting to deny service by filling up the entire disk with garbage.

- If you need to write temporary files to disk, consider using isolated storage.

- If you need to write files to disk but might not be fully trusted (because your executable is running from an intranet share, for instance) then use isolated storage.

❑ **Make Sensitive Objects Thread Safe**

- Consider the security implications of non-thread-safe code called from multiple threads. If there is a way to make state inconsistent or leak information that has security implications, then consider making the object threadsafe.

- You can get thread safety without writing a fully multithreaded object by checking for calls on an unexpected thread.

❑ **Be Careful with Delegates**

- If you are calling a delegate then remember that the code that gave you the delegate is not necessarily from the same trust level as the code that the delegate will invoke. In particular, never `Assert` a permission before calling a delegate.

- Try to avoid exposing highly trusted event handlers that do dangerous things. Hostile, less-trusted code could hook up your event handler to some event source. When the event source calls the delegate the less-trusted code is no longer on the stack.

Use this list as a starting point when reviewing your code and as a source of ideas, but remember:

Just because you have checked everything on the list, it does not mean your code has no security vulnerabilities.

Even Good Software Security is Not Enough

The aim of this book is not to teach you how to write perfectly secure code, because there is no such thing. Rather, the aim is to teach you how to raise the bar sufficiently so that attackers have to spend so much time and resources on attacking your code that they give up and look for an easier target. There are two more issues worth considering that aren't anything to do with software, physical security and whom you trust.

Physical Security

If an attacker really wants to obtain your users' data, there are some attack techniques that are difficult and expensive for the attackers but also difficult and expensive to mitigate. For example, suppose an attacker was after your company's internal financial data. They could try to defeat the building security and go through the files physically. That seems hard; those files are probably locked up somewhere.

What if they could get into the building and replace a user's keyboard with an identical looking keyboard that broadcasts every keystroke to a radio receiver outside the building? There are all manner of listening and viewing devices that could be used to capture passwords or other sensitive data. (In fact, while looking online for singing rubber fish for my own office the other day, I found a singing rubber fish with a hidden camera in it for sale! Go to http://AllActionAlarm.com/ if you need one.) Perhaps eventually some user will type in a name and password that could be used to attack the network and gain access to the financial data.

If you can make your software, so secure that attackers have to physically put themselves at risk by breaking into a building then you have given them a huge disincentive. Attackers prefer to attack over networks while sitting safely in their own homes.

If, however, you do not have good physical security and an attacker is willing to run the gauntlet then all the software security in the world will not help you. Attackers in the building can not only install modified hardware like keyboards or cameras; they can walk off with your machines. Even from outside the building they can spy on your wireless network traffic or try to get information from the radio noise generated by processors and monitors.

The danger of attacks like that is that you might not know that your security has been compromised until it is too late. If the attacker simply walks off with your laptop then they have all the time in the world to brute-force attack it, but at least you know that you have been compromised and can take appropriate steps.

> **Software security is not a panacea – your security is no stronger than the weaker of your physical security and software security.**

Trusting too Much

Another source of potential security problems comes from extending trust to people who are either not trustworthy because they are secretly hostile or not trustworthy because they lack the necessary defenses to protect themselves from attackers.

An enormous number of serious software-related security breaches are a result of attacks from within by disgruntled staff. No one likes to work in an environment of mutual distrust, but that does not change the fact that the people who are best able to mount attacks on your systems are the insiders who understand those systems and their vulnerabilities. The worst thing that can happen is to end up with a hostile administrator; they can access, copy, change, or delete any information they choose to, and cover up their tracks. The obvious way to cut down on the number of potentially hostile administrators is to grant administrative privileges to only a tiny number of highly trustworthy people.

Grant as few people "Power User" status as possible as well. Hostile users in the Power User group have a number of techniques that they may use to effectively become administrators. For example, the ability to install and modify software in the My Programs folder is an extremely powerful right which can be abused; imagine what would happen if a power user installed hostile code as "excel.exe" in the appropriate directory. If an administrator ever ran it then the hostile power-user's code could grant administrative rights to the hostile user.

The other large source of security hazards within an organization is the group of individuals who do not understand how to keep themselves or others secure. These are the people who download and run unmanaged executables from the Internet, leave their passwords written on yellow sticky notes on their monitors, throw away sensitive documents without shredding them, and tell people posing as administrators their passwords over the telephone. The obvious way to cut down on the number of walking security holes is to espouse a corporate culture that educates people about potential risks and how to mitigate them.

> **Grant the least privileges necessary for people to get their jobs done. Educate people about software and physical risks.**

Summary

We have covered rather a lot of ground in the last six chapters. Hopefully, you'll take away the following points:

- ❑ First, software security is *important.*

- ❑ Second, security is *not a feature* you can easily add to a complex program at the end of the development cycle. You need to have the security implications of your user scenarios worked out ahead of time and baked in early in the development cycle.

- ❑ Third, software security is *possible.* All that is required is a good working knowledge of the security system, some insights into how attackers think and what they want, and careful attention to detail when designing, implementing, and testing your software.

❑   Fourth, software security is just *one part of an overall security process.*

In the next and final chapter, we shall test what we've learned so far by providing some short, seemingly correct programs that could be much better from a security perspective.

VB.NET

Code Security

Handbook

7

7

Spot the Security Bug!

At Microsoft, there are thousands of internal e-mail lists; one of my personal favorites is called "Spot the Defect!" Twice a week the list moderator sends a code fragment (in any programming language) to the list members. Usually the code is from a real, live code base of some Microsoft product that recent required a bug fix. The list members each read the code fragment and analyze it to try to find flaws, not necessarily knowing anything about the initial problem or even the purpose of the code. They then e-mail their proposed flaws back to the moderator who compiles them into one big e-mail summarizing the findings.

It is quite amazing to see how many dozen distinct flaws the 643 people who read "Spot the Defect!" can find in a twenty line code fragment. Many of the flaws identified are simply irksome: poorly named variables, misleading comments, code that "reinvents the wheel" by solving a problem already handled by an available API, and so on. Most interesting though are the fatal coding flaws: rare-but-possible "corner cases" that lead to crashes, buffer overruns, infinite loops, and so on. Occasionally there are even code fragments that are "broken by design": correct implementations of algorithms that do not actually solve the problem intended to be solved.

Unsurprisingly, a large number of the "coding" and "design" flaws found on "Spot the Defect!" have obvious security implications. Even some of the "irksome" flaws have indirect security implications because they make the code harder to read, debug, and maintain.

There are many benefits of having an e-mail list like "Spot the Defect!". Reading other people's broken code to find the flaws is a fun mental challenge. It keeps you abreast of the various issues faced by people all over the company working on diverse projects. However, most importantly, it lets you **learn from the mistakes of others**. In addition, seeing what other people consider a defect improves one's own coding habits immensely and provides you with motivation to find them in your own code; if only to try to avoid having your own code show up on the list one day!

It is a cliché but it is true:

> **If you do not learn from mistakes then they will be repeated. When you find a flaw, do not just fix it tell others about it, look for similar flaws elsewhere, and set up tests to ensure that it does not come back.**

Bugs are learning opportunities. Almost all the "worst practices" in Chapter 5 were discussed on e-mail lists such as "Spot the Defect" (and other internal Microsoft lists specifically for promulgating information about security flaws). Many of them were discussions motivated by finding and fixing flaws in the actual .NET Framework implementation!

In this chapter, we will play "Spot the Defect!" ourselves. The code examples are somewhat contrived rather than being based on real code, but the point of the exercise remains valid: practice spotting defects in known-to-be broken code now so that you can effectively eliminate defects in your own code.

Spot the Security Flaw #1: Calling Unmanaged Code

Suppose you have an unmanaged DLL (`FooCorp.dll`), which contains some internal business logic. Perhaps it has a method that contacts a database, verifies that the current process is being run by a user authorized to read certain records from the database, and returns some salary information. You want to be able to write managed programs that call this method, so you tell your resident VB.NET programmer "Mort" to create a managed wrapper around the unmanaged DLL.

First, we shall present Mort's version. Then we'll analyze it, looking for security vulnerabilities as well as other general problems. Finally, we'll present a somewhat more robust version.

Mort begins by defining the unmanaged method he is going to call and the enumerated type it takes:

```vb
'Flaw1.vb

Imports System
Imports System.Runtime.InteropServices
Imports System.Security.Permissions

Enum SalaryType
    Gross = 1
    AfterTax = 2
End Enum
```

```
Class FooCorp
  <DllImport("foocorp.dll")> _
  Shared Function GetSalary(Employee As String, _
                     SType As Integer, _
                     <Out()> Salary As Decimal) As Boolean
  End Function
```

Next, he writes a managed wrapper method that simply calls the unmanaged version. He modifies the design slightly though so that the managed version throws an exception, unlike the unmanaged version that returns a Boolean success code. The return value is then available to return the salary information.

```
Shared Function GetEmployeeSalary(Employee As String, _
                     SType As SalaryType) As Decimal
```

Since this method must call unmanaged code but it has been determined that there is no possible luring attack, Mort asserts the right to call unmanaged code.

```
Dim P As New SecurityPermission( _
  SecurityPermissionFlag.UnmanagedCode)
Dim S As Decimal
Dim B As Boolean
P.Assert()
```

Finally, he actually does the unmanaged call and returns the result.

```
  B = GetSalary(Employee, SType, S)
  If Not B Then
    Throw New Exception( _
      "You are not authorized to get salary info for " _
      & Employee)
  End If
  GetEmployeeSalary = S
  End Function
End Class
```

This looks reasonable. You might compile it, run a few test cases, see that it works, and distribute it to anyone who needs to call this library from managed code. However, now you have been called in to do a security review on Mort's code.

Cast a critical eye over that code from the perspectives of an attacker looking for vulnerabilities, a future maintainer, and a consumer of the assembly. What defects can you see?

Do you have your list? Here is mine, with the defects classified into low, medium, and high seriousness. These classifications are somewhat arbitrary and may be judgment calls. Essentially, "high" means that either important functionality is broken or there are security issues that may lead to serious harm to users. "Low" issues are maintainability, fit-and-finish issues, or very mild vulnerabilities. "Medium" is everything in between.

Defect 1: (High)

This assembly is not strong named. This means that users of the assembly will essentially have no guarantee that they really are binding to your assembly instead of someone else's with the same name. This also means that their strong-named assemblies may not bind to your assembly. (Of course, assembly attributes might be in another file in this assembly.)

Defect 2: (Low)

This assembly does not document its security requirements with `RequestMinimum`. It always needs the right to call unmanaged code and to assert privileges. It should document these facts. (Though again, these attributes may be in another source file.)

Defect 3: (Low)

This assembly has no other attribute-level documentation. It has no version number, no copyright date, nothing. While this is not really a security problem, it should still be addressed.

Defects 4, 5, and 6: (Low)

```
Class FooCorp

    Shared Function GetSalary(Employee As String, _

    Shared Function GetEmployeeSalary(Employee As String)
```

Presumably, this class is intended to be public and not intended to be extended. If that is the case then it should be marked as `Public NonInheritable` so that there is no doubt about the programmer's intention. Since the DLL import method is not intended to be called by consumers of this assembly, it should be marked `Private`; only the public wrapper should be marked `Public`.

Defects 7, 8, and 9: (Low)

```
        Dim P As New SecurityPermission( _
            SecurityPermissionFlag.UnmanagedCode)
        Dim S As Decimal
        Dim B As Boolean
```

These are non-descriptive variable names, which makes maintenance harder. Again, this is not so much a security issue as a general code quality issue and poor quality code is almost never secure code.

Defect 10: (Low)

```
        P.Assert()
```

Since this method must always assert the right to call unmanaged code, and since the method does nothing else but call unmanaged code and then return, perhaps this should be a declarative assert rather than an imperative assert. Declarative security information is emitted as metadata that can be analyzed by the .NET Runtime or other tools. However, this is a minor stylistic point; the code is fine with an imperative demand.

Defect 11: (High)

This method asserts a powerful permission without demanding anything in return. This means that any code that can call your code can call this unmanaged method. Suppose you run some code off a web site; it might be able to learn what your salary is. That is privileged information that you might not want just any web site to know. For that matter, the same goes for any intranet site. A hostile coworker could send you a program that runs in the intranet zone and reports your salary back to them.

Once all of these scenarios have been analyzed and you have determined what users and what code has the right to call this method you can put the appropriate demands in the code. For instance, this would be a good place to make a role-based security demand to ensure that the current user is a manager with authority to obtain salary information. The correct demand to make depends on the business rules surrounding salary disclosures.

We shall discuss whether to demand full trust or not below.

Defect 12: (High)

```
B = GetSalary(Employee, SType, S)
```

No attempt is made to vet the string. What happens if the unmanaged code itself has a bug? Perhaps the underlying unmanaged object uses SQL to obtain the salary from a backend database but has a SQL injection bug. Perhaps it has a buffer overrun bug when given a large string. Untrustworthy code may pass in a bogus employee name to take advantage of these problems. Assume that your code is the only uncompromised code left standing that can prevent an exploit.

Similarly, no attempt is made to ensure that SType really is 1 or 2; it is possible to pass in any integer value to a method expecting an enum. Does the underlying unmanaged call do anything sensible or desirable if -34 is passed in? If not, then don't allow it to be passed through in the first place. Don't take the chance that some sloppy programmer wrote brittle code that crashes horribly when given bad input.

Defect 13: (Medium)

Is the underlying unmanaged code threadsafe? If not, then bad things might happen if untrusted code calls this method on multiple threads at once. Without knowing the details of the unmanaged code it is hard to say exactly what would happen if hostile code called it millions of times in a tight loop from multiple threads. There could be situations where data is lost, where memory is never freed, or where information from authorized threads leaks into unauthorized threads.

Defects 12 and 13 also imply that a detailed security analysis of the unmanaged code might be in order to ensure that the managed wrapper is secure.

Defect 14: (Medium)

```
Throw New Exception( _
    "You are not authorized to get salary info for " _
    & Employee)
```

If there is any hostile code on the call stack then it could be running exception filters or exception handlers that parse the employee name out of the exception. If that employee name was provided by code that is more trustworthy then information about a valid employee name has just been given to hostile code.

Defect 15: (High)

If this code is being run on a server, then there might be a cross-site scripting vulnerability introduced by echoing the employee name. Hostile code could have passed in a bogus employee name that contained some script. This script would then be echoed out on the error-reporting page served up to the client.

If this code is being run on a server then it is probably a good idea for the caller of this code to vet the data; however, again it is also wise to assume that your code is the last defense left standing.

Defect 16: (Low)

The exception's message is potentially misleading. All we know is that the call to unmanaged code returned False. We do not know why it returned False but this code assumes that it was for security reasons. Perhaps we have run out of memory. Perhaps the user is authorized but the database is down for maintenance. There is any number of possible reasons. Either the error message should be more generic or the code should call unmanaged routines such as GetLastError() to obtain more information.

That's sixteen defects in a program with only fourteen statements! – "End" lines do not count as statements in my opinion. Perhaps there are even more, which I missed, and yet at first glance it appears to be a perfectly reasonable program.

What is necessary to mitigate these defects? Defects 1 through 10, 15, and 16 are all easy "fit and finish" defects that can be addressed by simply adding the appropriate attributes and making other simple changes.

It is very tempting to say that the remainder of them can all be solved in one fell swoop: just demand full trust. After all, defects 11, 12, 13, and 14 are all essentially luring attacks. Just demand full trust and there will be no luring attack because there will not be any untrusted code on the stack. Alternatively, you could just strong-name the assembly and not add the "allow partially trusted callers" attribute.

Unfortunately, those are not necessarily good options, for several reasons.

First off, you might have good reasons to want this code to be able to run from, say, the Intranet zone. Perhaps you have considered the risks and benefits of allowing code like this to run from the Intranet zone and the benefits outweigh the risks.

Second, by essentially not fixing defects 12 and 13 you miss the chance to find flaws in your benign, buggy callers who do not know the right name format, and flaws in the threading model.

Third, and most important: to do so is to abandon our fundamental security model of multiply nested defenses. Get in the habit of locking down everything. Make the attackers have to do five impossible things rather than one, so that if one of them actually turns out to be possible you have not lost all your protection.

Here's a more robust way to write this wrapper:

We'll start by ensuring that all the assembly attributes are in place:

```
Imports System
Imports System.Runtime.InteropServices
Imports System.Security
Imports System.Security.Permissions
Imports System.Reflection
Imports System.Text.RegularExpressions

<Assembly: AssemblyKeyFile("public.snk")>
<Assembly: AssemblyDelaySign(true)>
<Assembly: AssemblyVersion("1.0.0.0")>
<Assembly: AssemblyTitle("FooCorp Managed Wrapper")>
<Assembly: AssemblyDescription( _
  "Managed wrapper for business logic DLL")>
<Assembly: AssemblyCompany("FooCorp")>
<Assembly: AssemblyCopyright("Copyright (C) FooCorp 2002")>
<Assembly: AllowPartiallyTrustedCallersAttribute()>
<Assembly: SecurityPermission(SecurityAction.RequestMinimum, _
  Assertion := True, UnmanagedCode := True)>
```

Next, we will declare the unmanaged function so that we can call it via interop. This time it is explicitly private:

```
Public Enum SalaryType
  Gross = 1
  AfterTax = 2
End Enum

Public NotInheritable Class FooCorp

  <DllImport("foocorp.dll")> _
  Private Shared Function GetSalary(Employee As String, _
  SType As Integer, _
  <Out()> Salary As Decimal) As Boolean
  End Function
```

The method now declares that its callers must have at least the permissions associated with the Intranet zone, since this code is only intended to be run within your organization. Hostile Internet code will probably not be able to call this method.

```
<PermissionSet(SecurityAction.Demand, Name := "LocalIntranet"), _
SecurityPermission(SecurityAction.Assert, UnmanagedCode := True)> _
Public Shared Function GetEmployeeSalary(Employee As String, _
SType As SalaryType) As Decimal
```

The variable names are now descriptive:

```
Dim Salary As Decimal
Dim Success As Boolean = False
```

We vet the employee name. For this example, we assume that a valid employee name consists of 1 to 50 letters and spaces. (A more sophisticated regular expression could be used to match different patterns.)

Note also that none of the exceptions echoes information now.

```
Dim RE As Regex = New Regex("^[a-zA-Z ]{1,50}$")
If Not RE.IsMatch(Employee)
  Throw New Exception("Invalid employee name")
End If
```

We also vet the enumerated type. (Note that this trades a potential security vulnerability for a potential maintenance problem. If you produce a new version of the unmanaged code that has more legal enumerated values then you will need to update the wrapper as well. Whether eliminating the security problem is worth taking on the maintenance problem needs to be decided on a case-by-case basis.)

```
If SType <> SalaryType.Gross And SType <> SalaryType.AfterTax Then
  Throw New Exception("Invalid salary type")
End If
```

The call to unmanaged code is synchronized. Any attempt to call this code via this class on multiple threads at once will do one entire call, then another, rather than interleaving the calls.

```
    SyncLock GetType(FooCorp)
      Success = GetSalary(Employee, SType, Salary)
    End SyncLock
    If Not Success Then
      Throw New Exception("Unable to obtain requested information")
    End If
    GetEmployeeSalary = Salary
  End Function
End Class
```

Spot the Security Flaw #2: Playing Games

Suppose you decide to quit your current job and go into the exciting, marginally legal world of offshore Internet gambling. You move to Bermuda, write up a few little client-side front ends to your server-side game logic, write some code to do credit card transactions and sit back to wait for the money to roll in.

Security flaws can hide in the most innocuous seeming code. Here is some code that uses a standard shuffling algorithm to put a simulated deck in random order. The algorithm works by choosing 52 random fractions. The order of these numbers is obviously random, so we just convert the smallest fraction into 1, the next smallest into 2, and so on. The numbers 1 through 52 can then be used to represent cards: 1 might be the deuce of clubs, up to 52 representing the ace of spades.

```vb
' flaw2.vb

Imports Microsoft.VisualBasic

Friend Class Deck

  Friend Cards(52) As Integer

  Friend Sub Shuffle()
    Dim CardOrder(52) As Double
    Dim Card As Integer
    Dim CurCard As Integer
    For CurCard = 1 To 52
      CardOrder(CurCard) = Rnd()
    Next
    For CurCard = 1 To 52
      Card = FindSmallest(CardOrder)
      CardOrder(Card) = 1
      Cards(CurCard) = Card
    Next
  End Sub

  Private Function FindSmallest(ByRef Arr() As Double) As Integer
    Dim I As Integer
    Dim Smallest As Double = 1
    Dim SmallestIndex As Integer
    For I = 1 To UBound(Arr)
      If Arr(I) < Smallest Then
        Smallest = Arr(I)
        SmallestIndex = I
      End If
    Next
    FindSmallest = SmallestIndex
  End Function

End Class
```

How could this possibly have any security vulnerabilities? This class does nothing except put an array of fifty-two integers representing cards in a randomly ordered array. A minor improvement might be documenting that fact: we could put some declarative `PermitOnly` attributes on the class, and so on. However, the likelihood of there being luring attacks in this code is almost zero; it does not call any other code! So surely, there is no serious vulnerability in this code, right?

Don't bet on it! This code returns the same sequence of cards every time. The Visual Basic "random number" generator is actually a pseudo-random number generator. It generates a pseudo-random sequence based on a seed value. This code uses the default seed value, so the sequence of cards chosen is always the same.

Just to clarify: the first, second, third, fourth, and so on decks generated will be different from each other but predictable from each other. A hostile player could play a game, note the order of the cards they received, and eventually deduce what each subsequent game's deck would be. At that point, it would be rather easy to beat the house.

The obvious way to mitigate the vulnerability is to put a `Randomize()` statement in the code, right?

```
Friend Sub Shuffle()
   Randomize()
```

After all, the VB.NET documentation says "`Randomize(n)` uses n to initialize the `Rnd()` function's random-number generator, giving it a new seed value. If you omit n, the value returned by the system timer is used as the new seed value." This will now return a different sequence every time because every time you generate a new deck the timer value will be different. Is it secure now?

It does raise the bar for the attacker but not very far. The seed is now generated by computing the current number of milliseconds since midnight. That means that in a given minute there are only 60,000 possible seed values. That is better than one possible seed value, but not much better.

There are over 300 million possible first five-card hands from a shuffled 52-card deck. This means that if the attacker knows what minute the deck was generated, they can generate the 60,000 possible decks on their home machine. If we are playing 5-card stud poker the attacker will know what the first five cards off the top of the deck are, and then essentially knows the order of the rest of the deck. It is very unlikely that two of those 60,000 possible decks will have the same first five cards, given that there are 300 million possibilities.

> **That is just one example of a potential technique; there are many well-known techniques for determining the behavior of a weak random number generator.**

The security flaw here is essentially that you are attempting to keep a secret: the security of this program depends on ensuring that the random number seed is secret. The solution here is to not use such a weak random number generator for applications where real randomness is critical.

The .NET Framework provides a cryptographically strong random number generator for use in cryptographic and other applications that require unguessable randomness.

We wish to generate a random number greater than or equal to 0 and less than 1. Suppose we could generate a very random number between 1 and 10. We could just generate a random number between 1 and 10, subtract 1 and divide by 10. However, that would only give 10 possible results (0.0, 0.1, ... 0.9), which is only a very small number of possibilities. We'd like as many possibilities as we can possibly get.

What then if we generate two random numbers between 1 and 10, subtract 1 from each, multiply one by 10 and add the other? That effectively generates a random number between 0 and 99, with each number equally likely. We could divide this number by 100 and get 100 possibilities between 0 and 1. If we wanted more, we could continue the process, adding more and more digits.

That is what the algorithm below does, except that we use base-255 arithmetic rather than base-10 arithmetic. The result is a random number between 0 and 1 with around four billion possibilities, each equally likely.

```
' flaw2fix.vb

Imports System.Security.Cryptography

' ...

Private Function StrongRandom() As Double
    Dim RandomBytes() As Byte = New Byte(3){}
    Dim RNG As New RNGCryptoServiceProvider()
    rng.GetNonZeroBytes(RandomBytes)
    StrongRandom = RandomBytes(0) - 1 + _
                (RandomBytes(1) - 1) * 255.0 + _
                (RandomBytes(2) - 1) * 255.0 * 255.0+ _
                (RandomBytes(3) - 1) * 255.0 * 255.0 * 255.0
    StrongRandom = StrongRandom / (255.0 * 255.0 * 255.0 * 255.0)
End Function
```

Lest you think that this is just a theoretical example, this pattern of attack against code that relies on weak random number generators has been used many times. One example is Paul Larson's victory against the "random" behavior of the machines running the 1980's CBS game show "Press Your Luck". He set a record for the most money ever won from a game show. Another is Ian Goldberg's and David Wagner's successful breaking of the Netscape Navigator 1.1 security system in 1995, by being able to predict the "random" behavior of one of its cryptography algorithms.

More information on each of these can be found at
http://www.snopes2.com/radiotv/tv/whammy.htm and
http://www.demailly.com/~dl/netscapesec/cypherp1.txt respectively.

Spot the Security Flaw #3: Server Code

Whether you go into offshore Internet gambling or more conventional e-commerce, it
is a good idea to log the behavior of users on your server. That way you can audit
problems and identify suspicious behaviors that might indicate attacks.

Since auditing is a security feature, you should be even more careful than usual when
implementing it. What are some of the security flaws in this server-side code?

First, we set up the page:

```
' flaw3.aspx

<%@ Page Language="vb" AutoEventWireup="false"
Codebehind="WebForm1.aspx.vb" Inherits="WebApplication2.WebForm1"%>
<%@ Import Namespace="System.IO" %>
<%@ Import Namespace="System.Data.SqlClient" %>
<%@ Import Namespace="Microsoft.VisualBasic" %>
<!DOCTYPE HTML PUBLIC "-//W3C//DTD HTML 4.0 Transitional//EN">
<script runat=server>
```

This method says hello to a user who has just logged on to the site. It also records
information about this user's behavior in a log file on the local disk:

```
Friend Sub GreetUser()
  Dim UserName As String
  UserName = Request.Params("Name")
  ' Open the global audit file, note user logged on.
  Dim LogFile As StreamWriter

  LogFile = File.AppendText("C:\logs\Global.log")
  LogFile.WriteLine("logon name=" & UserName & " time=" & Now)
  LogFile.Close()

  ' [BWhite] To prevent contention on
  ' the global audit file we have a per-user log.

  LogFile = File.AppendText("C:\logs\" & UserName & ".log")
  LogFile.WriteLine("logon time=" & Now)
```

Once the user logon has been audited, we want to fetch information about the user. In
particular, is this a "Mr." or a "Mrs." or a "Dr." or what?

```
    Dim myCommand As New SqlCommand()
    Dim myReader As SqlDataReader
```

250

```
myCommand.Connection = New SqlConnection( _
    "server=dbmachine;uid=sa;pwd=abracadabra;database=UserDB")
myCommand.CommandText = "SELECT Title FROM Users WHERE Name = '" & _
    UserName & "'"
myCommand.Connection.Open()
myReader = myCommand.ExecuteReader()
myReader.Read()
```

OK, we have the information so we'll write it out to the client stream, and add a time-based greeting while we are at it:

```
' "Good afternoon, Dr. Richard Kimble."
Response.Write("Good ")

Dim Morning As New TimeSpan(12, 0, 0)
Dim Afternoon As New TimeSpan(18, 0, 0)

If -1 = TimeSpan.Compare(DateTime.Now.TimeOfDay, Morning) Then
    Response.Write("morning")          .
ElseIf -1 = TimeSpan.Compare(DateTime.Now.TimeOfDay, Afternoon) Then
    Response.Write("afternoon")
Else
    Response.Write("evening")
End If
    Response.Write(", " & myReader.GetString(0) & " " & UserName)
    ' ...
</script>
```

This code has a litany of flaws, some directly security related and others mere run-of-the-mill flaws.

Defect 1

There are several defects involving static strings. For instance:

Defect 1a: (medium)

```
LogFile = File.AppendText("D:\logs\Global.log")
```

If the code is ever compromised, then the attacker has just learned something valuable: where you keep your security logs. An attacker wants to know where the logs are so that they can erase them or fill them with misleading information.

In addition, the log file name is hard-coded in the script as a literal string. Every piece of code that uses this log will have to replicate that string. That is a maintenance nightmare waiting to happen. What happens if you want to change the name or location of the log or turn logging off temporarily for some reason? That would require potentially hundreds of minor source code modifications.

Defect 1b: (high)

```
myCommand.Connection = New SqlConnection( _
    "server=dbmachine;uid=sa;pwd=abracadabra;database=UserDB")
```

If the source code is ever compromised then the attacker knows almost everything they need to know about your database. (Again, this is a potential maintenance problem in the future.)

Furthermore, the connection is made with the administration account. Run with least privilege; use an account that only has read access if you only need to read. The database server also has an extremely weak password. That would fall to a dictionary-based password attack.

For both security and maintenance reasons, information about logs, database, and so on should be in a configuration file, registry key, or other securable location. That way if the source code is lost then the attacker must also manage to compromise an ACL controlled file or key to obtain information about the log file location, database passwords, and so on.

Defect 2

The exception handling code seems to be, well, nonexistent.

Defect 2a: (low)

There is no exception handling for the case where the log file is for some reason unavailable. Whether that is intentional is unclear from this code. Does code higher up the call stack handle this situation? What happens if the file is locked or the disk is full? Is the correct thing to do to throw an exception and abort?

This is not necessarily a security hole, but it certainly seems like brittle code. The intended behavior for exceptional cases should be clearer.

Speaking of which, can a hostile client keep connecting over and over again to attempt to fill up your log file and hence your hard disk? Could this be used as a DoS attack? Once the log file is full then no users can use the server because every attempt throws an error.

The log file management code could first check the log file size, warning the administrator (by, say, sending an e-mail) when the log file is getting near a maximum size.

Defect 2b: (low)

```
myReader.Read()
```

Similarly, there is no error handling for the SQL code. What if there is no record returned for this query? That should probably set off some alarm bells, since it seems clear that the author of this code assumes that the name is good. What happens if two names are returned? Is it guaranteed that user names are unique?

Again, this is not necessarily a security hole, but better exception handling might help find attacks earlier. An attacker wishes to make the program behave in an unusual way, so put in checks to ensure that it is working as expected.

Defect 3

The code does not abstract away implementation details into helper methods. This is not explicitly a security vulnerability, but rather a code quality issue. Code intended specifically for security features such as auditing should be extremely maintainable and configurable.

Defect 3a: (low)

None of the logging code should be interspersed into the main-line code. There should be methods or an object that abstracts away the implementation of the logging. That way the calling code will be shorter, cleaner, and more easily maintained.

Defect 3b: (low)

This database code should probably also be isolated into a separate method or object. This code is cluttered and difficult to follow because it fails to abstract away details. For instance, you could have a `"GetTitle()"` function and call it rather than putting all this code in line.

Defect 4: (low)

```
' [BWhite] To prevent contention on
' the global audit file we have a per-user log.
```

Presumably, "BWhite" is the user name of the developer who wrote this code. If the source code is ever compromised then an attacker knows the name of someone whom they can impersonate as part of a social engineering attack. They can also make guesses at user names that are likely to have access to this server.

Defect 5

Some of the security problems in this code are a result of failing to vet the client-supplied user name.

Defect 5a: (medium)

```
LogFile.WriteLine("logon name=" & UserName & " time=" & Now)
```

Suppose a hostile client set the user name to:

```
"BobSmith time=10:35:00[embedded vbCRLF here]logon name=MaryJones"
```

The log file will then have an erroneous entry for Bob Smith because it will write out:

```
logon name=BobSmith time=10:35:00
logon name=MaryJones time=11:40:23
```

Whether that is a security problem depends on what you do with the log file; the attacker might have a good reason to make you think that Bob Smith and Mary Jones were involved in some attack on your server. Regardless, it is probably not a good idea to let an untrusted client write arbitrary text into your log file.

Defect 5b: (medium)

```
LogFile = File.AppendText("C:\logs\" & UserName & ".log")
```

Here is a similar attack involving a slightly different use of the unvetted user name. An attacker can append bits to any file on your C drive that ends in ".log". The user name could be

```
"..\otherfiles\foo"
```

This would then append a log file entry to the file foo.log. That is a weak attack, but still, there is no point in giving the attacker any undesired abilities.

Alternatively, the attacker could also attempt to mount a path disclosure attack. If writing to C:\logs\..\Program Files\Microsoft Office\foo.log succeeds then you probably have Office installed. (This is yet another good reason to not give detailed error information to clients.)

Defect 5c: (high)

```
myCommand.CommandText = "SELECT Title FROM Users WHERE Name = '" & _
    UserName & "'"
```

This code has a SQL injection vulnerability because the user name is not vetted. The username could contain arbitrary SQL that inserted records into your database or did other undesirable things. If the user name were:

```
Bob' UPDATE [SQL update query here] --
```

then an attacker could force custom queries to run in your database. It would be more secure (and likely give better performance) to call a stored procedure rather than building up a query like this.

Defect 5d: (high)

```
Response.Write(", " & myReader.GetString(0) & " " & UserName)
```

This code echoes a client-supplied string, which means that it could be part of a cross-site scripting attack. That user name could contain an HTML script block that posted site-specific data to the attacker's web site.

If somehow the attacker managed to get a custom string in the database for a user's title then that string could also be used as part of a CSS attack.

The code could encode the response to ensure that no unintended script blocks are written out.

Defect 6: (low)

The problem identified by BWhite (the possibility of many server threads all attempting to write to the same log file at the same time) is not solved very well. If there is a problem with too many threads accessing the global log file then going to a per-user log file may alleviate some of the contention but may introduce other problems. Now there are more files to manage, and there still may be contention on the main file. In addition, there is potential for inconsistent information here. What happens if the global log and the per-user logs get out-of-sync somehow?

We probably should use a database-driven auditing solution. Databases are designed to solve these sorts of contention problems. Well-designed databases offer good support for limiting table sizes, and so on.

If, as suggested above, the logging code is highly modularized then replacing a file-based solution with a database solution should be easy. As the code stands now, every call site for this logging code will have to be changed for even minor maintenance of the logging code. Put all that code in one class so that the callers can treat it as a black box.

Defect 7: (low)

```
If Time() < 0.5 Then
```

Finally, the coder has forgotten that the client and the server may be in different time zones. This should be checking the client's time, not the current server time. This is not a security hole, but may be incorrect. It would probably be wise to either omit this feature, or emit a client-side script block.

A better way to write this code might look something like this:

```
' flaw3fix.aspx

<%@ Page Language="vb" AutoEventWireup="false"
Codebehind="WebForm1.aspx.vb" Inherits="WebApplication2.WebForm1"%>
<%@ Import Namespace="System.IO" %>
<%@ Import Namespace="System.Data" %>
<%@ Import Namespace="System.Data.SqlClient" %>
<%@ Import Namespace="Microsoft.VisualBasic" %>
<!DOCTYPE HTML PUBLIC "-//W3C//DTD HTML 4.0 Transitional//EN">
<script runat=server>
```

First, we note the requirements on our caller. Next, we vet the user name. In this case, we'll say that a valid user name is between 1 and 50 letters, spaces, and periods.

```
' This method may throw exceptions for security problems or
' database problems; ensure that the caller can handle them.

Friend Sub GreetUser()

  Dim UserName As String
  UserName = Request.Params("Name")

  Dim UserRegEx As Regex = New Regex("^[\.a-zA-Z ]{1,50}$")
  If Not UserRegEx.IsMatch(UserName) Then
    ' This is unexpected.
    ' We may be under attack by a hostile client.
    ' Log this fact to a special security log and alert
    ' the administrator.
    AuditAttack(UserName)
    Throw New Exception("Bad user name")
  End If
  AuditLogon(UserName)
```

Next, we abstract away the database call into a method. If the method fails then we ignore the failure and use a sensible default.

```
  Dim Title As String
  Try
    Title = FetchTitle(UserName)
  Catch
    ' If we cannot get the title just default to nothing.
    Title = ""
  End Try
```

Finally, we write out an encoded string, ensuring that the user is protected, even if the title has somehow been compromised so that it contains script.

```
  Response.Write(Server.HTMLEncode("Hello " & Title & " " & UserName _
    & ","))

  ' ...
```

We then have several utility functions. For example, here is a method that calls into a stored procedure to fetch the title. It checks for the exceptional cases (that is, where there are zero or multiple matches) and throws an exception if that happens. In addition, it reads the connection string from the web.config file rather than embedding the password in the source code.

```
' This utility function can throw errors if something goes
' wrong in the database or if UserName is not unique. Callers
' must handle this case.

Private Function FetchTitle(UserName As String)
```

```
' Note: UserName must have already been validated by caller.

Dim myCommand As New SqlCommand()
Dim myReader As SqlDataReader
Dim myParameter As New SqlParameter("@Name", SqlDbType.NVarChar, 50)
myCommand.Connection = New SqlConnection( _
ConfigurationSettings.AppSettings("DBReadConnection"))
myCommand.CommandType = CommandType.StoredProcedure
myCommand.CommandText = "FetchTitle"
myParameter.Value = UserName
myCommand.Parameters.Add(myParameter)
myCommand.Connection.Open()
myReader = myCommand.ExecuteReader()
If Not myReader.Read() Then
   ' No records matched. Something is wrong.
   Throw New Exception("Bad user name")
End If
FetchTitle = myReader.GetString(0)
If myReader.Read() Then
   ' Two or more records matched. Something is wrong.
   Throw New Exception("Bad user name")
End If
myReader.Close()
End Function
</script>
```

Similarly, the AuditLogon() and AuditAttack() methods should use stored procedures to write information about the logon and the attack to the database. Since the log is in a database rather than a file, the problems associated with file contention and attackers writing confusing text into the file disappear. A clever implementation of AuditAttack() might also have features such as e-mailing the administrator if a potential attack is detected.

Be careful though; think about the vulnerabilities of your security code! It would probably be wise to also limit that behavior to a few e-mails per hour. A few thousand attacks over a period of one minute could result in a lot of e-mail all sent at once, which might be the attacker's intention.

Note that in the fixed version the main-line code is very short and understandable because it uses helper functions and objects. This also makes the code more maintainable; to change the storage used for the database or the auditing code only one place needs to be changed.

An even better helper function would be a generalized stored-procedure calling method so that the database code is not replicated between helper methods. Any time you write the same line of code twice there is an opportunity there for abstracting away the operation into a helper function.

Note also that all the methods clearly document their security semantics and error handling semantics. This will also help to keep the code maintainable.

Now Spot the Security Flaws in Your Code

Writing secure code has little to do with any theoretical knowledge of arcane cryptography or authentication protocols. Instead, the vast majority of security vulnerabilities come directly from careless implementations of code that seem to have little to do with security.

Perhaps a class containing useful information is left inheritable. Perhaps a secret is left embedded in code. Perhaps a game uses a predictable algorithm. Perhaps a server page trusts a client-supplied string. None of these things looks like a security vulnerability at first glance. With practice, however, they start to stand out.

The information in this book is just a start. Getting the right tools and the right attitude to get security flaws out of code is an important part of the security story. Applications in the future will increasingly be implemented by gluing together components from many sources that may be trusted to varying degrees by users; getting the end-to-end security story correct requires a good understanding of the security system and attention to detail.

VB.NET

Code Security

Handbook

Appendix A

A Brief Explanation of Public Key Cryptography

The .NET Runtime uses public key cryptography to ensure that publisher certificates and strong names are not forgeable by hostile attackers. Though it is not necessary to understand how PKC algorithms work to use strong names and publisher certificates, it may be helpful to understand how it works behind the scenes. This appendix gives a brief, nonmathematical explanation of public key cryptography.

The objects implementing the techniques discussed here are available in the System.Security.Cryptography namespace of the .NET Framework.

Jargon

There is a lot of jargon associated with cryptography, so let's get some of that out of the way first. A **cryptosystem** is a collection of technologies that, among other things are useful for **storing** and **transmitting** information. Cryptosystems have certain desirable characteristics: they provide **secrecy**, **authentication,** and **integrity**.

- ❑ **Secrecy** ensures that only the intended recipient of a message can read it.

- ❑ **Authentication** ensures that only the purported originator of a message could have actually originated it.

- ❑ **Integrity** ensures that the message recieved is the same message that was transmitted.

Information transmitted "in the clear" over an insecure system such as the Internet has none of these properties. It is not secret; if Alice sends an e-mail to Bob then Eve (the eavesdropper) can install a packet sniffer on the network and read the mail in transit. It does not guarantee integrity; Eve can tamper with the packets so that Bob receives a different e-mail than the one sent by Alice. Nor does it provide authentication; Eve can create fake e-mail packets that trick Bob's server into believing that it has received a message from Alice, which is actually from Eve.

> **Though the strong name system in .NET only uses cryptography to provide authentication and integrity (not secrecy) historically, cryptography has been motivated by the need to transmit information securely over an insecure channel. We will therefore digress for a moment and discuss some general ways to transmit secrets securely.**

Symmetric Cryptosystems

Algorithms to mitigate the vulnerabilities of insecure transmission systems have existed for thousands of years. Traditional cryptosystems are algorithms that encrypt and decrypt messages based on a parameter called the **key**. Traditional cryptosystems are often called **symmetric** cryptosystems for reasons that will become apparent.

If Alice and Bob agree upon an effective cryptosystem to use and come up with a shared key then they can communicate securely over an insecure medium. When Bob receives an encrypted message from Alice he knows that the only people who can read it are people who have the key. He knows that the only people who could have encoded the message are people who have the key. (Good traditional cryptosystems also provide integrity through mechanisms such as checksums to ensure that no attacker has changed the encrypted version of the data in transit.)

Since only Alice and Bob have the key, Bob knows that any message he can decrypt must have come from Alice (or himself, though you would think he would remember that!) and that no one else has read it. Of course, if Alice has accidentally revealed the secret key to a hostile party then an attacker could send Bob a message that appeared to come from Alice.

What if Alice and Bob are very careful with the key? By the **strength** of a cryptosystem, we mean the level of difficulty encountered by Eve when she tries to deduce what the key is based on analysis of the encrypted messages. There are extremely strong traditional cryptosystems, but all traditional cryptosystems have a major problem: Alice and Bob have to share the key. How do they do that? **The key must remain a secret for the cryptosystem to work.** Furthermore, if Alice and Bob have a way to share secret key information securely then why do they need a cryptosystem at all?

Look at the schematic diagram of a symmetric cryptosystem (Figure 1). Here Alice creates a secret key and securely transmits it to Bob. Perhaps they arrange to meet at a convenient time. Once the key is exchanged Alice can send a message to Bob over an insecure channel at any time. Only Bob can read the message because only Bob has the key – assuming that Eve has not stolen the key or cleverly deduced it through analysis of the encrypted message.

Figure 1

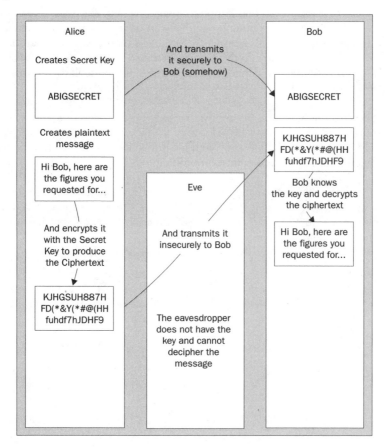

Asymmetric Cryptosystems

In the twentieth century, a new type of cryptography, called of **asymmetric** or **public key** cryptography, was invented to address some of the problems with traditional symmetric cryptosystems. In an asymmetric cryptosystem, there are two keys, not one: Bob has a **public key** and a **private key**. A message encrypted with a public key can only be decrypted with the corresponding private key, and vice versa. It is extremely difficult to deduce the private key if you only know the public key.

When Alice wants to send a message (called the **plaintext**) to Bob using an asymmetric cryptosystem, she first asks Bob for his public key. The public key is, as you might have assumed from the name, publicly available to everyone, including Eve.

Alice then encrypts the message with the public key and transmits it insecurely to Bob. The message can only be decrypted with the private key, and only Bob knows that key, so only Bob can decrypt the message.

Note that we have glossed over one important detail, namely that Alice must be certain that she is actually using Bob's public key. If Eve can trick Alice into encrypting the message with Eve's public key, thinking it is Bob's, and then clearly Eve can decrypt the message. Modern public-key cryptosystems also have systems in place whereby public keys can be securely exchanged; the details are not particularly relevant for the purposes of this discussion.

Now Bob decrypts the message. He knows that only he can decrypt it and that it was therefore transmitted securely, but Bob does not know who the message is from! Anyone could have encoded a message with his public key. So far we have solved the secrecy problem but not the authentication problem.

In Figure 2, you can see a schematic representation of the whole process: Alice generates a message, signs it with Bob's public key, and transmits the encrypted message over an insecure channel. Bob is able to read the message but has no guarantee that it came from Alice.

Figure 2

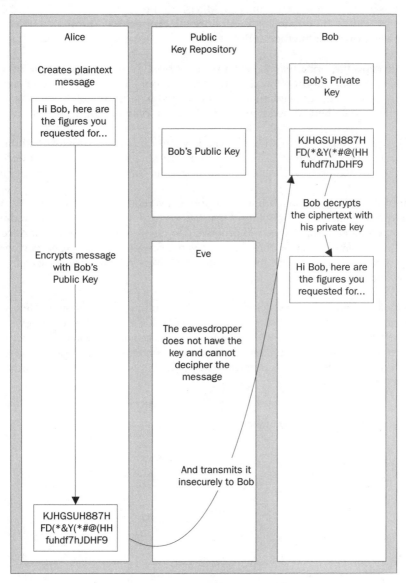

To solve the authentication problem we modify the algorithm somewhat. The first step is that Alice gets her own pair of public and private keys, different from Bob's. Alice then creates a **hash** of the plaintext. A hash is like a checksum, but the hash algorithm is a cleverly designed algorithm that generates a for-all-practical-purposes-unique number for every possible plaintext. The hash algorithm is designed so that it is extremely difficult to find two messages that produce the same hash. A hash is of fixed size, usually about a hundred bits, depending on the exact details of the algorithm.

Alice encrypts her hash with her private key to generate a different number called the **signed hash**. She then appends the signed hash to the plaintext and encrypts the whole thing with Bob's public key to produce the **ciphertext**. The ciphertext can then be transmitted over the Internet to Bob.

If Eve intercepts the ciphertext she cannot read it because she does not have Bob's private key. (She has Bob's public key, but that will only decode messages encrypted with Bob's private key; the ciphertext was encrypted with Bob's public key.) When Bob receives the ciphertext he knows that it is secret; only he can decrypt it.

Bob decrypts the ciphertext with his private key and obtains the plaintext and the signed hash. Since the signed hash was signed with Alice's private key Bob then decrypts the signed hash with Alice's public key to recover the hash.

Bob can now hash the plaintext himself. If the recovered hash and the newly generated hash match then Bob knows that the message has not been tampered with (because two different messages will produce two different hashes) and that Alice created the message (because only someone with access to Alice's private key could produce a hash decodable with Alice's public key). This system provides secrecy, integrity, and authentication.

Take a look at Figure 3 for a schematic view of the full public key system. Here we see Alice generating a message, hashing it, encoding the hash with her private key, appending the encoded hash to the message, and encoding the whole thing with Bob's public key. As before, Eve is unable to deduce the contents of the message she has overheard because she lacks Bob's private key and is unable to deduce it from the public key.

Figure 3

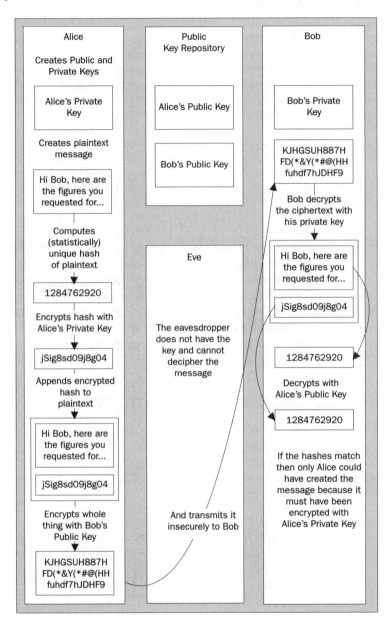

Performance Considerations

You might wonder why Alice does not simply encrypt the entire plaintext with her private key rather than adding the extra complexity of creating a hash. The reason is mostly practical; public key cryptosystems are computationally expensive for long messages compared to hash algorithms. Encrypting the entire plaintext would require two encryptions of a long message to send the message (once with Alice's private key and once with Bob's public key.) The hash system replaces one expensive encryption with an inexpensive hash operation and a relatively inexpensive encryption of a short fixed-length hash.

This performance improvement is particularly important in applications where secrecy is not important but integrity and authentication are important. If secrecy is not important then the number of expensive encryptions and decryptions is reduced to zero by using encrypted hashes.

> **This high-level description of public-key cryptosystems glosses over many important practical problems, such as "How does Alice know that she really has Bob's public key?", "What if Eve put her own public key in the key repository under Bob's name?", or "What if Eve breaks in to Bob's office and steals the computer that contains his private key?" We will not discuss the practical problems of key management in this text.**

Combining Symmetric and Asymmetric Cryptosystems

As a practical matter, most secure messaging systems (such as the Secure Socket Layer, for example) use a combination of symmetric and asymmetric cryptosystems. Asymmetric cryptosystems are usually far more computationally intensive than symmetric cryptosystems.

Asymmetric cryptosystems answer the question raised in our discussion of symmetric cryptosystems: how do Alice and Bob exchange the key securely in the first place? Alice and Bob can securely transmit a short symmetric cryptosystem key using an asymmetric cryptosystem, allowing them to later use the fast, efficient symmetric cryptosystem for longer messages.

Public Key Cryptography and Strong Names

It should now be clear why the strong name system uses public key cryptography. The strong name system must provide integrity (no one has tampered with the code in this assembly) and authentication (this assembly was actually written by a particular publisher) but must do so without sharing a secret! A public key cryptosystem provides all these characteristics.

Secure Transmission is Not Important

Suppose that Alice wants to send a message to Bob but really does not care whether it is secret or not. All Alice cares about is that Bob knows that the message is from her. This is straightforward: Alice hashes her message, encrypts the hash with her private key, and transmits the message and the signed hash in the clear. Bob, or anyone else for that matter, can read the message and verify that Alice's public key decrypts the hash.

Now suppose that you are Alice, your customer is Bob and the "message" you want to send is a .NET assembly. "Bob" would like very much to know that the assembly came from you, not from some attacker.

> Since the strong name and Authenticode technologies are concerned with authentication and integrity, not keeping secrets, we will not discuss the problems of sending secret messages further.

We now have the conceptual background necessary to understand strong names and Authenticode certificates.

A strong name, as we know, consists of a regular name, a cultural identifier, a version number, and a digital signature. We can now expand that last one: a digital signature consists of a **public key** and an **encrypted assembly hash**.

The .NET Runtime can verify that a strong name is valid by attempting to decrypt the encrypted hash with the provided public key. The .NET Runtime will compute the actual hash of the assembly and compare it to the decrypted hash. If they match then integrity is established: not a single bit of the assembly has changed. The customer is also guaranteed that any assembly with a particular public key must have come from only the owner of the private key.

The policy system therefore allows administrators to configure their policy to trust certain public keys. For example, one of the default policies is "fully trust any local-machine assembly with a valid strong name that references the Microsoft public key". Only assembly hashes actually strong-named with the Microsoft private key will be successfully decryptable by the public key, so this is effectively a guarantee that a particular file actually came from Microsoft.

VB.NET

Code Security

Handbook

Appendix B

Using ILDASM to View IL

You can look at the IL associated with an executable by running the `ILDASM.EXE` utility (ILDASM is short for "Instruction Language Disassembler"). For example, compile up this "Hello World" program and look at it with ILDASM:

```
'Hello.vb
Imports Microsoft.VisualBasic
Public Module HelloExample
  Public Sub Main()
    Interaction.MsgBox("Hello, world!")
  End Sub
End Module
```

Compile that up with debugging information:

```
c:\> vbc /debug hello.vb
```

ILDASM has a graphical mode, but for now, we will just look at a straight text dump:

```
c:\> ildasm /text /source hello.exe > hello.il
```

We will not look at every line of the disassembled file, as that would take us rather far a field. Here are some highlights:

```
// Hello.il
.class public auto ansi sealed HelloExample
       extends [mscorlib]System.Object
{
  .custom instance void
[Microsoft.VisualBasic]Microsoft.VisualBasic.CompilerServices.
  StandardModuleAttribute::.ctor() = ( 01 00 00 00 )
```

First off, we note that Visual Basic .NET generates modules as sealed classes. In case anyone needs to know that this class is really a VB module it is marked with a custom attribute.

Next, we can look at the implementation of the body of the class, consisting of a single method. The method is "shared" (also known as "static" in other languages). Note that anything following two slashes is a comment.

```
    .method public static void  Main() cil managed
// Source File 'C:\hello.vb'
//000003:    Public Sub Main()
    IL_0000:  nop
//000004:        Interaction.MsgBox("Hello, world!")
    IL_0001:  ldstr       "Hello, world!"
    IL_0006:  ldc.i4.0
    IL_0007:  ldnull
    IL_0008:  call        valuetype
[Microsoft.VisualBasic]Microsoft.VisualBasic.MsgBoxResult
[Microsoft.VisualBasic]Microsoft.VisualBasic.Interaction::MsgBox(
object,
valuetype [Microsoft.VisualBasic]Microsoft.VisualBasic.MsgBoxStyle,
object)
    IL_000d:  pop
//000005:    End Sub
    IL_000e:  nop
    IL_000f:  ret
    } // end of method HelloExample::Main
} // end of class HelloExample
```

Even if you do not know any kind of machine language this program should be quite straightforward. The "nop" instruction is a "no operation" instruction included so that if you put a breakpoint on the first line of the subroutine the debugger has a specific instruction to break on. The program then loads the string with "ldstr" and the default values (with "ldc.i4.0" and "ldnull") for the two missing arguments onto the stack. The defaults are zero (a constant four-byte integer) for the style and null for the title. It then calls the method, pops the ignored result off the stack, and returns.

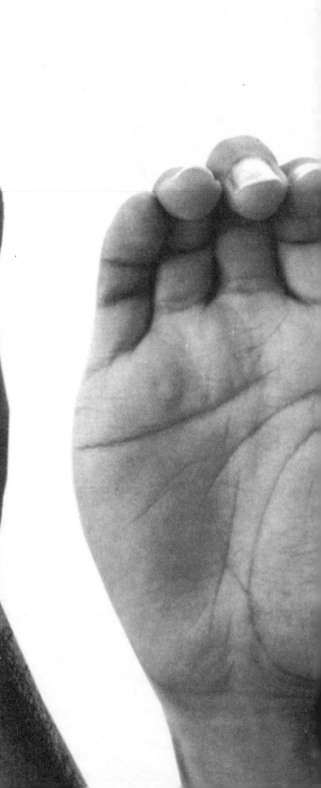

VB.NET

Code Security

Handbook

Appendix C

Support, Errata, and Code Download

We always value hearing from our readers, and we want to know what you think about this book and series: what you liked, what you didn't like, and what you think we can do better next time. You can send us your comments, either by returning the reply card in the back of the book, or by e-mailing us at feedback@wrox.com. Please be sure to mention the book title in your message.

How to Download the Sample Code for the Book

When you log on to the Wrox site, http://www.wrox.com/, simply locate the title through our Search facility or by using one of the title lists. Click on Download Code on the book's detail page.

The files that are available for download from our site have been archived using WinZip. When you have saved the attachments to a folder on your hard-drive, you will need to extract the files using WinZip, or a compatible tool. Inside the Zip file will be a folder structure and an HTML file that explains the structure and gives you further information, including links to e-mail support, and suggested further reading.

Errata

We've made every effort to ensure that there are no errors in the text or in the code. However, no one is perfect and mistakes can occur. If you find an error in this book, like a spelling mistake or a faulty piece of code, we would be very grateful for feedback. By sending in errata, you may save another reader hours of frustration, and of course, you will be helping us to provide even higher quality information. Simply e-mail the information to support@wrox.com; your information will be checked and if correct, posted to the Errata page for that title.

To find errata, locate this book on the Wrox web site (http://www.wrox.com/ACON11.asp?ISBN=1861007477), and click on the Book Errata link on the book's detail page:

E-Mail Support

If you wish to query a problem in the book with an expert who knows the book in detail then e-mail support@wrox.com, with the title of the book, and the last four numbers of the ISBN in the subject field of the e-mail. A typical e-mail should include the following:

❑ The name, last four digits of the ISBN (7477), and page number of the problem, in the Subject field

❑ Your name, contact information, and the problem, in the body of the message

We won't send you junk mail. We need the details to save your time and ours. When you send an e-mail message, it will go through the following chain of support:

❑ **Customer Support**

Your message is delivered to our customer support staff. They have files on most frequently asked questions and will answer anything general about the book or the web site immediately.

❑ **Editorial**

More in-depth queries are forwarded to the technical editor responsible for the book. They have experience with the programming language or particular product, and are able to answer detailed technical questions on the subject. Once an issue has been resolved, the editor can post any errata to the web site.

❑ **The Author**

Finally, in the unlikely event that the editor cannot answer your problem, they will forward the request to the author. We do try to protect the author from any distractions to their writing (or programming); but we are quite happy to forward specific requests to them. All Wrox authors help with the support on their books. They will e-mail the customer and the editor with their response, and again all readers should benefit

The Wrox support process can only offer support for issues that are directly pertinent to the content of our published title. Support for questions that fall outside the scope of normal book support, is provided via our P2P community lists – http://p2p.wrox.com/forum.

p2p.wrox.com

For author and peer discussion, join the P2P mailing lists. Our unique system provides Programmer to Programmer™ contact on mailing lists, forums, and newsgroups, all in addition to our one-to-one e-mail support system. Be confident that the many Wrox authors and other industry experts who are present on our mailing lists are examining any queries posted. At http://p2p.wrox.com/, you will find a number of different lists that will help you, not only while you read this book, but also as you develop your own applications.

To subscribe to a mailing list follow this these steps:

- ❑ Go to http://p2p.wrox.com/
- ❑ Choose the appropriate category from the left menu bar
- ❑ Click on the mailing list you wish to join
- ❑ Follow the instructions to subscribe and fill in your e-mail address and password
- ❑ Reply to the confirmation e-mail you receive
- ❑ Use the subscription manager to join more lists and set your mail preferences

VB.NET

Code Security

Handbook

Index

Index

A Guide to the Index

he index is arranged hierarchically, in alphabetical order, with symbols preceding the
tter A. Most second-level entries and many third-level entries also occur as first-level
ntries. This is to ensure that users will find the information they require however they
noose to search for it.